# McGraw-Hill's
# Essential
# American Idioms
# Dictionary

## Second Edition

## Richard A. Spears, Ph.D.

New York   Chicago   San Francisco   Lisbon   London   Madrid   Mexico City
Milan   New D(   ney   Toronto

**Library of Congress Cataloging-in-Publication Data**

Spears, Richard A.
 [Essential American idioms]
 McGraw-Hill's essential American idioms dictionary / Richard A. Spears;
[illustrations by Luc Nisset]. — [Rev. and updated ed.].
   p.   cm. — (McGraw-Hill's essential American dictionaries)
 Rev. ed. of: 4th ed. of McGraw-Hill's American idioms Dictionary, ©2007.
 ISBN-13: 978-0-07-149784-8 (alk. paper)
 ISBN-10:   0-07-149784-6 (alk. paper)
 1. English language—United States—Idioms—Dictionaries.   2. Americanisms—
Dictionaries.   I. Nisset, Luc.   II. Title.   III. Title: Essential American idioms.

 PE2839.S63   2008
 423'.130973—dc22                                              2007038241

1 2 3 4 5 6 7 8 9 10 11 12 13 14 15 16 17 18 19 20   FGR/FGR   0 9 8 7

ISBN 978-0-07-149784-8
MHID    0-07-149784-6

Illustrations by Luc Nisset
Interior design by Terry Stone

McGraw-Hill books are available at special quantity discounts to use as premiums and
sales promotions or for use in corporate training programs. To contact a representative,
please visit the Contact Us pages at www.mhprofessional.com.

**Also in this series:**

*McGraw-Hill's Essential American Slang Dictionary*
*McGraw-Hill's Essential Phrasal Verb Dictionary*

This book is printed on acid-free paper.

# Contents

# Introduction

Every language has phrases that cannot be understood literally. Even if you know the meanings of all the words in such a phrase and you understand the grammar completely, the total meaning of the phrase may still be confusing. English has many such idiomatic expressions. This dictionary is a selection of the frequently encountered idiomatic expressions found in everyday American English. The collection is small enough to serve as a useful study guide for learners, and large enough to serve as a reference for daily use.

This second edition contains 2,000 idiomatic phrases. This edition also has a Hidden Key Word Index that allows the user to find a particular idiom by looking up the words found "inside the idiom," which is useful in finding the key words that do not occur at the beginning of the idiomatic phrase.

This dictionary should prove useful for people who are learning how to understand idiomatic English and for all speakers of English who want to know more about their language.

# How the Dictionary Works

The following sections are numbered sequentially, since there is cross-referencing between the sections. Here is a directory:

1. Terms, Symbols, and Type Styles
2. Fixed and Variable Idioms
3. Optional Elements
4. Variable Elements
5. Movable Elements and the Dagger
6. Someone vs. One
7. The Asterisk, Swung Dash, and Shared Idiomatic Core
8. Brackets and Extra Information
9. Alphabetization, Organization, and Synonym Clusters

## 1. Terms, Symbols, and Type Styles

☐ (a square) is found at the beginning of an example. Examples are printed in *italic* type. Words emphasized within an example are printed in roman (not italic) type.

† (a dagger) follows a movable element. (See #5.)

\* (an asterisk) stands for a short list of words or phrases that are part of an entry head, as with **\*above suspicion** where the **\*** stands for **be, keep, remain**. (See #7.)

~ (a swung dash) stands for any entry head at the beginning of the entry block in which the swung dash is used. (See #7.)

**( )** (parentheses) enclose **optional elements** and explanatory comments such as origins, etymologies, cross-referencing, and additional entry heads formed with the swung dash. (See #3.)

**[ ]** (brackets) enclose information in a definition that is necessary for the understanding of the entry head. (See #8.)

**AND** introduces **synonymous** entry heads or additional entry heads after a sense number. Additional synonymous entry heads are separated by semicolons (;). (See #9.)

**Fig.** means figurative or nonliteral.

**Euph.** means euphemism or euphemistic.

**Go to** means to locate and move to the entry head named after **Go to**. This does not indicate synonymy. An entry head being pointed to by a **Go to** is in sans serif type.

**Inf.** means informal.

**Lit.** means literal.

**movable element** is an adverb or other particle that can either follow or precede a direct object. In entry heads movable elements follow the direct object and are followed by the dagger (†). (See #5.)

**optional element** is a word, phrase, or **variable element** that may or may not be present in an entry head. Optional elements are enclosed in parentheses. (See #3.)

**Rur.** means rural.

**See also** means to consult the entry head named after **See also** for additional information or to find expressions similar in form or meaning. An entry head being pointed to by a **See also** is in sans serif type.

**sense** is the definition of an entry head. Some entry heads have two or more senses, and in this case, the senses are numbered. Some senses have *additional* entry heads for that sense only. These appear after the sense number and are preceded by the word AND in light type. (See #9.)

**Sl.** means slang or highly informal.

**synonymous** means having the same meaning. **Synonymy** is the quality of having the same meaning.

**typeface: bold** is used for the introduction of entry heads.

*typeface: italic* is used for examples and to single out individual words for comment.

**typeface: sans serif** is used for entry heads that are referred to, such as with cross-referencing.

typeface: light, condensed sans serif is used for variable elements.

**variable element** is a "word" in an entry head that can stand for an entire list or class of words or phrases. Variable elements are in light, condensed sans serif type. (See #4.)

# 2. Fixed and Variable Idioms

Although idioms are usually described as "fixed phrases," most of them exhibit some type of variation. A much larger number of idioms present different kinds of variation, and much of the symbolic and typographic apparatus used here describes the details of this variation. The majority of the idioms found in this dictionary—and in the real world—allow four kinds of variation, as represented by optional elements, variable elements, movable elements, and grammatical variation. Optional elements are enclosed in parentheses within an entry head. Variable elements are printed in a light, condensed sans serif typeface in an entry head. Movable elements, mostly in idiomatic phrasal verbs, are followed by the dagger (†). Grammatical variation—as with differences in tense, aspect, voice, irregular forms, number, and pronoun case and gender—can cause some confusion in identifying the dictionary form of the idiom. A knowledge of basic English grammar provides the ability to reduce nouns to their singular form, verbs to their infinitive or bare form, and passive voice to active.

# 3. Optional Elements

An example of an optional element is the word *two* in the following entry head:

**alike as (two) peas in a pod.**

This idiom is actually two variant forms:

**alike as peas in a pod**
**alike as two peas in a pod**

# 4. Variable Elements

Variable elements stand for the classes or lists of the possible words or phrases that can occur in entry heads. They are sort of wild cards. The most common variable elements used here are: so = someone; sth = something; so/sth = someone or something; one = the same person as the agent of the utterance (see #6); some place = a location. There are others that are more specific, such as an amount of money; some quality; some time; doing sth; etc.

# 5. Movable Elements and the Dagger

The dagger (†)will be found in the following sequence, typically called a phrasal verb:

**Verb + Object + Particle** (†)
Put + your hat + on. (†)
Take + the trash + out. (†)

The dagger indicates that the particle can also occur before the object. This means that there is an alternate form of the idiom:

**Verb + Particle + Object**
Put + on + your hat.
Take + out + the trash.

# 6. Someone vs. One

Two of the variable elements discussed above, so and one, are quite distinct from one another and need further explanation. The use of the word *one* in a sentence seems very stilted, and many people would feel uncomfortable using it in the company of their peers. Do not worry about that; it is just a stand-in for a class of variables. Used as a variable element here, it refers to the same human being that is named as the agent or subject of the sentence in which the variable element one is found. The variable element oneself works the same way. For an example, look at the following idiom:

**able to** do sth **standing on** one's **head**

Here are some sentences containing this idiom:

> <u>He</u> is able to bake cookies standing on <u>his</u> head.
> <u>She</u> is able to bake cookies standing on <u>her</u> head.
> <u>Those guys</u> are able to bake cookies standing on <u>their</u> heads.

Now look at this incorrect representation of the idiom:

*X* **able to** do sth **standing on** so's **head**

Here are some sentences containing this incorrect representation:

> *X* <u>He</u> is able to bake cookies standing on <u>her</u> head.
> *X* <u>She</u> is able to bake cookies standing on <u>Tom's friends'</u> head.

Native speakers of English know instinctively that the X-marked sentences are wrong, but language learners do not have this knowledge and require these details to be spelled out. This dictionary spells out the required knowledge by showing the difference between one and someone.

# 7. The Asterisk, Swung Dash, and Shared Idiomatic Core

Examine the following idiomatic expressions:

**be against the grain**
**cut against the grain**
**go against the grain**
**run against the grain**
**saw against the grain**

They all share a common idiomatic core, **against the grain**. In this dictionary, the shared idiomatic core (in this case, **against the grain**) is defined one time in one place, and the words that enhance the meaning are represented by an asterisk (**\***). Look up **\*against the grain** in the dictionary to see how this is done. The asterisk (**\***) in the entry head is explained within the entry block at "**\*Typically:,**" where the variant phrases **be against the grain**, **cut against the grain**, **go against the grain**, **run against the grain**, and **saw against the grain** are listed. To save space, the swung dash (~) is used as an abbreviation for the entry head, so that ~ = against the grain. The shared idiomatic core is defined only once, and the variants are listed at the same place. This saves space, displays variation, and brings all the related forms together in one place. Similarly, "**\*Also**" is used to explain a variant of the entry head.

# 8. Brackets and Extra Information

Occasionally, it is useful to add additional contextual information to the definition to make it more specific. This added information appears within brackets because it is not actually present in the wording of the entry head.

# 9. Alphabetization, Organization, and Synonym Clusters

In alphabetizing, an initial the, a, or an is ignored, and the entry head is alphabetized on the second word. All punctuation is ignored, as are the major variable element symbols.

Many of the entry blocks contain more than a single sense. In that case, the senses are numbered. Often, sense number one is more literal than the others and is listed first. When the subsequent senses are figuratively based on the first sense it is noted with Fig. In some instances, one of the senses may have one or more variants in addition to the entry head at the top of the entry block. In that case, the additional sense(s) are listed after the sense number preceded by and. This means in addition to the entry head, not instead of the entry head.

# A

**abandon ship 1.** to leave a sinking ship. □ *The captain ordered the crew and passengers to abandon ship.* **2.** *Fig.* to leave a failing enterprise. □ *A lot of the younger people are abandoning ship because they can get jobs elsewhere easily.*

**able to cut** sth *Inf.* to be able to manage or execute something. (Often negative. *Able to* is often *can*.) □ *We thought he could handle the new account, but he is simply not able to cut it.*

**able to fog a mirror** *Inf.* alive, even if just barely. (Usually jocular. Refers to the use of a small mirror placed under the nose to tell if a person is breathing or not. *Able to* is often *can*.) □ *Look, I don't need an athlete to do this job! Anybody able to fog a mirror will do fine!*

**able to take a joke** *Fig.* to be able to accept ridicule good-naturedly; to be able to be the object or butt of a joke willingly. (*Able to* is often *can*.) □ *Better not tease Ann. She can't take a joke.*

**above par** *Fig.* better than average or normal. □ *His work is above par, so he should get paid better.*

**above the fray** *Fig.* not involved in the fight or argument; aloof from a fight or argument. □ *The president tried to appear above the fray, but he couldn't keep out of things, no matter how nasty they got.*

**above the law** *Fig.* not subject to the law; immune to the law. □ *None of us is above the law. We have to obey all of them.*

**according to Hoyle** *Fig.* according to the rules; in keeping with the way something is normally done. (Refers to the rules for playing games. Edmond Hoyle wrote a widely used book with rules for card games.) □ *That's wrong. According to Hoyle, this is the way to do it.*

**ace in(to** sth**)** *Fig.* to be lucky in getting admitted to something. □ *I aced into the history class at the last minute.*

**ace out** *Inf.* to be fortunate or lucky. □ *Freddy aced out at the dentist's office with only one cavity.*

**ace** so **out**† *Inf.* to maneuver someone out; to win out over someone. □ *Martha aced out Rebecca to win the first place trophy.*

**ace out (of** sth**)** *Inf.* to get out of something through luck; to evade or avoid something narrowly. □ *I just aced out of having to take the math test!*

**Achilles' heel** *Fig.* a weak point or fault in someone or something otherwise perfect or excellent. (From the legend of the Greek hero Achilles, who had only one vulnerable part of his body, his heel. As an infant his mother had held him by one heel to dip him in the River Styx to make him invulnerable.) □ *He was very brave, but fear of spiders was his Achilles' heel.*

an **act of faith** *Fig.* an act or deed demonstrating religious faith; an act or deed showing trust in someone or something. □ *For him to trust you with his safety was a real act of faith.*

**Act your age!** *Fig.* Behave more maturely! (A rebuke for someone who is acting childish. Often said to a child who is acting like an even younger child.) □ *Child: Aw, come on! Let me see your book! Mary: Be quiet and act your age. Don't be such a baby!*

**afraid of** one's **own shadow** *Fig.* easily frightened; always frightened, timid, or suspicious. □ *After Tom was robbed, he was even afraid of his own shadow.*

**after hours** *Fig.* after the regular closing time; after any normal or regular time, such as one's bedtime. □ *John got a job sweeping floors in the library after hours.*

**after the fact** *Fig.* after something has happened; after something, such as a crime, has taken place. □ *John is always making excuses after the fact.*

***against the grain 1.** across the alignment of the fibers of a piece of wood. (*Typically: **be** ~; **cut** ~; **go** ~; **run** ~; **saw** ~.) □ *You sawed it wrong. You sawed against the grain when you should have cut with the grain.* **2.** *Fig.* running counter to one's feelings or ideas. (Fig. on ①. *Typically: **be** ~; **go** ~.) □ *The idea of my actually taking something that is not mine goes against the grain.*

**Age before beauty.** *Fig.* a jocular way of encouraging someone to go ahead of oneself; a comical, teasing, and slightly grudging way of indicating that someone else should or can go first. □ *"No, no. Please, you take the next available seat," smiled Tom. "Age before beauty, you know."*

**agree to disagree** *Fig.* [for two or more parties] to calmly agree not to come to an agreement in a dispute. □ *We have accomplished nothing except that we agree to disagree.*

***ahead of the game** *Fig.* being early; having an advantage in a competitive situation; having done more than necessary. (*Typically: **be** ~; **get** ~; **keep** ~; **remain** ~; **stay** ~.) □ *Without the full cooperation of my office staff, I find it hard to stay ahead of the game.*

**aid and abet** so *Cliché* to help someone; to incite someone to do something, possibly something that is wrong. □ *He was scolded for aiding and abetting the boys who were fighting.*

**all agog** *Fig.* surprised and amazed. □ *He sat there, all agog, as the master of ceremonies read his name as the winner of first prize.*

**all and sundry** *Cliché* everyone; one and all. □ *Cold drinks were served to all and sundry.*

**all around Robin Hood's barn** going somewhere by an indirect route; going way out of the way [to get somewhere]; by a long and circuitous route. □ *We had to go all around Robin Hood's barn to get to the little town.*

**all ears** *Fig.* listening eagerly and carefully. □ *Well, hurry up and tell me. I'm all ears.*

**all eyes and ears** *Fig.* listening and watching eagerly and carefully. □ *Be careful what you say. The children are all eyes and ears.*

**\*all hours (of the day and night)** *Fig.* very late in the night or very early in the morning. (\*Typically: **until** ~; **till** ~; **at** ~.) □ *Why do you always stay out until all hours of the day and night?* □ *I like to stay out till all hours.*

**all in a day's work** *Fig.* part of what is expected; typical or normal. □ *I don't particularly like to cook, but it's all in a day's work.*

**(all) in one breath** *Fig.* spoken very rapidly, usually while one is very excited. □ *Jane was in a play, and she was so excited that she said her whole speech in one breath.*

**(all) in the family** *Fig.* restricted to one's own family or closest friends, as with private or embarrassing information. □ *Don't tell anyone else. Please keep it all in the family.*

**all of the above** everything named in the list of possibilities just listed or recited. □ *Q: What's wrong, Sally? Are you sick, tired, frightened, or what? A: All of the above. I'm a mess!*

**all or nothing** everything or nothing at all. □ *Sally would not accept only part of the money. She wanted all or nothing.*

**all over town 1.** *Fig.* in many places in town. □ *Jane looked all over town for a dress to wear to the party.* **2.** *Fig.* known to many; widely known. □ *In a short time the secret was known all over town.*

**all sweetness and light** *Fig. Cliché* very kind, innocent, and helpful. □ *At the reception, the whole family was all sweetness and light, but they argued and fought after the guests left.*

**All systems (are) go.** *Fig.* Everything is ready. (Originally said when preparing to launch a rocket.) □ *The rocket is ready to blast off—all systems are go.*

**all talk (and no action)** *Fig.* talking often about doing something, but never actually doing it. □ *The car needs washing, but Bill is all talk and no action on this matter.*

**all thumbs** *Fig.* very awkward and clumsy, especially with one's hands. □ *Poor Bob can't play the piano at all. He's all thumbs.* □ *Mary is all thumbs when it comes to gardening.*

**all to the good** *Fig.* for the best; to one's benefit. □ *He missed the train, but it was all to the good because the train had a wreck.*

**all told** *Fig.* totaled up; including all parts. □ *All told, he earned about $700 last week.* □ *All told, he has many fine characteristics.*

**all walks of life** *Fig.* all social, economic, and ethnic groups. □ *The people who came to the street fair represented all walks of life.*

**all wool and a yard wide** *Fig.* trustworthy and genuinely good. (A description of good quality wool cloth.) □ *I won't hear another word against Bill. He's all wool and a yard wide.*

*an **all-out effort** *Fig.* a very good and thorough effort. (*Typically: **begin** ~; **have** ~; **make** ~; **start** ~.) □ *We need to make an all-out effort to get this job done on time.*

the **almighty dollar** *Fig.* the U.S. dollar, or the acquisition of money, when viewed as more important than anything else. □ *It's the almighty dollar that drives Wall Street thinking.*

**alpha and omega** *Fig.* the essentials, from the beginning to the end; everything, from the beginning to the end. □ *He was forced to learn the alpha and omega of corporate law in order to even talk to the lawyers.*

**alphabet soup** initialisms and acronyms, especially when used excessively. □ *Just look at the telephone book! You can't find anything, because it's filled with alphabet soup.*

**ambulance chaser** *Inf.* a lawyer who hurries to the scene of an accident to try to get business from injured persons. □ *The insurance companies are cracking down on ambulance chasers.*

**\*American as apple pie** *Cliché* quintessentially American. (\*Also: **as ~.**) □ *A small house with a white picket fence is supposed to be as American as apple pie.*

the **American dream** *Fig.* financial stability as well as physical and emotional comfort. (From the notion that Americans are preoccupied with obtaining certain materialistic goals.) □ *The American dream of home ownership with a car in the garage and a chicken in every pot started in the early 1930s.*

**ancient history** *Fig.* someone or something from so long ago as to be completely forgotten or no longer important, as a former relationship. □ *Bob? I never think about Bob anymore. He's ancient history.*

**and change** *Fig.* plus a few cents; plus a few hundredths. (Used in citing a price or other decimal figure to indicate an additional fraction of a full unit.) □ *The New York Stock Exchange was up seven points and change for the third broken record this week.*

**and what have you** *Fig.* and more things; and other various things. □ *The merchant sells writing paper, pens, string, and what have you.*

**answer for** so **1.** *Fig.* to vouch for someone; to tell of the goodness of someone's character. □ *Mr. Jones, who had known the girl all her life, answered for her. He knew she was innocent.* **2.** to speak for another person; to speak for oneself. □ *I can't answer for Chuck, but I do have my own opinion.*

**answer for** so/sth *Fig.* to explain or justify the actions of someone or something; to take responsibility or blame for someone or something. □ *I will answer only for my own misdeeds.*

**answer the call 1.** *Euph.* to die. □ *Our dear brother answered the call and has gone to his eternal rest.* **2.** AND **answer the call (of nature)** *Euph.* to find and use the toilet. □ *We stopped the car long enough for Jed to answer the call of nature.*

**answer to** so **1.** to explain or justify one's actions to someone. (Usually with *have to*.) □ *If John cannot behave properly, he'll have to answer to me.* **2.** *Fig.* [in the hierarchy of the workplace] to be under the supervision of someone; to report to someone. □ *I answer only to the boss.*

***ants in** one's **pants** *Fig.* the imaginary cause of nervousness and agitation. (From the image of someone suffering great discomfort as if having actual ants in the pants. *Typically: **get** ~; **have** ~; **give** one ~.) □ *I always get ants in my pants before a test.*

**appear in court** to go to a court of law as a participant. □ *I have to appear in court for my traffic violation.*

the **apple of** so's **eye** *Fig.* someone's favorite person or thing; a boyfriend or a girlfriend. □ *Tom is the apple of Mary's eye. She thinks he's the greatest.*

**apple-polisher** *Fig.* a flatterer. □ *Doesn't that wimpy apple-polisher know how stupid he looks?*

***an **arm and a leg** *Fig.* a great amount of money; more money than the value of the purchase warrants. (*Typically: **charge** ~; **cost** ~; **pay** ~.) □ *I had to pay an arm and a leg for these seats.* □ *They charge an arm and a leg for a gallon of gas these days!*

***armed and dangerous** *Cliché* [of someone who is suspected of a crime] having a gun or other lethal weapon and not being reluctant to use it. (This is part of a warning to police officers who might try to capture an armed suspect. *Typically: **be** ~; **be**

**regarded as** ~**; be presumed to be** ~.) □ *The murderer is at large, presumed to be armed and dangerous.*

**armed to the teeth** *Fig.* heavily armed with deadly weapons. (Armed so heavily that even a knife was carried in the teeth.) □ *The bank robber was armed to the teeth when he was caught.*

**article of faith** *Fig.* a statement or element of strong belief. (Refers to a religious tenet.) □ *With Chuck, believing that the oil companies are cheating people is an article of faith.*

**as a matter of course** *Fig.* normally; as a normal procedure. □ *You are expected to make your own bed as a matter of course.*

**as a token (of** sth) *Fig.* symbolic of something, especially of gratitude; as a memento of something. □ *Here, take this gift as a token of my appreciation.*

**as good as** one's **word** obedient to one's promise; dependable in keeping one's promises. □ *She said she would babysit, and she was as good as her word.*

**as is** a state of goods for purchase wherein there may or may not be concealed or unknown defects in the goods. □ *I purchased this car "as is" and so far, everything has been all right.*

**as it were** *Fig.* as one might say; as could be said. (Sometimes used to qualify an assertion that may not sound reasonable.) □ *He carefully constructed, as it were, a huge submarine sandwich.*

**as luck would have it** *Fig.* by good or bad luck; as it turned out; by chance. □ *As luck would have it, the check came in the mail today.*

**as the crow flies** [of a route] straight. □ *Yes, the old cemetery is about two miles west, as the crow flies. There ain't no proper road, though.*

**ask for the moon** *Fig.* to make outlandish requests or demands for something, such as a lot of money or special privileges. □ *She's asking for the moon, and she's not going to get it.*

**\*asleep at the switch** *Fig.* not attending to one's job; failing to do one's duty at the proper time. (Fig. on the image of a technician or engineer on a train sleeping instead of turning whatever switches are required. \*Typically: **be** ~; **fall** ~.) □ *If I hadn't been asleep at the switch, I'd have noticed the car being stolen.*

**\*asleep at the wheel** asleep while behind the steering wheel of a car or other vehicle. (\*Typically: **be** ~; **fall** ~.) □ *He fell asleep at the wheel and crashed.*

**assault the ear** *Fig.* [for sound or speech] to be very loud or persistent. □ *I can't hear you with all that traffic noise assaulting my ears.*

**at a dead end** *Fig.* having reached an impasse; able to go no further forward. □ *We are at a dead end; the project is hopelessly stalled.*

**at a premium** *Fig.* at a high price; priced high because of something special. □ *This new sports car sells at a premium because so many people want to buy it.*

**at a stretch** *Fig.* continuously; without stopping. □ *We all had to do eight hours of duty at a stretch.*

**at** so's **beck and call** *Fig.* ready to obey someone. □ *What makes you think I wait around here at your beck and call? I have to leave for work, you know!*

**at close range** *Fig.* very near; in close proximity. (Usually used in regard to shooting.) □ *The powder burns tell us that the gun was fired at close range.*

**at cross-purposes** *Fig.* with opposing viewpoints; with goals that interfere with each other. □ *Bill and Tom are working at cross-purposes. They'll never get the job done right.*

**at death's door** *Fig.* very near the end of one's life. (Often an exaggeration.) □ *I was so ill that I was at death's door for three days.*

**at** one's **fingertips** *Fig.* very close to one's hands; within one's immediate reach. (Usually a bit of an exaggeration.) □ *I had my pen right here at my fingertips. Now where did it go?*

**at first blush** *Fig.* when first examined or observed. □ *At first blush, the whole idea appealed to us all. Later on we saw its flaws.*

**\*at great length** *Fig.* for a long period of time. (\*Typically: **explain** ~; **question** so ~; **speak** ~.) □ *The lawyer questioned the witness at great length.*

**at loggerheads (with** so**) (over** sth**)** AND **at loggerheads (with** so**) (about** sth**)** *Fig.* in conflict with someone; having reached an impasse with someone about something. □ *The twins were at loggerheads over who should take the larger room.*

**\*at loose ends** *Fig.* restless and unsettled; unemployed. (\*Typically: **be** ~; **leave** so ~.) □ *Just before school starts, all the children are at loose ends.* □ *Jane has been at loose ends ever since she lost her job.*

**at peace 1.** *Fig.* relaxed and happy. □ *When the warm breeze is blowing, I am at peace.* **2.** *Euph.* dead. □ *It was a long illness, but she is at peace now.*

**at sixes and sevens** *Fig.* lost in bewilderment; at loose ends. □ *Bill is always at sixes and sevens when he's home by himself.*

**at the drop of a hat** *Fig.* immediately; instantly; on the slightest signal or urging. (Fig. on the dropping of a hat as a signal.) □ *John was always ready to go fishing at the drop of a hat.*

**at the end of** one's **rope** AND **at the end of** one's **tether** *Fig.* at the limits of one's endurance. (*Tether* is more U.K. and U.S.) □ *I'm at the end of my rope! I just can't go on this way!* □ *I can't go on! I'm at the end of my tether.*

**at the end of the day 1.** at the time when work or one's waking hours end. (Very close to **by the end of the day.** See also **late in the day.**) □ *Will this be finished at the end of the day or before?*

at the end of one's rope

**2.** *Fig.* when everything else has been taken into consideration. □ *The committee interviewed many applicants for the post, but at the end of the day made no appointment.*

**at the last gasp** *Fig.* at the very last; at the last chance; at the last minute. (*Fig.* on the idea of someone's last breath before death.) □ *She finally showed up at the last gasp, bringing the papers that were needed.*

**at the last minute** *Fig.* at the last possible chance; in the last few minutes, hours, or days. □ *Please don't make reservations at the last minute.*

**at the mercy of** so AND **at** so's **mercy** *Fig.* under the control of someone; without defense against someone. □ *We were left at the mercy of the arresting officer.*

**at the top of** one's **game** *Fig.* good and as good as one is likely to get. (Usually of sports.) □ *I guess I was at the top of my game last year. This year, I stink.*

**at this juncture** *Fig.* at this point; at this pause. □ *There is little more that I can say at this juncture.*

**at** one's **wit's end** *Fig.* at the limits of one's mental resources. □ *I'm at my wit's end with this problem. I cannot figure it out.*

**avail** oneself **of** sth to take advantage of something. □ *You would be wise to avail yourself of the resources offered to you.*

**avenue of escape** *Fig.* the pathway or route along which someone or something escapes. □ *Bill saw that his one avenue of escape was through the back door.*

**avoid** so/sth **like the plague** *Fig.* to avoid someone or something completely. (As if contact would transmit the plague.) □ *I hate candied sweet potatoes and avoid them like the plague.*

**\*away from** one's **desk** *Fig.* not available for a telephone conversation; not available to be seen or spoken to. (Sometimes said by the person who answers a telephone in an office. It means that the person whom the caller wants is not immediately available due to personal or business reasons. \*Typically: **be** ~; **step** ~.) □ *I'm sorry, but Ann is away from her desk just now. Can you come back later?* □ *Tom has stepped away from his desk, but if you leave your number, he will call you right back.*

# B

a **babe in the woods** *Fig.* a naive or innocent person; an inexperienced person. (Like a child lost in the woods.) □ *Bill is a babe in the woods when it comes to dealing with plumbers.*

**back and fill** *Fig.* to act indecisively; to change one's direction repeatedly; to reverse one's course. (Originally nautical, referring to trimming the sails so as to alternately fill them with wind and release the wind, in order to maneuver in a narrow space.) □ *The president spent most of his speech backing and filling on the question of taxation.*

**back in the game 1.** back playing the game with the other members of the team. □ *After a bit of a rest, I was back in the game again.* **2.** *Fig.* back doing things as one was before; in action again; back in circulation. □ *Now that final exams are over, I'm back in the game. Wanna go out tonight?*

the **back of the beyond** *Fig.* the most remote place; somewhere very remote. □ *Mary likes city life, but her husband likes to live in the back of the beyond.*

**back to basics** *Fig.* return to basic instruction; start the learning process over again. □ *Class, you seem to have forgotten the simplest of facts, so it's back to basics for the first week of classes.*

**back to square one** *Fig.* back to the beginning. (As with a board game.) □ *Negotiations have broken down, and it's back to square one.*

**back to the drawing board** *Fig.* time to start from the start; it is time to plan something over again. (Plans or schematics are drawn on a drawing board.) □ *It didn't work. Back to the drawing board.*

**back to the salt mines** *Cliché* time to return to work, school, or something else that might be unpleasant. (The phrase implies that the speaker is a slave who works in the salt mines.) □ *School starts in the fall, so then it's back to the salt mines again.*

**backfire on** so *Fig.* [for something, such as a plot] to fail unexpectedly; to fail with an undesired result. (Fig. on the image of an explosion coming out of the breech of a firearm, harming the person shooting rather than the target.) □ *I was afraid that my scheme would backfire on me.*

**backseat driver** *Fig.* an annoying passenger who tells the driver how to drive; someone who tells others how to do things. □ *Stop pestering me with all your advice. Nobody likes a backseat driver!*

**\*bad blood (between** people) *Fig.* unpleasant feelings or animosity between people. (\*Typically: **be** ~; **have** ~.) □ *There is no bad blood between us. I don't know why we should quarrel.*

a **bad hair day** *Inf.* a bad day in general. (As when one's inability to groom one's hair in the morning seems to color the events of the day.) □ *I'm sorry I am so glum. This has been a real bad hair day.*

a **bad penny** *Fig.* a worthless person. □ *Wally is a bad penny. Someday he'll end up in jail.*

**bag of bones** *Inf.* an extremely skinny person or animal with bones showing. (The skin is the figurative bag.) □ *I've lost so much weight that I'm just turning into a bag of bones.*

**bag of tricks** *Fig.* a collection of special techniques or methods. □ *What have you got in your bag of tricks that could help me with this problem?*

**bait and switch** *Fig.* a deceptive merchandising practice where one product is advertised at a low price to get people's attention [the bait], but pressure is applied to get the customer to purchase a more expensive item. □ *Wilbur accused the merchant of bait-and-switch practices and stalked out of the store.*

a **baker's dozen** *Fig.* thirteen. (Bakers often added an extra item to an order for a dozen.) □ *We ended up with a baker's dozen each of socks and undershirts on our shopping trip.*

**ball and chain 1.** *Inf.* a wife. (Mostly jocular.) □ *I've got to get home to my ball and chain.* **2.** *Inf.* a person's special burden; a job. (Prisoners sometimes were fettered with a chain attached to a leg on one end and to a heavy metal ball on the other.) □ *Tom wanted to quit his job. He said he was tired of that old ball and chain.*

the **ball is in** so's **court** *Fig.* someone is responsible for the next move in some process; someone has to make the next response. □ *There was no way that Liz could avoid responding. The ball was in her court.*

**ball of fire** *Fig.* an energetic and ambitious person; a go-getter. □ *I was a real ball of fire until my heart attack.*

a **ballpark figure** *Fig.* an estimate; an off-the-cuff guess. □ *I don't need an exact number. A ballpark figure will do.*

**baptism of fire** *Fig.* a first experience of something, usually something difficult or unpleasant. □ *My son's just had his first visit to the dentist. He stood up to this baptism of fire very well.*

**bare-bones** *Cliché* limited; stripped down; lacking refinements or extras. □ *This one is the bare-bones model. It has no accessories at all.*

**bargaining chip** *Fig.* something to be used (traded) in negotiations. □ *I want to use their refusal to meet our terms as a bargaining chip in future negotiations.*

**bark up the wrong tree** *Fig.* to make the wrong choice; to ask the wrong person; to follow the wrong course. (Fig. on the image of a dog in pursuit of an animal, where the animal is in one tree and the dog is barking at another tree.) □ *If you think I'm the guilty person, you're barking up the wrong tree.*

a **basket case** *Fig.* a person who is a nervous wreck. (Formerly referred to a person who is physically disabled and must be transported in a basket on wheels.) □ *After that all-day meeting, I was practically a basket case.*

**batten down the hatches 1.** to seal a ship's deck hatches against storm damage. □ *Batten down the hatches, lads! She's blowing up a good one!* **2.** *Fig.* to prepare for difficult times. (Fig. on ①. Fixed order.) □ *Batten down the hatches; Congress is in session again!*

**battle of the bulge** *Inf.* the attempt to keep one's waistline slim. (Jocular here. This is the U.S. name for the German Ardennes Offensive, December 16, 1944, to January 25, 1945, involving over a million men.) □ *She appears to have lost the battle of the bulge.*

a **battle royal** *Fig.* a classic, hard-fought battle or argument. (The word order is typical of French order, as is the plural, **battles royal**. *Battle Royale* with an *e* is the name of a film.) □ *The meeting turned into a battle royal, and everyone left angry.*

**Be my guest.** *Fig.* Help yourself.; After you. (A polite way of indicating that someone else should go first, take a serving of something, or take the last one of something.) □ *Mary: I would just love to have some more cake, but there is only one piece left. Sally: Be my guest. Mary: Wow! Thanks!*

**Be there or be square.** *Sl.* Attend or be at some event or place or be considered uncooperative or not "with it." □ *There's a bunch of people going to be at John's on Saturday. Be there or be square!*

**bear arms** to carry and display weapons, usually firearms. □ *He claims that he has the right to bear arms any place at any time.*

**bear fruit** *Fig.* to yield results. □ *We've had many good ideas, but none of them has borne fruit.*

**beat a (hasty) retreat** *Fig. Cliché* to withdraw from a place very quickly. □ *We went out into the cold weather, but quickly beat a retreat to the warmth of our fire.*

**beat a path to** so's **door** *Fig.* [for people] to arrive (at a person's place) in great numbers. (The image is that so many people will wish to come that they will wear down a pathway to the door.) □ *I have a new product so good that everyone will beat a path to my door.*

**beat around the bush** AND **beat about the bush** *Fig.* to avoid answering a question; to stall; to waste time. □ *Stop beating around the bush and answer my question.*

**beat** one's **brains out**† **(to** do sth**)** *Inf.* to try very hard to do something. □ *If you think I'm going to beat my brains out to do this, you are crazy.*

**beat** one's **gums** *Inf.* to waste time talking a great deal without results. (As if one were toothless.) □ *You're just beating your gums. No one is listening.*

**beat the clock** *Fig.* to do something before a deadline; to finish before the time is up. (Fig. on accomplishing something before a clock reaches a specific time.) □ *Sam beat the clock, arriving a few minutes before the doors were locked.*

**beat the gun** *Fig.* to manage to do something before the ending signal. (Originally from sports, referring to scoring in the last seconds of a game just before the signal for the end of the game. See also **beat the clock.**) □ *Tom kicked and tried to beat the gun, but he was one second too slow.*

**beat** so **to the draw** Go to next.

**beat** so **to the punch** AND **beat** so **to the draw** *Fig.* to do something before someone else does it. □ *I planned to write a book about using the new software program, but someone else beat me to the draw.*

the **beauty of** sth *Fig.* the cleverness or ingenuity of something. □ *The beauty of my plan is that it does much and costs little.*

a **bed of roses** *Inf. Fig.* a luxurious situation; an easy life. (Fig. on a soft mattress made of rose petals.) □ *Who said life would be a bed of roses?*

*a **bee in** one's **bonnet** *Fig.* a single idea or a thought that remains in one's mind; an obsession. (*Typically: **get** ~; **have** ~; **give** one ~; **put** ~.) □ *I have a bee in my bonnet over that cool new car I saw, and I can't stop thinking about it.*

**begin to see daylight** *Fig.* to begin to see the end of a long task. □ *I've been so busy. Only in the last week have I begun to see daylight.*

***behind bars** *Fig.* in jail. (*Typically: **be** ~; **put** so ~.) □ *Very soon, you will be behind bars for your crimes.*

***behind the eight ball 1.** *Inf.* in trouble; in a weak or losing position. (Referring to the eight ball in billiards, which in certain games cannot be touched without penalty. *Typically: **be** ~; **get** ~; **have** so ~; **put** so ~.) □ *John is behind the eight ball because he started writing his term paper far too late.* **2.** *Inf.* broke. (*Typically: **be** ~; **get** ~; **have** so ~; **put** so ~.) □ *I was behind the eight ball again and couldn't make my car payment.*

**belabor the point** *Fig.* to spend too much time on one item of discussion. □ *If the speaker would agree not to belabor the point further, I will place it on the agenda for resolution at the next meeting.*

**bells and whistles** *Fig.* extra, fancy add-ons or gadgets. (Fig. on steam locomotives enhanced with added bells and whistles.) □ *I like cars that are loaded with all the bells and whistles.*

**below** so's **radar (screen)** *Fig.* outside of the consciousness or range of observation of someone. (Fig. on flying lower than can be seen on radar.) □ *It's not important right now. It's completely below my radar.*

**belt the grape** *Sl.* to drink wine or liquor heavily and become intoxicated. □ *He has a tendency to belt the grape—every afternoon after work.*

**bend the law** AND **bend the rules** *Fig.* to cheat a little bit without breaking the law. (Jocular.) □ *I didn't break the rules. I just bent the rules a little.* □ *Nobody ever got arrested for bending the law.*

**bend the rules** Go to previous.

*the **benefit of the doubt** *Fig.* a judgment in one's favor when the evidence is neither for one nor against one. (*Typically: **get** ~; **have** ~; **give** so ~.) □ *I thought I should have had the benefit of the doubt, but the judge made me pay a fine.*

**bent out of shape 1.** *Inf.* angry; insulted. □ *I'm bent out of shape because of the way I was treated.* **2.** *Inf.* intoxicated by alcohol or drugs. □ *I've been drunk, but never as bent out of shape as this.*

one's **best bib and tucker** *Rur.* one's best clothing. □ *Put on your best bib and tucker, and let's go to the city.*

**Better late than never.** It is better to do something late than to never do it at all. □ *You were supposed to be here an hour ago! Oh, well. Better late than never.*

**better safe than sorry** better to take extra precautions than to take risks and suffer the consequences. □ *I know I probably don't need an umbrella today, but better safe than sorry.*

**betwixt and between 1.** *Fig.* between (people or things). □ *I liked the soup and the dessert and all that came betwixt and between.* **2.** *Fig.* undecided about someone or something. □ *I wish she would choose. She has been betwixt and between for three weeks.*

**beyond** one's **ken** *Fig.* outside the extent of one's knowledge or understanding. □ *Why she married that shiftless drunkard is beyond my ken.*

**beyond measure** *Fig.* in an account or to an extent more than can be quantified; in a very large amount. □ *They brought in hams, turkeys, and roasts, and then they brought vegetables and salads beyond measure.*

**beyond the pale** *Fig.* unacceptable; outlawed. (Fig. on a *pale* as a barrier made of wooden stakes.) □ *Your behavior is simply beyond the pale.*

the **Big Apple** *Fig.* New York City. (Originally a nickname used of New York area racetracks as being the best. Much has been written on the origin of this expression. There are entire websites devoted to advocating and demolishing new and old theories of origin.) □ *We spent the weekend in the Big Apple.*

a **big frog in a small pond** *Fig.* an important person in the midst of less important people. (Fig. on the idea of a large frog that dominates a small pond with few challengers.) □ *The trouble with Tom is that he's a big frog in a small pond. He needs more competition to make him do even better.*

**big man on campus** *Sl.* an important male college student. (Often derisive or jocular.) □ *Hank acts like such a big man on campus.*

**binge and purge** *Fig.* to overeat and vomit, alternatively and repeatedly. (A symptom of the condition called bulimia.) □ *She had binged and purged a number of times before she finally sought help from a doctor.*

a **bird's-eye view 1.** *Fig.* a view seen from high above. □ *From the top of the church tower you get a splendid bird's-eye view of the village.* **2.** *Fig.* a brief survey of something; a hasty look at something. (Fig. on ①. Alludes to the smallness of a bird's eye.) □ *The course provides a bird's-eye view of the works of Mozart, but it doesn't deal with them in enough detail for your purpose.*

the **birds and the bees** *Euph.* sex and reproduction. (See also the facts of life.) □ *He's twenty years old and doesn't understand about the birds and the bees!*

**bite** so's **head off** *Fig.* to speak sharply and with great anger to someone. (Fixed order.) □ *I'm very sorry I lost my temper. I didn't mean to bite your head off.*

**bite off more than** one **can chew 1.** to take a larger mouthful of food than one can chew easily or comfortably. □ *I bit off more than I could chew and nearly choked.* **2.** *Fig.* to take (on) more than one can deal with; to be overconfident. (Fig. on ①.) □ *Ann is exhausted again. She's always biting off more than she can chew.*

**bite the bullet** *Sl.* to accept something difficult and try to live with it. □ *You are just going to have to bite the bullet and make the best of it.*

**bite the dust 1.** *Sl.* to die. □ *A shot rang out, and another cowboy bit the dust.* **2.** *Sl.* to break; to fail; to give out. □ *My old car finally bit the dust.*

**bite** one's **tongue** *Fig.* to struggle not to say something that you really want to say. □ *I had to bite my tongue to keep from telling her what I really thought.* □ *I sat through that whole silly conversation biting my tongue.*

**black and blue** *Fig.* "bruised," physically or emotionally. □ *I'm still black and blue from my divorce.*

**black and white** *Fig.* [describing] a clear choice; this one or that one. □ *It's not just black and white. It's a hard, complex choice.*

*a **black eye 1.** *Fig.* a bruise near the eye from being struck. (*Typically **have** ~; **get** ~; **give** so ~.) □ *I have a black eye where John hit me.* **2.** *Fig.* harm done to one's character. (Fig. on ①. *Typically **have** ~; **get** ~; **give** so ~.) □ *The whole group now has a black eye, and it will take years to recover our reputation.*

a **blank check** freedom or permission to act as one wishes or thinks necessary. □ *He's been given a blank check with regard to reorganizing the workforce.*

**blood and guts 1.** *Inf. Fig.* strife; acrimony. □ *There is a lot of blood and guts around here, but we get our work done anyway.*

**2.** *Inf. Fig.* acrimonious. (This is hyphenated before a nominal.) □ *Old blood-and-guts Albert is making his threats again.*

**blood, sweat, and tears** *Fig.* the signs of great personal effort. □ *After years of blood, sweat, and tears, Timmy finally earned a college degree.*

**blow** so **a kiss** *Fig.* to pantomime the sending of a kiss to a person visible nearby by kissing one's hand and "blowing" the kiss off the hand toward the person. □ *As she boarded the train she blew him a kiss, and he waved back.*

**blow hot and cold** *Fig.* to be changeable or uncertain (about something). □ *He blows hot and cold about this. I wish he'd make up his mind.*

**blow** one's **nose** to expel mucus and other material from the nose using air pressure from the lungs. □ *Bill blew his nose into his handkerchief.*

**blow the whistle (on** so/sth**) 1.** *Fig.* to report someone's wrongdoing to someone (such as the police) who can stop the wrongdoing. (Fig. on blowing a whistle to attract the police.) □ *The citizens' group blew the whistle on the street gangs by calling the police.* **2.** to report legal or regulatory wrongdoing of a company, especially one's employer, to authorities. □ *She was fired for blowing the whistle on the bank's mismanagement of accounts, but she then sued the bank.*

**blow** so/sth **to pieces** Go to next.

**blow** so/sth **to smithereens** AND **blow** so/sth **to bits; blow** so/sth **to pieces 1.** to explode someone or something into tiny pieces. □ *The bomb blew the ancient church to smithereens.* □ *The explosion blew the tank to bits.* **2.** to destroy an idea or plan by exposing its faults. (Fig. on ①.) □ *The opposing lawyer blew my case to smithereens.*

**blue blood 1.** *Fig.* the blood [heredity] of a noble family; aristocratic ancestry. □ *The earl refuses to allow anyone who is not of* *blue blood to marry his son.* **2.** *Fig.* a person of aristocratic or wealthy ancestry. □ *Because his great-grandparents made millions, he is regarded as one of the city's blue bloods.*

**blue-collar** *Fig.* of the lower class or working class; of a job or a worker, having to do with manual labor. (Compare this with **white-collar.** Refers to the typical color of work shirts worn by mechanics, laborers, etc.) □ *His parents were both blue-collar workers. He was the first person in his family to go to college.*

the **body politic** *Fig.* the people of a country or state considered as a political unit. □ *The body politic was unable to select between the candidates.*

**bolster** so **up**† *Fig.* to give someone emotional support and encouragement. □ *We bolstered her up the best we could, but she was still unhappy.*

a **bolt from the blue** *Fig.* a sudden surprise. (Fig. on the image of a stroke of lightning from a cloudless sky.) □ *The news that Mr. and Mrs. King were getting a divorce struck all their friends as a bolt from the blue.*

**bone of contention** *Fig.* the subject or point of an argument; an unsettled point of disagreement. □ *We've fought for so long that we've forgotten what the bone of contention is.*

**booby prize** *Fig.* a mock prize given to the worst player or performer. □ *Bob should get the booby prize for the worst showing in the race.*

**born lazy** very lazy indeed. (This means the same as *bone lazy* to which it could be related, but there is no evidence for any such derivation.) □ *You are not suffering from any sickness at all! You're just born lazy!*

**born with a silver spoon in** one's **mouth** *Fig.* born into wealth and privilege. □ *James doesn't know anything about working for a living; he was born with a silver spoon in his mouth.*

**bosom buddy** AND **bosom pal** *Fig.* a close friend; one's closest friend. □ *Of course I know Perry. He is one of my bosom pals.*

**bottom out** *Fig.* to reach the lowest or worst point of something. (Fig. on a car making a loud noise when going over a bump because the bottom of the car or its suspension gets hit.) □ *Interest rates bottomed out last February.*

**bound and determined** *Cliché* very determined; very committed or dedicated (to something). □ *We were bound and determined to get there on time.*

**bound hand and foot** *Fig.* with hands and feet tied up. □ *We remained bound hand and foot until the police found us and untied us.*

**bow and scrape** *Fig.* to be very humble and subservient. □ *The salesclerk came in, bowing and scraping, and asked if he could help us.*

the **boys in the backroom** AND the **backroom boys** *Fig.* any private group of men who make decisions, usually political decisions. □ *The boys in the backroom picked the last presidential candidate.*

the **brains behind** sth *Fig.* the originator of the plans for something; the operator or manager of a complex matter. □ *Fred was the brains behind the scheme and made sure that all went well.*

so's **bread and butter** *Fig.* the source of someone's basic income; someone's livelihood—the source of one's food. □ *I can't miss another day of work. That's my bread and butter.*

**bread and water** *Fig.* the most minimal meal possible; the meal that was once given to prisoners. (Usually used in reference to being in prison or jail.) □ *Wilbur knew that if he got in trouble again it would be at least a year on bread and water.*

**break a story** *Fig.* [for a media outlet] to be the first to broadcast or distribute the story of an event. □ *The* Tribune *broke the story before the* Herald *could even send a reporter to the scene.*

**break bread with** so *Fig.* to eat a meal with someone. (Stilted or religious.) □ *Please come by and break bread with us sometime.*

**break ground (for** sth**)** *Fig.* to signal the building of a new structure by a ceremony in which an important person digs out the first shovelful of earth. □ *When do they expect to break ground at the new site?*

**break** so's **heart** *Fig.* to cause someone great emotional pain. □ *It just broke my heart when Tom ran away from home.* □ *Sally broke John's heart when she refused to marry him.*

**break** sth **in**† **1.** to crush or batter something (such as a barrier) to pieces. □ *Why are you breaking the door in? Here's the key!* □ *Who broke in the barrel?* **2.** *Fig.* to use a new device until it runs well and smoothly; to wear shoes, perhaps a little at a time, until they feel comfortable. □ *I can't drive at high speed until I break this car in.* □ *Her feet hurt because her new shoes were not yet broken in.*

**break new ground** *Fig.* to begin to do something that no one else has done; to pioneer [in an enterprise]. □ *Dr. Anderson was breaking new ground in cancer research.*

**break out in a cold sweat** *Fig.* to become frightened or anxious and begin to sweat. □ *I was so frightened, I broke out in a cold sweat.*

**break ranks with** so/sth *Fig.* to disagree with or dissociate oneself from a group in which one is a member. (Fig. on leaving a line or rank of soldiers.) □ *I hate to break ranks with you guys, but I think you are all completely wrong.*

**break silence** *Fig.* to give information about a topic that no one was mentioning or discussing. □ *The press finally broke silence on the question of the plagiarized editorial.*

**break the bank** *Fig.* to use up all one's money. (Fig. on the image of casino gambling, in the rare event that a gambler wins more money than the house [bank] has on hand.) □ *It will hardly break*

break the bank

*the bank if we go out to dinner just once.* □ *Buying a new dress at a discount price won't break the bank.*

**break the ice** *Fig.* to initiate social interchanges and conversation; to get something started. □ *It's hard to break the ice at formal events.* □ *Sally broke the ice at the auction by bidding $20,000 for the painting.*

**break the silence** *Fig.* to make a noise interrupting a period of silence. □ *The wind broke the silence by blowing the door closed.*

**break the spell 1.** *Fig.* to put an end to a magic spell. □ *The wizard looked in his magic book to find out how to break the spell.* **2.** *Fig.* to do something that ends a desirable period of [figurative] enchantment. □ *At the end of the second movement, some idiot broke the spell by applauding.*

**break with tradition 1.** *Fig.* to deviate from tradition; to cease following tradition. □ *The media broke with tradition and completely ignored Groundhog Day to devote more space to serious news.* **2.** *Fig.* a deviation from tradition. □ *In a break with tradition, Groundhog Day was totally ignored by the media.*

*a **breath of fresh air 1.** *Fig.* a portion of air that is not "contaminated" with unpleasant people or situations. □ *You people are disgusting. I have to get out of here and get a breath of fresh air.* **2.** *Fig.* a new, fresh, and imaginative approach (to something). (*Typically: **like** ~.) □ *Sally, with all her wonderful ideas, is a breath of fresh air.*

**breathe easy** *Fig.* to assume a relaxed state after a stressful period. □ *After this crisis is over, I'll be able to breathe easy again.*

**breathe new life into** sth *Fig.* to revive something; to introduce something new or positive into a situation. □ *Her positive attitude breathed new life into the company.*

**bricks and mortar** *Fig.* buildings; the expenditure of money on buildings rather than something else. (The buildings referred to can be constructed out of anything.) □ *Sometimes people are happy to donate millions of dollars for bricks and mortar, but they never think of the additional cost of annual maintenance.*

**bridge the gap** *Fig.* to do or create something that will serve temporarily. (The "gap" is temporal.) □ *We can bridge the gap with a few temporary employees.*

**bright-eyed and bushy-tailed** *Fig.* awake and alert. (The idea is that one is like a frisky animal, such as a squirrel.) □ *Despite the early hour, Dennis was bright-eyed and bushy-tailed.*

**bring home the bacon** *Inf.* to earn a salary; to bring home money earned at a job. □ *I've got to get to work if I'm going to bring home the bacon.*

**bring** sth **home to** so *Fig.* to cause someone to realize something. □ *My weakness was brought home to me by the heavy work I had been assigned to do.*

**bring** so **into the world 1.** *Fig.* to deliver a baby; to attend the birth of someone. □ *I was brought into the world by a kindly old doctor.* **2.** *Fig.* to give birth to a baby. □ *Son, when I brought you into the world, you weighed only five pounds.*

**bring** sth **out**† *Fig.* to issue something; to publish something; to present something [to the public]. □ *I hear you have brought out a new edition of your book.*

**bring** sth **out**† **(in** so**)** *Fig.* to cause a particular quality to be displayed by a person, such as virtue, courage, a mean streak, selfishness, etc. □ *This kind of thing brings out the worst in me.*

**bring** sth **out of mothballs 1.** to remove something from storage in mothballs. □ *He brought his winter coat out of mothballs to wear to the funeral in Canada. Wow, did it stink!* **2.** *Fig.* to bring something out of storage and into use; to restore something to active service. (Fig. on ①.) □ *They were going to bring a number of ships out of mothballs, but the war ended before they needed them.*

**bring the house down**† **1.** to cause a house to collapse or at least be heavily damaged. □ *The most severe earthquake in years finally brought the house down.* **2.** *Fig.* [for a performance or a performer] to excite the audience into making a great clamor of approval. (Fig. on ①. *House* = audience.) □ *Karen's act brought the house down.*

**bring** sth **to a head** *Fig.* to cause something to come to the point when a decision has to be made or action taken. □ *The latest disagreement between management and the union has brought matters to a head. There will be an all-out strike now.*

**bring** sth **to fruition** *Fig.* to make something come into being; to achieve a success. □ *The plan was brought to fruition by the efforts of everyone.*

**bring** sth **to the fore** to move something forward; to make something more prominent or noticeable. □ *All the talk about costs brought the question of budgets to the fore.*

**bring up the rear** *Fig.* to move along behind everyone else; to be at the end of the line. (Originally referred to marching soldiers. Fixed order.) □ *Hurry up, Tom! Why are you always bringing up the rear?*

**broad in the beam 1.** [of a ship] wide at amidships. □ *This old tub is broad in the beam and sits like a ball in the water, but I love her.* **2.** *Inf.* with wide hips or large buttocks. (Fig. on ①.) □ *I am getting a little broad in the beam. It's time to go on a diet.*

**broken dreams** *Fig.* wishes or desires that cannot be fulfilled. □ *We all have our share of broken dreams, but they were never all meant to come true anyway.*

**brown out 1.** *Fig.* [for the electricity] to diminish in power and dim the lights, causing a brownout. (Something less than a *blackout*, when there is no power.) □ *The lights started to brown out, and I thought maybe there was a power shortage.* **2.** *Fig.* a period of dimming or fading of the electricity. (Spelled **brownout**.) □ *They keep building all these expensive power stations, and then we still have brownouts!*

a **brush with death** *Fig.* an instance of nearly dying. □ *After a brush with death in an automobile accident, Claire seemed more friendly and outgoing.*

The **buck stops here.** *Fig.* The need to act or take responsibility, that other people pass on to still other people, ultimately ends up here. (An expression made famous by U.S. President Harry Truman, about the decisions a president must make. See also **pass the buck.**) □ *After everyone else has avoided making the decision, I will have to do it. The buck stops here.*

**build a better mousetrap** *Fig.* to develop or invent something superior to a device that is widely used. (From the old saying, "If you build a better mousetrap, the world will beat a path to your door.") □ *Harry thought he could build a better mousetrap, but everything he "invented" had already been thought of.*

**build castles in Spain** Go to next.

**build castles in the air** AND **build castles in Spain** *Fig.* to daydream; to make plans that can never come true. □ *Ann spends most of her waking hours building castles in Spain.* □ *I really like to sit on the porch in the evening, just building castles in the air.*

**bulldoze through** sth *Fig.* to push clumsily and carelessly through something. □ *Don't just bulldoze through your work!*

*a **bum steer** *Inf.* misleading instructions or guidance; a misleading suggestion. (*Bum* = false; phony. *Steer* = guidance, as in the steering of a car. *Typically: **get** ~; **have** ~; **give** so ~.) □ *Wilbur gave Ted a bum steer, and Ted ended up in the wrong town.*

**bumper to bumper** *Fig.* [of traffic] close together and moving slowly. □ *The traffic is bumper to bumper from the accident up ahead.*

**burn** so **at the stake 1.** to set fire to a person tied to a post as a form of execution. □ *They used to burn witches at the stake.* **2.** *Fig.* to chastise or denounce someone severely or excessively. (Fig. on ①.) □ *Stop yelling! I made a simple mistake, and you're burning me at the stake for it!*

**burn** one's **bridges (behind** one**) 1.** *Fig.* to cut off the way back to where you came from, making it impossible to retreat. □ *By blowing up the road, the spies had burned their bridges behind them.* **2.** *Fig.* to act unpleasantly in a situation that you are leaving, ensuring that you'll never be welcome to return. (Fig. on ①.) □ *If you get mad and quit your job, you'll be burning your bridges behind you.* □ *No sense burning your bridges. Be polite and leave quietly.*

**burn** so **in effigy** to burn a dummy or other figure that represents a hated person. □ *For the third day in a row, they burned the king in effigy.*

**burn the candle at both ends** *Fig.* to work very hard and stay up very late at night. (Fig. one end of the candle is work done in the daylight, and the other end is work done at night.) □ *No wonder Mary is ill. She has been burning the candle at both ends for a long time.*

**burn the midnight oil** *Fig.* to stay up working, especially studying, late at night. (Fig. on working by the light of an oil lamp late in the night.) □ *I have a big exam tomorrow, so I'll be burning the midnight oil tonight.*

**burned to a cinder** *Fig. Lit.* burned very badly. □ *I stayed out in the sun too long, and I am burned to a cinder.* □ *This toast is burnt to a cinder.*

**burst** so's **bubble** *Fig.* to destroy someone's illusion or delusion; to destroy someone's fantasy. □ *I hate to burst your bubble, but Columbus did not discover Canada.*

**bury the hatchet** *Fig.* to make peace. (Fig. on the image of warring tribes burying a tomahawk as a symbol of ending a war.) □ *Let's stop arguing and bury the hatchet.*

**business as usual** *Fig.* having things go along as usual. □ *Even right after the flood, it was business as usual in all the stores.* □ *Please, everyone, business as usual. Let's get back to work.*

the **business end of** sth *Fig.* the part or end of something that actually does the work or carries out the procedure. □ *Keep away from the business end of the electric drill so you won't get hurt.* □ *Don't point the business end of that gun at anyone. It might go off.*

the **butt of a joke** *Fig.* the reason for or aim of a joke, especially when it is a person. (*Butt* = target.) □ *Poor Fred was the butt of every joke told that evening.*

**\*butterflies in** one's **stomach** *Fig.* a nervous feeling in one's stomach. (\*Typically: **get** ~; **have** ~; **give** one ~.) □ *Whenever I have to speak in public, I get butterflies in my stomach.*

**buy a pig in a poke** *Fig.* to buy something without looking inside first. (Fig. on the notion of buying a pig in a sack [*poke* is a folksy word for a sack or bag], without looking at it to see how good a pig it is.) □ *If you don't get a good look at the engine of a used car before you buy it, you'll wind up buying a pig in a poke.*

**by a show of hands** *Fig.* [of a vote taken] expressed by people raising their hands. □ *Bob wanted us to vote on paper, not by a show of hands, so that we could have a secret ballot.*

**by and large** *Fig.* generally; usually. (Originally a nautical expression.) □ *I find that, by and large, people tend to do what they are told to do.*

**by brute strength** *Fig.* by great muscular strength. □ *The men moved the heavy door by brute strength.*

**by force of habit** *Fig.* owing to a tendency to do something that has become a habit. □ *After I retired, I kept getting up and getting dressed each morning by force of habit.*

**by shank's mare** *Fig.* by foot; by walking. (*Shank* refers to the shank of the leg.) □ *My car isn't working, so I'll have to travel by shank's mare.*

**by the nape of the neck** by the back of the neck. (Mostly said in threats.) □ *If you do that again, I'll pick you up by the nape of the neck and throw you out the door.*

**by the same token** *Cliché* a phrase indicating that the speaker is introducing parallel or closely contrasting information. □ *Tom: I really got cheated! Bob: You think they've cheated you, but, by the same token, they believe that you've cheated them.*

**\*by the seat of** one's **pants** *Fig.* by sheer luck and use of intuition. (\*Typically: **fly** ~; **make it** ~.) □ *I got through school by the seat of my pants.*

**by the skin of** one's **teeth** *Fig.* just barely. (By an amount equal to the thickness of the [imaginary] skin on one's teeth.) □ *I got through calculus class by the skin of my teeth.*

**by the sweat of** one's **brow** *Fig.* by one's efforts; by one's hard work. □ *Tom raised these vegetables by the sweat of his brow.*

**by word of mouth** *Fig.* by speaking rather than writing. □ *I need it in writing. I don't trust things I hear about by word of mouth.*

**call a spade a spade** *Fig.* to call something by its right name; to speak frankly about something, even if it is unpleasant. (This, in its history and origins has no racial connotations but has recently been misinterpreted as relating to the slang pejorative *spade* = Negro.) □ *Well, I believe it's time to call a spade a spade. We are just avoiding the issue.*

**call** so's **bluff** *Fig.* to demand that someone prove a claim or is not being deceptive. □ *Tom said, "You've made me really angry, and I'll punch you if you come any closer!" "Go ahead," said Bill, calling his bluff.*

**call hogs** to snore. □ *I couldn't sleep at all last night, with Cousin Joe calling hogs in the next room.* □ *Joe calls hogs so loudly the windows rattle.*

**call** so **to account** *Fig.* to ask one to explain and justify one's behavior, policy, performance, etc. □ *The sergeant called the police officer to account.*

**\*a can of worms** *Fig.* a very difficult issue or set of problems; an array of difficulties. (\*Typically: **be** ~; **open (up)** ~.) □ *This political scandal is a real can of worms.* □ *Let's not open that can of worms!*

**can take it to the bank** *Fig.* able to depend on the truthfulness of the speaker's statement: it is not counterfeit or bogus. □ *Believe me. What I am telling you is the truth. You can take it to the bank.*

can't carry a tune in a bucket

**cannot hear** oneself **think** *Fig.* [a person] cannot concentrate. (Often following an expression something like *It's so loud here. . . .*) □ *Quiet! You're so loud I can't hear myself think!*

**can't carry a tune in a bucket** Go to next.

**can't carry a tune (in a bushel basket)** AND **can't carry a tune in a bucket; can't carry a tune in a paper sack** *Rur.* unable to sing or hum a melody. (Also with *cannot.*) □ *I don't know why Mary's in the choir. She can't carry a tune in a bushel basket.* □ *I'd try to hum the song for you, but I can't carry a tune in a paper sack.*

**can't carry a tune in a paper sack** Go to previous.

**can't hit the (broad) side of a barn** *Rur.* cannot aim something accurately. (Also with *cannot.*) □ *Please don't try to throw the paper into the wastebasket. You can't hit the side of a barn.*

**can't see** one's **hand in front of** one's **face** *Fig.* [to be] unable to see very far, usually due to darkness or fog. (Also with *cannot.*) □ *Bob said that the fog was so thick he couldn't see his hand in front of his face.*

**can't unring the bell** *Fig.* cannot undo what's been done. □ *I wish I wasn't pregnant, but you can't unring the bell.*

**card-carrying member** *Fig.* an official member of some group, originally, the U.S. Communist Party. □ *Bill is a card-carrying member of the electricians union.*

**carry (a lot of) weight (with** so/sth**)** *Fig.* to be very influential with someone or some group of people. □ *Your argument does not carry a lot of weight with me.*

**carry the weight of the world on** one's **shoulders** *Fig.* to appear or behave as if burdened by all the problems in the whole world. □ *Look at Tom. He appears to be carrying the weight of the world on his shoulders.*

**\*carte blanche** *Fig.* freedom or permission to act as one wishes or thinks necessary. (\*Typically: **get** ~; **have** ~; **give** so ~.) □ *He's been given carte blanche with the reorganization of the workforce.* □ *The manager has been given no instructions about how to train the staff. He has carte blanche from the owner.*

**carve out a niche** *Fig.* to have developed and mastered one's own special skill. □ *John, you have carved out a niche for yourself as the most famous living scholar on the Akkadian language.*

**carve out a reputation** *Fig.* to have developed a reputation for doing something well. □ *I worked for years to carve out a reputation as a careful and thoughtful scholar.*

a **case in point** *Fig.* a specific example of what one is talking about. □ *Now, as a case in point, let's look at 19th-century England.*

**cast a pall on** sth AND **cast a pall over** sth *Fig.* to make an event less enjoyable; to place an unpleasant aura on an event. □ *The death of the bride's grandmother cast a pall over the wedding.*

**cast in the same mold** *Fig.* [of two or more people or things] very similar. □ *The two sisters are cast in the same mold—equally mean.*

**cast (**one's**) pearls before swine** *Fig.* to waste something good on someone who doesn't care about it. (From a biblical quotation.) □ *To serve them French cuisine is like casting one's pearls before swine.*

**cast the first stone** *Fig.* to make the first criticism; to be the first to attack. (From a biblical quotation.) □ *John always casts the first stone. Does he think he's perfect?*

**cast** one's **vote** *Fig.* to vote; to place one's ballot in the ballot box. □ *The wait in line to cast one's vote was almost an hour.*

the **cat is out of the bag** *Fig.* the secret has been made known. □ *Now that the cat is out of the bag, there is no sense in pretending we don't know what's really happening.*

**catch** one's **breath** *Fig.* to struggle for normal breathing after strenuous activity. □ *It took Jimmy a minute to catch his breath after being punched in the stomach.*

**catch** one **with** one's **pants down** *Fig.* to discover someone in the act of doing something that is normally private or hidden. (Figurative, although literal uses are possible.) □ *Some council members were using tax money as their own. But the press caught them with their pants down, and now the district attorney will press charges.*

**catch-as-catch-can** *Fig.* the best one can do with whatever is available. □ *There were ten children in our family, and every meal was catch-as-catch-can.*

**cause (some) tongues to wag** *Fig.* to cause people to gossip; to give people something to gossip about. □ *The way John was looking at Mary will surely cause some tongues to wag.*

**center around** so/sth *Fig.* to focus broadly on the details related to someone or something; to **center on** so/sth. (A seeming contradiction.) □ *The novel centers around the friends and activities of an elderly lady.*

the **center of attention** *Fig.* the focus of people's attention; the thing or person who monopolizes people's attention. □ *She had a way of making herself the center of attention wherever she went.*

a **certain party** *Fig.* someone you know but whom I do not wish to name. □ *If a certain party finds out about you-know-what, what on earth will you do?*

the **chain of command** *Fig.* the series or sequence of holders of responsibility in a hierarchy. □ *The only way to get things done in the military is to follow the chain of command. Never try to go straight to the top.*

**chain of events** *Fig.* a sequence of things that happened in the past, in order of occurrence. □ *An odd chain of events led up to our meeting on the plane. It was like some unseen force planned it.*

a **change of pace** an addition of some variety in one's life, routine, or abode. □ *Going to the beach on the weekend will be a change of pace.*

**change** so's **tune** to change someone's manner or attitude, usually from bad to good, or from rude to pleasant. □ *The teller was most unpleasant until she learned that I'm a bank director. Then she changed her tune.*

**chapter and verse** *Fig.* very specifically detailed, in reference to sources of information. □ *He gave chapter and verse for his reasons for disputing that Shakespeare had written the play.*

**charm the pants off** so *Inf.* to use very charming behavior to persuade someone to do something. □ *He will try to charm the pants off you, but you can still refuse to take the job if you don't want to do it.*

**cheap at half the price** nicely priced; fairly valued; bargain priced. (This is the way that many people seem to use this phrase. The meaning does not follow logically from the wording of the phrase. There are other interpretations, but none is clearly correct. One thought is that it is a play on "cheap at twice the price" = if the price were doubled, it would still be cheap for the value received.) □ *I only paid $12 for this ring. Wow! It would be cheap at half the price!*

**checks and balances** *Fig.* a system, as in the U.S. Constitution, where power is shared between the various branches of government. □ *The newspaper editor claimed that the system of checks and balances built into our Constitution has been subverted by party politics.*

**cheek by jowl** *Fig.* side by side; close together. □ *The pedestrians had to walk cheek by jowl along the narrow streets.*

**chew** one's **cud** to think deeply; to be deeply involved in private thought. (Fig. on the cow's habit of bringing food back from the stomach to chew it further. The cow appears to be lost in thought while doing this.) □ *He's chewing his cud about what to do next.*

**chicken feed** *Fig.* a small amount of anything, especially of money. (See also **for chicken feed**.) □ *It may be chicken feed to you, but that's a month's rent to me!*

**chief cook and bottle washer** *Fig.* the person in charge of practically everything (such as in a very small business). □ *I'm the chief cook and bottle washer around here. I do everything.*

**chin music** *Inf.* talk; conversation. □ *Whenever those two get together, you can be sure there'll be plenty of chin music.*

a **chip off the old block** *Fig.* a person (usually a male) who behaves in the same way as his father or who resembles his father. □ *John looks like his father—a real chip off the old block.*

**chock full of** sth *Fig.* very full of something. □ *These cookies are chock full of big chunks of chocolate.*

a **chunk of change** *Fig.* a lot of money. □ *Tom's new sports car cost a real big chunk of change!*

**claim a life** *Fig.* [for something] to take the life of someone. □ *The killer tornado claimed the lives of six people at the trailer park.*

so's **claim to fame** *Fig.* someone's reason for being well-known or famous. □ *Her claim to fame is that she can recite the entire works of Shakespeare from memory.*

**clean** one's **act up**† to reform one's conduct; to improve one's performance. □ *I cleaned up my act, but not in time. I got kicked out.*

a **clean sweep** *Fig.* a broad movement clearing or affecting everything in its pathway. □ *The manager and everybody in accounting got fired in a clean sweep of that department.*

**clear the air 1.** to get rid of stale or bad air. □ *Open some windows and clear the air. It's stuffy in here.* **2.** *Fig.* to get rid of doubts or hard feelings. □ *All right, let's discuss this frankly. It'll be better if we clear the air.*

**clear** one's **throat** to vocalize in a way that removes excess moisture from the vocal cords and surrounding area. □ *I had to clear my throat a lot today. I think I'm coming down with something.*

**climb the wall(s)** *Fig.* to be very agitated, anxious, bored, or excited. (Fig. on the image of a nervous wild animal trying to climb up a wall to escape.) □ *He was home for only three days; then he began to climb the wall.*

**cloak-and-dagger** *Fig.* involving secrecy and plotting. □ *A great deal of cloak-and-dagger stuff goes on in political circles.*

**\*close as two coats of paint** *Cliché* close and intimate. (\*Also: **as** ~.) □ *All their lives, the cousins were close as two coats of paint.*

**Close, but no cigar.** *Cliché* Some effort came close to succeeding, but did not succeed. (Fig. on the idea of failing to win a contest for which a cigar is a prize.) □ *Jill: How did you do in the contest? Jane: Close, but no cigar. I got second place.*

**close ranks** *Fig.* to move closer together in a military formation. □ *The soldiers closed ranks and marched on the enemy in tight formation.*

**close up shop** to quit working, for the day or forever. (Fixed order.) □ *It's five o'clock. Time to close up shop.*

**clown around (with** so**)** *Fig.* to join with someone in acting silly; [for two or more people] to act silly together. □ *The kids are having fun clowning around.*

**coat and tie** [for men] a jacket or sports coat and necktie. (A respectable but less than formal standard of dress.) □ *My brother was not wearing a coat and tie, and they would not admit him into the restaurant.*

**cock-and-bull story** *Fig.* a hard-to-believe, made-up story; a story that is a lie. □ *I asked for an explanation, and all I got was your ridiculous cock-and-bull story!*

**coffee and Danish** *Fig.* a cup of coffee and a Danish sweet roll. □ *Coffee and Danish is not my idea of a good breakfast!*

**coin a phrase** *Fig.* to create a new expression that is worthy of being remembered and repeated. (Often jocular.) □ *He is "worth his weight in feathers," to coin a phrase.*

**cold, hard cash** *Inf.* cash, not checks or credit. □ *I want to be paid in cold, hard cash, and I want to be paid now!*

**collect** one's **thoughts** *Fig.* to take time to think through an issue; to give some thought to a topic. □ *I'll speak to the visitors in a moment. I need some time to collect my thoughts.*

**come a cropper** *Fig.* to have a misfortune; to fail. (Meaning "fall off one's horse." More U.K. than U.S.) □ *Bob invested all his money in the stock market just before it fell. Boy, did he come a cropper.*

**come down in the world** *Fig.* to lose one's social position or financial standing. □ *Mr. Jones has really come down in the world since he lost his job.*

**come down to earth 1.** *Lit.* to arrive on earth from above. □ *An angel came down to earth and made an announcement.* **2.** *Fig.* to become realistic; to become alert to what is going on around one. (Fig. on ①.) □ *You are having a spell of enthusiasm, John, but you must come down to earth. We can't possibly afford any of your suggestions.*

**come full circle** *Fig.* to return to the original position or state of affairs. □ *The family sold the house generations ago, but things have come full circle and one of their descendants lives there now.*

**come hell or high water** *Inf.* no matter what happens. □ *I'll be there tomorrow, come hell or high water.*

**come home (to roost) 1.** [for a fowl or other bird] to return to its home, as for a night's rest. □ *The chickens come home to roost in the evening.* **2.** *Fig.* [for a problem] to return to cause trouble [for someone]. (Fig. on ①. See also **come home (to** so**).** □ *As I feared, all my problems came home to roost.*

**come into the world** *Fig.* to be born. □ *Little Timmy came into the world on a cold and snowy night.*

**come out in the wash** *Fig.* to work out all right. (Fig. on the image of a clothing stain that can be removed by washing.) □ *Don't worry about that problem. It'll all come out in the wash.*

**come out on top** *Fig.* to end up being the winner. □ *I knew that if I kept trying, I would come out on top.* □ *Harry came out on top as I knew he would.*

**come to a bad end** *Fig.* to have a disaster, perhaps one that is deserved or expected; to die an unfortunate death. □ *The dirty crook came to a bad end!*

**come to a boil 1.** *Fig.* [for a problem or situation] to reach a critical or crucial stage. (Fig. on the image of water reaching an active boil.) □ *Everything came to a boil after Mary admitted her guilt.* **2.** *Fig.* [for someone] to get very angry. (Fig. on the heat of anger.) □ *Fred was coming to a boil, and clearly he was going to lose his temper.*

**come to a pretty pass** *Fig.* to encounter a difficult situation. (Older. Here *pretty* expresses irony.) □ *This project has come to a pretty pass. I don't know how we can possibly finish on time.*

**come to grief** *Fig.* to experience something unpleasant or damaging. □ *In the end, he came to grief because he did not follow instructions.*

**come to grips with** so/sth *Fig.* to begin to deal with someone or something; to face the challenge posed by someone or something. □ *I found it hard to come to grips with Crystal and her problems.*

**come to** one's **senses** *Fig.* to begin thinking sensibly. □ *I'm glad he finally came to his senses and went on to college.*

**come unglued** *Inf.* to lose emotional control; to break out into tears or laughter. □ *When Sally heard the joke, she almost came unglued.*

**come up for air 1.** *Fig.* to stop what one is doing for a different activity or rest. □ *Whenever you get off the phone and come up for air, I have a question for you.* **2.** *Fig.* to stop kissing for a moment and breathe. (Fig. on ①.) □ *Don't those kids ever come up for air?*

**come what may** *Cliché* no matter what might happen. □ *I'll be home for the holidays, come what may.*

**come within an ace of** sth *Inf.* to come very close to [doing] something. □ *I came within an ace of leaving school. I'm glad you talked me out of it.*

**come within an inch of** doing sth *Fig.* almost to do something; to come very close to doing something. (Can also be literal.) □ *I came within an inch of going into the army.* □ *I came within an inch of falling off the roof.*

**come-hither look** *Fig.* an alluring or seductive look or glance, usually done by a woman. □ *She had mastered the come-hither look, but was not ready for the next part.*

**commit** sth **to memory** *Fig.* to memorize something. □ *The dress rehearsal of the play is tomorrow night. Please make sure you have committed all your lines to memory by that time.*

**compare apples and oranges** *Fig.* to compare two entities that are not similar. (Used especially in reference to comparisons of unlike things.) □ *Talking about her current book and her previous bestseller is like comparing apples and oranges.*

**cook** so's **goose** *Inf.* to damage or ruin someone. □ *I cooked my own goose by not showing up on time.*

***cool as a cucumber** extremely calm; imperturbable. (*Also: as ~.) □ *The politician kept cool as a cucumber throughout the interview with the aggressive journalist.*

**cop a plea** *Inf.* to plead guilty to a lesser charge to avoid a more serious charge or lessen time of imprisonment. □ *He copped a plea and got off with only two months in the slammer.*

a **couch potato** a lazy individual, addicted to television-watching. □ *All he ever does is watch TV. He's become a real couch potato.*

**count** one's **blessings** to recognize and appreciate one's good fortune and providential gifts. □ *Whenever I see someone really in need, I always count my blessings.*

**count** one's **chickens before they hatch** *Fig.* to plan how to utilize good results of something before those results have occurred. □ *You may be disappointed if you count your chickens before they hatch.*

**cover a lot of ground 1.** to travel over a great distance; to investigate a wide expanse of land. □ *The prospectors covered a lot of ground, looking for gold.* **2.** *Fig.* to deal with much information and many facts. (Fig. on ①.) □ *The history lecture covered a lot of ground today.*

**cover the waterfront** to deal with every detail concerning a specific topic. □ *Her talk really covered the waterfront. By the time she finished, I knew much more than I wanted to know.*

**cow juice** *Inf.* milk. □ *Here's a little cow juice to pour on your cereal.*

**crack a book** *Inf.* to open a book to study. (Typically in the negative.) □ *Sally didn't crack a book all semester and still passed the course.*

**crack a joke** *Fig.* to tell a joke. □ *Every time Tom cracked a joke, his buddies broke up laughing.*

**crack under the strain** *Fig.* to have a mental or emotional collapse because of continued work or stress. □ *He worked 80-hour weeks for a month and finally cracked under the strain.*

**crack** sth **(wide) open** to expose and reveal some great wrongdoing. □ *The police cracked the drug ring wide open.*

**cramp** so's **style** *Fig.* to limit someone in some way. □ *I hope this doesn't cramp your style, but could you please not hum while you work?* □ *To ask Bob to keep regular hours would cramp his style.*

**crazy in the head** *Inf.* stupid or insane. □ *Am I crazy in the head, or did I just see someone walking a leopard on a leash?*

the **cream of the crop** *Fig.* the best of all. □ *These three students are very bright. They are the cream of the crop in their class.*

**creature comforts** *Fig.* things that make people comfortable. □ *The hotel room was a bit small, but all the creature comforts were there.*

a **crick in** one's **back** a twisted or cramped place in the back that causes pain or immobility. □ *I had a crick in my back all night and I couldn't sleep.*

a **crick in** one's **neck** a twisted place or a cramp in the neck that causes pain. □ *I got a crick in my neck from sleeping in a draft.*

**cross swords (with so)** *Fig.* to become the adversary of someone. □ *Gloria loved an argument and was looking forward to crossing swords with Sally.*

**cross that bridge before** one **comes to it** AND **cross bridges before** one **comes to them** *Fig.* to worry excessively about something before it happens. □ *There is no sense in crossing that bridge before you come to it.* □ *She's always crossing bridges before coming to them. She needs to learn to relax.*

**cross that bridge when** one **comes to it** *Fig.* to delay worrying about something that might happen until it actually does happen. □ *Alan: Where will we stop tonight? Jane: At the next town. Alan: What if all the hotels are full? Jane: Let's cross that bridge when we come to it.*

**cry before** one **is hurt** *Fig.* to cry or complain needlessly, before one is injured. □ *There is no point in crying before one is hurt.*

**cry over spilled milk** *Fig.* to be unhappy about what cannot be undone. □ *He is always crying over spilled milk. He cannot accept reality.* □ *It can't be helped. Don't cry over spilled milk.*

**cry wolf** *Fig.* to cry or complain about something when nothing is really wrong. (From the story wherein a child sounds the alarm frequently about a wolf when there is no wolf, only to be ignored when there actually is a wolf.) □ *Pay no attention. She's just crying wolf again.*

**curry favor with** so to try to win favor from someone. □ *The lawyer tried to curry favor with the judge.*

**cut (so) a check** *Fig.* to write a check; to have a computer print a check. (Used in business especially of machine-made checks.) □ *We will cut a check for the balance due you later this afternoon.*

**cut and dried** *Fig.* fixed; determined beforehand; usual and uninteresting. (Can be hyphenated before nominals.) □ *I find your writing quite boring. It's too cut and dried.* □ *The lecture was, as usual, cut and dried.*

**cut and paste 1.** to cut something out of paper with scissors and paste it onto something else. □ *The teacher told the little children that it was time to cut and paste, and they all ran to the worktables.* **2.** *Fig.* something trivial, simple, or childish. (Fig. on ①.) □ *I don't mind doing things that have to be done, but I hate to waste my time on cut and paste.* **3.** to move computer data section by section in a document. □ *It's simple to cut and paste. Just highlight this section and move it to where you want it.*

**cut and run** *Sl.* to run away quickly. (Fig. on the image of cutting loose a ship's or boat's anchor and sailing away in a hurry.) □ *As soon as I finish what I am doing here, I'm going to cut and run. I've got to get home by six o'clock.*

**cut corners** *Fig.* to take shortcuts; to save money or effort by finding cheaper or easier ways to do something. □ *I won't cut corners just to save money. I put quality first.*

**cut** one's **(eye)teeth on** sth *Fig.* to grow up experiencing something; to have had the experience of dealing with something [successfully] at a very early age. □ *My grandfather taught me how to fish, so I cut my eyeteeth on fishing.*

**cut no ice (with** so**)** *Sl.* to have no influence on someone; to fail to convince someone. □ *So you're the mayor's daughter. It still cuts no ice with me.*

**cut off** one's **nose to spite** one's **face** *Fig.* to harm oneself while attempting to harm someone else. □ *Why do you want to fire your best worker? That's just cutting off your nose to spite your face.*

**cut** one's **(own) throat** *Fig.* [for someone] to bring about one's (own) failure. □ *If I were to confess, I'd just be cutting my throat.*

**cut the deadwood out**† *Fig.* to remove unproductive persons from employment. (Fig. on pruning trees and bushes.) □ *When we cut the deadwood out, all our departments will run more smoothly.*

**cut the ground out**† **from under** so *Fig.* to destroy the foundation of someone's plans or someone's argument. □ *The politician cut the ground out from under his opponent.*

**cut through red tape** *Fig.* to eliminate or neutralize something complicated, such as bureaucratic rules and procedures. (Fixed order.) □ *I will try to cut through all the red tape for you so you get your visa on time.* □ *I am sure someone can help us cut through all this red tape.*

**cut to the chase** *Sl.* to focus on what is important; to abandon the preliminaries and deal with the major points. □ *After a few introductory comments, we cut to the chase and began negotiating.*

the **daily grind** [someone's] everyday work routine. □ *When my vacation was over, I had to go back to the daily grind.*

**damn** so/sth **with faint praise** *Fig.* to criticize someone or something indirectly by not praising enthusiastically. □ *The critic did not say that he disliked the play, but he damned it with faint praise.*

**dance on air** *Fig.* to be very happy; to be euphoric enough as if to dance on air. □ *She was just dancing on air, she was so happy.*

**dance with death** *Fig.* to attempt to do something that is very risky. □ *The crossing of the border into enemy territory was like dancing with death.*

the **dark side of** so/sth *Fig.* the negative and often hidden aspect of someone or something. □ *I had never seen the dark side of Mary before, and I have to tell you that I was horrified when she lost her temper.*

**dead ahead** *Fig.* straight ahead; directly ahead. □ *The farmer said that the town we were looking for was dead ahead.*

**dead center** *Fig.* at the exact center of something. □ *The arrow hit the target dead center.*

**dead certain** *Fig.* very sure. (*Dead* means *absolutely.*) □ *I didn't believe the rumor at first, but Bill's dead certain that it's true.*

**dead from the neck up 1.** *Fig.* stupid. (With a "dead" head.) □ *She acts like she is dead from the neck up.* **2.** *Fig.* no longer open to new ideas. □ *Everyone on the board of directors is dead from the neck up.*

49

\*a **(dead) ringer (for** so) *Fig.* very closely similar in appearance to someone else. (There are a few entertaining origins made up for this phrase, all of which include a person who has rigged a coffin with a device that will ring a bell in case of burial before death. The concern was real and such devices were invented, but they have no connection with this phrase. \*Typically: **be** ~; **look like** ~.) □ *You are sure a dead ringer for my brother.*

**death on** sth **1.** *Fig.* very harmful; very effective in acting against someone or something. □ *This road is terribly bumpy. It's death on tires.* **2.** *Fig.* accurate or deadly at doing something requiring skill or great effort. □ *The boxing champ is really death on those fast punches.*

a **diamond in the rough** *Fig.* a person who has good qualities despite a rough exterior; a person with great potential. □ *Sam looks a little scruffy, but he's a diamond in the rough.*

**die laughing 1.** to meet one's death laughing—in good spirits, revenge, or irony. □ *Sally is such an optimist that she'll probably die laughing.* **2.** *Fig.* to laugh very long and hard. (Fig. on ①. An exaggeration.) □ *The play was meant to be funny, but the audience didn't exactly die laughing.*

**die of a broken heart** *Fig.* to die of emotional distress. □ *I was not surprised to hear of her death. They say she died of a broken heart.*

**dig** one's **own grave** *Fig.* to be responsible for one's own downfall or ruin. □ *Those politicians have dug their own grave with their new tax bill. They won't be reelected.*

**dig some dirt up**† **(on** so) *Fig.* to find out something bad about someone. □ *If you don't stop trying to dig some dirt up on me, I'll get a lawyer and sue you.*

**dip into** one's **savings** *Fig.* to use part of the money one has been saving. □ *I had to dip into my savings in order to pay for my vacation.*

a **disaster of epic proportions** *Cliché* a very large disaster. (Often jocular.) □ *The earthquake was responsible for a disaster of epic proportions.*

the **disease to please** an obsessive need to please people. □ *I, like so many, am afflicted with the disease to please. I am just too nice for my own good.*

**divide and conquer** *Fig.* to cause the enemy to divide and separate into two or more factions, and then move in to conquer all of them. □ *Sam led his men to divide and conquer the enemy platoon, and his strategy succeeded.*

**do a land-office business** *Fig.* to do a large amount of buying or selling in a short period of time. □ *The tax collector's office did a land-office business on the day that taxes were due.*

**do a slow burn** *Fig.* to be quietly angry. □ *I did a slow burn while I was waiting in line for a refund.*

**do a snow job on** so *Sl.* to deceive or confuse someone. □ *She thought she did a snow job on the teacher, but it backfired.*

**do** one's **damnedest** *Fig.* to do as well as one can, not sparing energy or determination. □ *I know you can win the contest. Just get out there and do your damnedest.*

**do justice to** sth **1.** *Fig.* to do something well; to represent or portray something accurately. (Often negative.) □ *This photograph doesn't do justice to the beauty of the mountains.* **2.** *Fig.* to eat or drink a great deal. □ *The party didn't do justice to the roast pig. There were nearly 10 pounds left over.*

**do the honors** *Fig.* to act as host or hostess and serve one's guests by pouring drinks, slicing meat, making (drinking) toasts, etc. □ *All the guests were seated, and a huge juicy turkey sat on the table. Jane turned to her husband and said, "Bob, will you do the honors?" Bob smiled and began slicing thick slices of meat from the turkey.*

**do the trick** *Fig.* to do exactly what is needed. □ *This new paint scraper really does the trick.*

**do** sth **up brown** *Fig.* to do something just right or with great effect. (Fixed order.) □ *Whenever they put on a party, they do it up brown.*

**dog and pony show** *Fig.* a display, demonstration, or exhibition of something—such as something one is selling. (As in a circus act where trained dogs leap onto and off of trained ponies.) □ *Gary went into his standard dog and pony show, trying to sell us on an upgrade to our software.*

**dog in the manger** *Fig.* one who unreasonably prevents other people from doing or having what one does not wish them to do or have. (From one of Aesop's fables in which a dog—which cannot eat hay—lay in the hayrack [manger] and prevented the other animals from eating the hay.) □ *If Martin were not such a dog in the manger, he would let his brother have that dinner jacket he never wears.*

a **doggy bag** *Fig.* a bag or other container used to carry uneaten food home from a restaurant. (As if it is for the dog.) □ *I can't eat all of this. Can I have a doggy bag, please?*

**dollar for dollar** *Fig.* considering the amount of money involved; considering the cost or value. (Often seen in advertising.) □ *Dollar for dollar, this laundry detergent washes cleaner and brighter than any other product on the market.*

**done by mirrors** AND **done with mirrors** *Fig.* illusory; purposefully deceptive. □ *The company's self-review was done by mirrors and didn't come off too bad, despite our falling stock price.*

**Don't bet on it!** *Fig.* Do not be at all sure! □ *So, you think I will be at your house at 5:00 A.M.? Don't bet on it!*

**Don't call us, we'll call you.** *Cliché* a formulaic expression said to applicants who have just interviewed or auditioned for a job or part. □ *Stupendous, Gloria, just stupendous. What glamour and radiance! Don't call us, we'll call you.*

**Don't give up the ship!** *Fig.* Do not give up yet!; Do not yield the entire enterprise! (Fixed order. Based on the words on a flag made by Captain Oliver Hazard Perry in the Battle of Lake Erie during the War of 1812.) □ *Bill: I'm having a devil of a time with calculus. I think I want to drop the course. Sally: Keep trying. Don't give up the ship!*

**don't know beans (about** sth) *Fig.* does not know anything about something. □ *Bill doesn't know beans about car engines.*

**Don't speak too soon.** I think you may be wrong. Don't speak before you know the facts. □ *Bill: It looks like it'll be a nice day. Mary: Don't speak too soon. I just felt a raindrop.*

**Don't stand on ceremony.** *Fig.* Do not wait for a formal invitation.; Please be at ease and make yourself at home. (Some people read this as "Don't remain standing because of ceremony," and others read it "Don't be totally obedient to the requirements of ceremony.") □ *Come in, Tom. Don't stand on ceremony. Get yourself a drink and something to eat and introduce yourself to everyone."*

**Don't waste your breath.** *Inf.* You will not get a positive response to what you have to say, so don't even say it.; Talking will get you nowhere. □ *Alice: I'll go in there and try to convince her otherwise. Fred: Don't waste your breath. I already tried it.*

**down in the mouth** *Fig.* sad-faced; depressed and unsmiling. □ *Since her dog died, Barbara has been down in the mouth.*

**downhill all the way** *Fig.* easy the entire way. □ *Don't worry about your algebra course. It's downhill all the way after this chapter.*

**drag** one's **feet (on** or **over** sth) AND **drag** one's **heels (on** or **over** sth) *Fig.* to progress slowly or stall in the doing of something. □ *Why is she taking so long? I think she is just dragging her feet on* *this matter.* □ *If the planning department had not dragged their heels, the building would have been built by now.*

**drag** one's **heels (on** or **over** sth) Go to previous.

**drag** so **through the mud** *Fig.* to insult, defame, and debase someone. □ *The newspapers dragged the actress through the mud week after week.*

**draw blood 1.** to remove blood from a person using a hypodermic needle as for a medical laboratory test. □ *A nice lady came into my hospital room at dawn to draw blood for some tests.* **2.** to injure someone severely enough to cause bleeding. □ *It was a nasty bite and it drew blood, but not a lot.* **3.** *Fig.* to anger or insult a person. □ *Sally screamed out a terrible insult at Tom. Judging by the look on his face, she really drew blood.*

**draw straws for** sth *Fig.* to decide who gets something or must do something by choosing straws from an unseen set of straws of different lengths. (The person who gets the shortest straw is chosen.) □ *We drew straws for the privilege of going first.*

**\*drawn and quartered** *Fig.* to be dealt with very severely. (Now fig. except in historical accounts; refers to a former practice of torturing someone guilty of treason, usually a male, by disemboweling and then dividing the remaining body into four parts. \*Typically: **be** ~; **have** so ~. Fixed order.) □ *Todd was practically drawn and quartered for losing the Wilson contract.*

**drive a coach and horses through** sth *Fig.* to expose weak points or "wide gaps" in an argument, alibi, or criminal case by "driving a horse and carriage through" them. (Emphasizes the large size of the holes or gaps in the argument.) □ *The opposition will drive a coach and horses through the wording of that government bill.*

**drop a brick** *Fig.* to commit a social error. □ *When he ignored the hostess, he really dropped a brick!*

**drop like flies** *Fig.* to faint, sicken, collapse, or die in great numbers like houseflies dying in a large group. □ *It was a terrible year for the flu. People were dropping like flies.*

**drop the ball** *Fig.* to make a blunder; to fail in some way. □ *Everything was going fine in the election until my campaign manager dropped the ball.*

**drop the other shoe** *Fig.* to do the deed that completes something; to do the expected remaining part of something. □ *Tommy has just failed three classes in school. We expect him to drop the other shoe and quit altogether any day now.*

**dry run** *Fig.* an attempt; a practice or rehearsal. □ *The children will need another dry run before their procession in the pageant.*

**duck and cover 1.** *Fig.* to bend down and seek protection against an attack. □ *When the gunfire started, we had to duck and cover or get killed.* **2.** *Fig.* to dodge something, such as an issue or a difficult question, and attempt to shield oneself against similar issues or questions. (Fig. on ①.) □ *The candidate's first reaction to the question was to duck and cover.*

**dyed-in-the-wool** *Fig.* [of someone] permanent or extreme. □ *My uncle was a dyed-in-the-wool farmer. He wouldn't change for anything.*

**dying to** do sth AND **dying to have** sth *Fig.* very eager to do something, such as to have, get, or ingest something. □ *After a long hot day like this one, I'm just dying to drink a cold beer.* □ *After a long hot day, I'm just dying to have a cold beer.*

# E

**eager beaver** *Fig.* someone who is very enthusiastic; someone who works very hard. □ *The young assistant gets to work very early. She's a real eager beaver.*

**early bird 1.** *Fig.* a person who gets up early. □ *I never miss sunrise. I'm an early bird.* **2.** *Fig.* a person who arrives early. □ *The early birds get the best seats.* **3.** *Fig.* having to do with early arrival. □ *The early-bird special this week is a free six-pack of iced tea for the first 100 visitors.*

**easy come, easy go** *Cliché* said to explain the loss of something that required only a small amount of effort to acquire in the first place. □ *John spends his money as fast as he can earn it. With John it's easy come, easy go.*

**Easy does it. 1.** *Fig.* Move slowly and carefully. □ *Bill (holding one end of a large crate): It's really tight in this doorway. Bob (holding the other end): Easy does it. Take your time.* **2.** *Fig.* Calm down.; Don't lose your temper. □ *Sue (frantic): Where is my camera? My passport is gone too! Fred: Easy does it, Sue. I think you have someone else's purse.*

**eat crow 1.** *Fig.* to display total humility, especially when shown to be wrong. □ *Well, it looks like I was wrong, and I'm going to have to eat crow.* **2.** *Fig.* to be shamed; to admit that one was wrong. □ *When it became clear that they had arrested the wrong person, the police had to eat crow.*

eat crow

**eat** one's **hat** *Fig.* a phrase telling the kind of thing that one would do if a very unlikely event really happens. □ *I'll eat my hat if you get a raise.*

**eat** one's **heart out 1.** *Fig.* to grieve; to be sorrowful. (Fixed order.) □ *She has been eating her heart out over that jerk ever since he ran away with Sally.* **2.** *Fig.* to suffer from envy or jealousy. (Usually a command.) □ *Yeah, the reward money is all mine. Eat your heart out!*

**eat humble pie** *Fig.* to act very humble when one is shown to be wrong. (*Umbles* is an old generic term for edible animal innards and does not necessarily involve humility. Nonetheless some writers tell us that only the humble poor ate such things—without regard to the elegant yuletide boar's head. The similarity between *umbles* and *humble* may then have given rise to the "pie of humility," *humble pie*, the expression being essentially a pun.) □ *I think I'm right, but if I'm wrong, I'll eat humble pie.*

**eat like a bird** *Fig.* to eat only small amounts of food; to peck at one's food. □ *Jane is very slim because she eats like a bird.*

**eat like a horse** *Fig.* to eat large amounts of food. □ *John works like a horse and eats like a horse, so he never gets fat.*

**eat** one's **words** *Fig.* to have to take back one's statements; to confess that one's predictions were wrong. □ *John was wrong about the election and had to eat his words.*

**elbow grease** *Fig.* hard scrubbing. □ *Tom: What did you use to get your car so shiny? Mary: Just regular wax and some elbow grease.*

**enough to keep body and soul together** *Fig.* very little; only enough to survive. (Usually refers to money.) □ *When he worked for the library, Marshall only made enough to keep body and soul together.*

the **eternal triangle** a sexual or emotional relationship involving two women and one man or two men and one woman. (Typically, a couple [man and woman] and another man or woman.) □ *Henry can't choose between his wife and his mistress. It's the eternal triangle.*

**even steven** *Inf.* to be even (with someone or something) by having repaid a debt, replied in kind, etc. □ *Bill hit Tom; then Tom hit Bill. Now they are even steven.*

**every nook and cranny** *Fig.* every small, out-of-the-way place or places where something can be hidden. □ *We looked for the tickets in every nook and cranny. They were lost. There was no doubt.*

**every trick in the book** *Fig.* every deceptive method known. □ *I used every trick in the book, but I still couldn't manage to get a ticket to the game Saturday.*

**every walk of life** *Fig.* every status and occupation. □ *We invited people from every walk of life, but only those who could afford the long drive could possibly come.*

**Everything's coming up roses.** *Fig.* Everything is really just excellent. Life is prosperous. □ *Life is wonderful. Everything is coming up roses.*

**eyeball to eyeball** *Fig.* face-to-face and often very close; in person. □ *They approached each other eyeball to eyeball and frowned.*

# F

**face (the) facts** *Fig.* to confront the (unpleasant) truth about someone or something; to confront and accept the consequences of something. □ *Eventually, you will have to face the facts. Times are hard.*

**face the music** *Fig.* to receive punishment; to accept the unpleasant results of one's actions. □ *Mary broke a dining-room window and had to face the music when her father got home.*

the **facts of life 1.** *Euph.* the facts of sex and reproduction, especially human reproduction. □ *My parents told me the facts of life when I was nine years old.* **2.** *Fig.* the truth about the unpleasant ways that the world works. □ *Mary really learned the facts of life when she got her first job.*

**fair and impartial** *Fig.* just and unbiased. (Usually referring to some aspect of the legal system, such as a jury, a hearing, or a judge.) □ *We demand that all of our judges be fair and impartial in every instance.*

**fair and square** *Fig.* completely fair(ly); justly; within the rules. □ *The division of the money should be fair and square.*

**fair to middlin'** *Rur.* mediocre; not bad but not good. (*Middling* = of average quality.) □ *Tom: How are you feeling today? Bill: Fair to middlin'.*

**fall between two stools** *Fig.* to come somewhere between two possibilities and so fail to meet the requirements of either. □ *The material is not suitable for an academic book or for a popular one. It falls between two stools.*

**fall into the wrong hands** *Fig.* to become associated with the wrong person; to become the possession of the wrong person. □ *I don't want these plans to fall into the wrong hands.*

**fall on deaf ears** *Fig.* [for talk or ideas] to be ignored by the persons they were intended for. □ *Her pleas for mercy fell on deaf ears; the judge gave her the maximum sentence.*

**fall on hard times** *Fig.* to experience difficult times, especially financially. □ *We fell on hard times during the recession.*

a **false move** AND **one false move** *Fig.* [even] a single movement that indicates that one is disobeying an order to remain still or in a nonthreatening posture. □ *The robber threatened to shoot us if we made one false move.*

**famous last words** *Fig.* assertions that are almost immediately countered. (Sarcastic.) □ *A: I said I would never speak to her again in my entire life! B: Famous last words! You just said hello to her.*

**fancy footwork 1.** *Fig.* clever and intricate dance steps. □ *The old man was known for his fancy footwork when he was on Broadway.* **2.** *Fig.* adroit movements of the feet that help someone retain balance or move through treacherous territory. □ *It took some fancy footwork to get down the mountain carrying the injured child.* **3.** *Fig.* a clever and intricate strategy that helps someone get out of trouble. □ *The governor did some fancy footwork to keep from getting blamed for the scandal.*

**Fancy meeting you here!** *Fig.* I am very surprised to meet you here! □ *"Fancy meeting you here," said Mr. Franklin when he bumped into the company president at the racetrack.*

**\*far and wide** *Fig.* to arrive from everywhere; to arrive from many directions and great distances. (\*Typically: **scattered** ~; **come from** ~; **found** ~.) □ *People came from far and wide to attend the annual meeting.*

a **far cry from** sth *Fig.* a thing that is very different from something else. □ *What you did was a far cry from what you said you were going to do.*

**far from the madding crowd** *Fig.* in a quiet, restful place. (From Thomas Gray's poem, "Elegy Written in a Country Churchyard.") □ *Julia sat daydreaming at her desk, wishing she were far from the madding crowd.*

**fat and happy** *Fig.* content, as if from being well-fed. □ *Since all the employees were fat and happy, there was little incentive to improve productivity.*

**fat and sassy** *Fig.* in good health and spirits. □ *She came back from her vacation all fat and sassy.*

a **feast for the eyes** AND a **feast for** one's **eyes** *Fig.* a delight for someone to look at. (Can be used to describe a fine-looking display of prepared food or anything that looks good.) □ *Ah, my dear, you are a feast for the eyes!*

a **feather in** one's **cap** *Fig.* an honor; a reward for something. □ *John earned a feather in his cap by getting an A in physics.*

**feather** one's **(own) nest** *Fig.* to use power and prestige to provide for oneself selfishly. (Said especially of politicians who use their offices to make money for themselves.) □ *The mayor seemed to be helping people, but she was really feathering her own nest.*

**feed the kitty** *Fig.* to contribute money. (A *kitty* here is a small collection of money.) □ *Please feed the kitty. Make a contribution to help sick children.*

**feel blue** *Fig.* to feel sad. □ *You look like you feel blue. What's wrong?*

**feeling no pain** *Inf.* numbed by alcohol and feeling nothing; intoxicated. □ *He drank the whole thing, and he's feeling no pain.*

**fiddle while Rome burns** *Fig.* to do nothing or something trivial while knowing that something disastrous is happening. (From a legend that the Roman emperor Nero played the lyre while

Rome was burning.) □ *The lobbyists don't seem to be doing anything to stop this tax bill. They're fiddling while Rome burns.*

a **fifth wheel** *Fig.* an unwelcome or extra person. □ *I don't like living with my son and daughter-in-law. I feel like a fifth wheel.*

**find** one's **tongue** *Fig.* to be able to talk; to figure out what to say. □ *Tom was speechless for a moment. Then he found his tongue.*

**fine and dandy** *Inf.* nice; good; well. □ *Well, that's just fine and dandy. Couldn't be better.*

a **fine kettle of fish** *Fig.* a troublesome situation; a vexing problem. □ *What a fine kettle of fish! My husband is not here to meet me at the train station, and there's no phone here for me to call him.* □ *Alan: Oh, no! I've burned the roast. We don't have anything to serve our guests as a main dish. Jane: But they'll be here any minute! This is a fine kettle of fish.*

**fish for a compliment** *Fig.* to try to get someone to pay oneself a compliment. □ *When she showed me her new dress, I could tell that she was fishing for a compliment.*

**fish in troubled waters** *Fig.* to involve oneself in a difficult, confused, or dangerous situation, especially with a view to gaining an advantage. □ *Frank is fishing in troubled waters by buying more shares of that company. They are supposed to be in financial difficulties.*

**fish or cut bait** *Fig.* either perform the task at hand or withdraw to a supporting position so that someone else can do the job unhampered. □ *You're not doing a good job, Tom. Get going. You need to fish or cut bait!*

**fish story** AND **fish tale** *Fig.* a great big lie. (As with a fisherman who exaggerates the size of the fish that got away.) □ *That's just a fish story. Don't try to fool me.*

**fish tale** Go to previous.

**\*fits and starts** *Fig.* with irregular movement; with much stopping and starting. (\*Typically: **by** ~; **in** ~; **with** ~.) □ *By fits and starts, the old car finally got us to town.*

**Flattery will get you nowhere.** *Fig. Cliché* Flattering me will not increase your chances of success. □ *A: Gee, you can do almost anything, can't you? B: Probably, but flattery will get you nowhere.*

**flex** so's/sth's **muscles** *Fig.* to do something that shows potential strength, power, or ability. (Fig. on someone demonstrating muscular development, and presumably strength, by displaying tensed or pumped muscles, usually biceps.) □ *The music committee is flexing its muscles again by threatening to make the choir wear robes even during the summer months.*

**flight of fancy** an idea or suggestion that is out of touch with reality or possibility. □ *What is the point in indulging in flights of fancy about exotic vacations when you cannot even afford the rent?*

**flirt with disaster** *Fig.* to take a great risk; to **tempt fate**. (Fig. on flirting with a person.) □ *Building a city below sea level is just flirting with disaster.*

**flirt with the idea of** doing sth *Fig.* to think about doing something; to toy with an idea; to consider something, but not too seriously. □ *I flirted with the idea of going to Europe for two weeks.*

**float a loan** *Fig.* to get a loan of money; to arrange for a loan of money. □ *I couldn't afford to pay cash for the car, so I floated a loan.*

**follow suit** to follow in the same pattern; to follow someone else's example. (From card games.) □ *Mary went to work for a bank, and Jane followed suit. Now they are both head cashiers.*

**food for thought** *Fig.* something for someone to think about; issues to be considered. □ *Your essay has provided me with some interesting food for thought.*

a **fool's paradise** *Fig.* a state of being happy for foolish or unfounded reasons. □ *Fred is confident that he'll get a big raise this year, but I think he's living in a fool's paradise.*

**for better or (for) worse** *Fig.* under any conditions; no matter what happens. □ *For better or for worse, I'm going to quit my job.* □ *I know I married you for better or worse, but I didn't really know how bad worse could be!*

**for old time's sake** *Fig.* [to do something] because of memories of better times and relationships in the past. □ *I stopped and had a drink with him for old time's sake, even though he was no longer a good friend.*

**for the birds** *Inf.* worthless; undesirable. (Older.) □ *Winter weather is for the birds.*

**for the duration** *Fig.* for the whole time that something continues; for the entire period of time required for something to be completed; for as long as something takes. □ *We are in this war for the duration.* □ *However long it takes, we'll wait. We are here for the duration.*

**For two cents I would** do sth. *Fig.* If someone would give me two cents, I would do something. □ *What a jerk. For two cents I'd poke him in the nose.*

**forty winks** *Fig.* a nap; some sleep. □ *I could use forty winks before I have to get to work.*

**fraught with danger** *Fig. Cliché* [of something] full of something dangerous or unpleasant. □ *My escape from the kidnappers was fraught with danger.*

a **free ride** *Fig.* an easy time; participation without contributing anything. □ *You've had a free ride long enough. You have to do your share of the work now.*

A **friend in need is a friend indeed.** A true friend is a person who will help you when you really need help. □ *When Bill helped* *me with geometry, I really learned the meaning of "A friend in need is a friend indeed."*

**friend or foe** *Fig.* a friend or an enemy. □ *I can't tell whether Jim is friend or foe.* □ *"Who goes there? Friend or foe?" asked the sentry.*

\*a **frog in** one's **throat** *Fig.* a feeling of hoarseness or a lump in one's throat. (Often regarded as a sign of fear. \*Typically: **get** ~; **have** ~.) □ *I feel like I'm getting a frog in my throat when I have to speak in public.*

**from A to Z** *Fig.* of a complete and wide variety. □ *We have just about everything from A to Z.*

**from Missouri** *Fig.* requiring proof; needing to be shown something in order to believe it. (From the nickname for the state of Missouri, the Show Me State.) □ *You'll have to prove it to me. I'm from Missouri.*

**from pillar to post** *Fig.* from one place to a series of other places; from person to person, as with gossip. □ *My father was in the army, and we moved from pillar to post year after year.*

**from rags to riches** *Fig.* from poverty to wealth; from modesty to elegance. □ *The princess used to be quite poor. She certainly moved from rags to riches.*

\***from scratch** *Fig.* [making something] by starting with the basic ingredients. (\*Typically: **bake** sth ~; do sth ~; **make** sth ~.) □ *We made the cake from scratch, using no prepared ingredients.*

**from stem to stern 1.** from the front of a boat or ship to the back. □ *He inspected the boat from stem to stern and decided he wanted to buy it.* **2.** *Fig.* from one end to another. (Fig. on ①.) □ *I polished my car carefully from stem to stern.*

**from the cradle to the grave** *Fig.* from birth to death. □ *The government promised to take care of us from the cradle to the grave.*

**from the sublime to the ridiculous** *Fig.* from something fine and uplifting to something ridiculous or mundane. □ *After Mr.*

*Jones had introduced my wife to his wife, he jokingly turned to introduce me and said, "From the sublime to the ridiculous."*

the **fruits of** one's **labor(s)** *Fig.* the results of one's work. □ *What have you accomplished? Where is the fruit of your labors?*

**fudge factor** *Fig.* a margin of error. □ *I never use a fudge factor. I measure correctly, and I cut the material exactly the way I measured it.*

**full of holes** *Fig.* [of an argument or plan] that cannot stand up to challenge or scrutiny. (See also **not hold water; pick holes in** sth.) □ *This plan is full of holes and won't work.*

**fun and games** *Fig.* playing around; doing pointless things. □ *All right, Bill, the fun and games are over. It's time to get down to work.*

**funny ha-ha** *Fig.* amusing; comical. (As opposed to **funny peculiar.**) □ *I didn't mean that Mrs. Peters is funny ha-ha. She's weird— funny peculiar, in fact.*

**funny peculiar** *Fig.* odd; eccentric. (As opposed to **funny ha-ha.**) □ *I didn't mean that Mrs. Peters is funny ha-ha. She's weird— funny peculiar, in fact.*

**gales of laughter** *Fig.* repeated choruses of laughter. □ *As the principal strode down the hall, she could hear gales of laughter coming from Mrs. Edwards's room.*

a **game that two can play** *Fig.* a manner of competing that two competitors can use; a strategy that competing sides can both use. (Said when about to use the same ploy that an opponent has used.) □ *The mayor shouted at the city council, "Politics is a game that two can play."*

**get** so **around the table** *Fig.* to collect people together for discussion or bargaining. □ *We have to get everyone around the table on this matter.*

**get away with murder 1.** to commit murder and not get punished for it. □ *Don't kill me! You can't get away with murder!* **2.** *Fig.* to do something very bad and not get punished for it. (Fig. on ①.) □ *You will spoil your son if you let him get away with murder. You should punish him for his backtalk.*

**get down to business** AND **get down to work** *Fig.* to begin to get serious; to begin to negotiate or conduct business. □ *All right, everyone. Let's get down to business. There has been enough chit-chat.*

**get down to cases** *Fig.* to begin to discuss specific matters; to get down to business. □ *When we've finished the general discussion, we'll get down to cases.*

**get down to the facts** *Fig.* to begin to talk about things that matter; to get to the truth. □ *Let's get down to the facts, Mrs. Brown. Where were you on the night of January 16?*

**get down to the nitty-gritty** *Inf.* to get down to the basic facts. □ *Stop messing around and get down to the nitty-gritty.*

**get down to the nuts and bolts** *Fig.* to get down to the basic facts. (See also nuts and bolts.) □ *Stop fooling around. Get down to the nuts and bolts.*

**get down to work** Go to get down to business.

**get** one's **fingers burned** AND **burn** one's **fingers** *Fig.* to receive harm or punishment for one's actions. □ *I had my fingers burned the last time I questioned the company policy.*

**get** one's **foot in the door** *Fig.* to complete the first step in a process. (Fig. on the image of people selling things from door-to-door and blocking the door with a foot so it cannot be closed on them.) □ *I think I could get the job if I could only get my foot in the door.*

**get in(to) the act** *Fig.* to participate in something; to try to be part of whatever is going on. (As if someone were trying to get onstage and participate in a performance.) □ *Everybody wants to get into the act! There is not room here for everyone.*

**get it (all) together** *Fig.* to become fit or organized; to organize one's thinking; to become relaxed and rational. (Fixed order.) □ *Bill seems to be acting more normal now. I think he's getting it all together.*

**get off the dime** *Sl.* to start moving; to get out of a stopped position. □ *As soon as the board of directors gets off the dime on this proposal, we will have some action.*

**get out of** one's **face** *Inf.* to stop bothering or intimidating someone. □ *Look, get out of my face, or I'll poke you in yours!*

**get out of** so's **hair** *Inf.* to stop annoying someone. □ *Will you get out of my hair! You are a real pain!*

**get** sth **out of** one's **system 1.** to get something like food or medicine out of one's body, usually through natural elimination. □ *He'll be more active once he gets the medicine out of his system.* **2.** *Fig.* to be rid of the desire to do something; to do something that you have been wanting to do so that you aren't bothered by wanting to do it anymore. (Fig. on ①.) □ *I bought a new car. I've been wanting to for a long time. I'm glad I finally got that out of my system.* **3.** *Fig.* to do so much of something that one does not want or need to do it anymore. (Fig. on ①.) □ *I got riding roller coasters out of my system when I was young.*

**get** one's **teeth into** sth AND **sink** one's **teeth into** sth; **get** one's **teeth in; sink** one's **teeth in**† *Fig.* to begin to do something; to get completely involved in something. □ *I can't wait to get my teeth into that Wallace job.* □ *Here, sink your teeth into this and see if you can't manage this project.*

**get the kinks (ironed) out** *Fig.* to fix a problem associated with something. □ *That'll be a right nice car, when you get the kinks ironed out in the engine.*

**get the wrinkles out (of** sth) *Fig.* to eliminate some initial, minor problems with an invention, a procedure, a computer program, or a mechanical device. □ *I need more time working with this system to get the wrinkles out.*

**get to first base (with** so/sth) AND **reach first base (with** so/sth) *Fig.* to make a major advance with someone or something. (Fig. on the notion that arrival at first base is the first step to scoring in baseball.) □ *I wish I could get to first base with this business deal.* □ *John adores Sally, but he can't even reach first base with her. She won't even speak to him.*

**get under** so's **skin** *Fig.* to bother or irritate someone. □ *John is so annoying. He really gets under my skin.*

**get up on** one's **hind legs** *Fig.* to get angry and assertive. (Refers to the action of a horse when it is excited or frightened.) □ *She got up on her hind legs and told them all to go to blazes.*

**get with the program** *Fig.* follow the rules; do what you are supposed to do. (Implies that there is a clearly known method or "program" that is usually followed.) □ *Jane just can't seem to get with the program. She has to do everything her way, right or wrong.*

**Getting there is half the fun.** *Fig.* The time spent traveling and the route taken is a major part of the entertainment of the entire journey. (Often sarcastic.) □ *The road is rough, the air-conditioning is broken, and the kids are fighting. Sure, getting there is half the fun!*

a **ghost of a chance** even the slightest chance. (Usually negative.) □ *There is just a ghost of a chance that I'll be there on time.*

**give** so **a red face** *Fig.* to make someone visibly embarrassed. □ *We really gave him a red face when we caught him eavesdropping.*

**Give** one **an inch and** one **will take a mile.** *Fig.* Yield just a small amount to a person and that person will demand even more. □ *When I agreed to pay an advance of 10 percent, he suddenly wanted 25 percent. Give some people an inch and they'll take a mile.*

**give birth to** sth *Fig.* to bring forth a new idea, an invention, a nation, etc. □ *The basic idea of participatory democracy gave birth to a new nation.*

**give currency to** sth *Fig.* to grant acceptance to a story or idea; to believe something. (With a negative if there is doubt about what is said.) □ *His actions gave currency to the rumor that he was about to leave.*

**give free rein to** so AND **give** so **free rein** *Fig.* to allow someone to be completely in charge (of something). □ *The boss gave the manager free rein with the new project.*

**Give it a rest!** *Inf.* Stop talking so much. Give your mouth a rest. □ *Mary: So, I really think we need to discuss things more and go* *over all our differences in detail. Bill: Stop! I've heard enough. Give it a rest!*

**Give me a break!** AND **Gimme a break! 1.** *Inf.* Don't be so harsh to me!; Give me another chance! □ *I'm sorry! I'll do better! Give me a break!* **2.** *Inf.* That is enough, you're bothering me!; Stop it! □ *Do you have to go on and on? Give me a break!* **3.** *Inf.* I don't believe you!; You don't expect anyone to believe that! □ *You say a gorilla is loose in the city? Gimme a break!*

**give the devil his due** AND **give the devil her due** *Fig.* to give your foe proper credit (for something). (This usually refers to a person who has been evil—like the devil.) □ *She's very messy in the kitchen, but I have to give the devil her due. She bakes a terrific cherry pie.*

**give** so **the shirt off** one's **back** *Fig.* to give anything that is asked for, no matter the sacrifice required. □ *You can always count on Mark when you're in trouble. He'd give you the shirt off his back.*

**give** so **up**† **for dead 1.** *Fig.* to give up hope for someone who is dying; to abandon a dying person as already dead. □ *The cowboys gave up their comrade for dead and rode off.* **2.** *Fig.* to abandon hope for someone to appear or arrive. (Fig. on ①.) □ *We were delighted to see you. We had almost given you up for dead.*

**give up the ghost** *Fig. Euph.* to die; [for something] to break down. (Fixed order. Biblical, Acts 12.) □ *The old man gave up the ghost.* □ *My poor old car finally gave up the ghost.*

**gloom and doom** *Fig.* unpleasant predictions, statements, or atmosphere. □ *All we hear these days from the government is gloom and doom. Isn't there any good news?*

a **glutton for punishment** *Fig.* someone who is eager for a burden or some sort of difficulty; someone willing to accept a difficult task. □ *I enjoy managing difficult projects, but I am a glutton for punishment.*

**go begging** *Fig.* to be left over, unwanted, or unused. (As if a thing were begging for an owner or a user.) □ *There is still food left. A whole lobster is going begging. Please eat some more.*

**go by the board** *Fig.* to get ruined or lost. (This is originally a nautical expression meaning "to fall or be washed overboard.") □ *I hate to see good food go by the board. Please eat up so we won't have to throw it out.*

**go cold turkey 1.** to stop taking an addictive drug without tapering off. □ *She tried to break her heroin habit by going cold turkey.* **2.** *Fig.* to stop (doing something) without tapering off. □ *I had to stop eating chocolate, so I went cold turkey. It's awful!*

**go down in flames** *Fig.* to fail spectacularly. □ *Todd went down in flames in his efforts to win the heart of Marsha.*

**go down in the annals of history** AND **go down in the history books** *Fig.* [of sufficient significance] to be recorded in history books. □ *His remarks will go down in the annals of history.*

**go down in the history books** Go to previous.

**go fifty-fifty (on** sth**)** *Fig.* to divide the cost of something in half with someone. □ *Todd and Jean decided to go fifty-fifty on dinner.*

**go from one extreme to the other** *Fig.* to change from one thing to its opposite. □ *You go from one extreme to another about Tom—one day angry, the next day perfectly happy.*

**go haywire** to go wrong; to malfunction; to break down. □ *I was talking to Mary when suddenly the telephone went haywire. I haven't heard from her since.* □ *There we were, driving along, when the engine went haywire. It was two hours before the tow truck came.*

**go home in a box** *Sl.* to be shipped home dead. (Often said in exaggeration.) □ *You had better be careful on this camping trip, or you'll go home in a box.*

**go in one ear and out the other** *Cliché Fig.* [for something] to be heard and then soon ignored or forgotten. □ *Everything I say to you seems to go in one ear and out the other. Why don't you pay attention?*

**go over like a lead balloon** *Fig.* to fail completely; to *go over* badly. □ *Your joke went over like a lead balloon.* □ *Her suggestion went over like a lead balloon.*

**go overboard 1.** to fall out of a boat or off of a ship; to fall overboard. □ *Be careful or you will go overboard.* **2.** *Fig.* to do too much; to be extravagant. □ *Look, Sally, let's have a nice party, but don't go overboard. It doesn't need to be fancy.*

**go stag** *Fig.* to go to an event (which is meant for couples) without a member of the opposite sex. (Originally referred only to males.) □ *Is Tom going to take you, or are you going stag?*

**go through the motions** *Fig.* to make a feeble effort to do something; to do something insincerely or in cursory fashion. □ *Jane isn't doing her best. She's just going through the motions.*

**go through the roof 1.** *Inf.* to become very angry. □ *She saw what had happened and went through the roof.* **2.** *Inf.* [for prices] to become very high. □ *These days, prices for gasoline are going through the roof.*

**go to hell in a bucket** AND **go to hell in a handbasket** *Fig.* to get rapidly worse and worse. □ *His health is going to hell in a handbasket ever since he started drinking again.*

**go to hell in a handbasket** Go to previous.

**go to town** *Inf.* to work hard or very effectively. □ *Look at all those ants working. They are really going to town.*

**go under the knife** *Inf.* to submit to surgery; to have surgery done on oneself. □ *Frank lives in constant fear of having to go under the knife.*

**go whole hog** *Inf.* to do everything possible; to be extravagant. □ *Let's go whole hog. Order steak* and *lobster.*

**going great guns** *Fig.* going fast or energetically. □ *I'm over my cold and going great guns.*

a **gold mine of information** *Fig.* someone or something that is full of information. □ *Grandfather is a gold mine of information about World War I.*

a **golden opportunity** *Fig.* an excellent opportunity that is not likely to be repeated. □ *When I failed to finish college, I missed my golden opportunity to prepare myself for a good job.*

**gone but not forgotten** *Cliché* gone or dead and still remembered. □ *Uncle Harry is gone but not forgotten. The stain where he spilled the wine is still visible in the parlor carpet.*

**gone with the wind** *Fig.* gone as if taken away by the wind. (A phrase made famous by the Margaret Mitchell novel and subsequent film *Gone with the Wind.* The phrase is used to make *gone* have a stronger force.) □ *Everything we worked for was gone with the wind.*

**good riddance (to bad rubbish)** *Cliché* [it is] good to be rid of worthless persons or things. □ *She slammed the door behind me and said, "Good riddance to bad rubbish!"*

**good to go** *Fig.* all ready to go; all checked and pronounced ready to go. □ *Everything's good to go, and we will start immediately.*

a **grandfather clause** *Fig.* a clause in an agreement that protects certain rights granted in the past even when conditions change in the future. □ *The contract contained a grandfather clause that protected my pension payments against claims such as might arise from a future lawsuit.*

**Great balls of fire!** *Inf.* Good heavens!; Wow! □ *Mary got up to play the fiddle, and great balls of fire! That girl can play!*

the **greatest thing since indoor plumbing** AND the **greatest thing since sliced bread** *Rur.* the most wonderful invention or useful item in a long time. □ *As far as I'm concerned, this new food processor is the greatest thing since indoor plumbing.* □ *Joe thinks Sally is the greatest thing since sliced bread. You can tell just by the way he looks at her.*

the **greatest thing since sliced bread** Go to previous.

**the grim reaper** *Fig.* death. □ *I think I have a few years to go yet before the grim reaper pays me a call.*

**grunt work** *Fig.* work that is menial and thankless. □ *I did all of the grunt work on the project, but my boss got all of the credit.*

**gut feeling** AND **gut reaction; gut response** a personal, intuitive feeling or response. □ *I have a gut feeling that something bad is going to happen.*

**gut reaction** Go to previous.

**gut response** Go to gut feeling.

# H

**hail a cab** AND **hail a taxi** *Fig.* to signal to a taxi that you want to be picked up. □ *See if you can hail a cab. I don't want to walk home in the rain.*

**hail a taxi** Go to previous.

**half a loaf** *Fig.* a small or incomplete portion of something. (From the proverb "Half a loaf is better than none.") □ *Why do you think I will be satisfied with half a loaf? I want everything that's due me.*

**hand over fist** *Fig.* [for money and merchandise to be exchanged] very rapidly. □ *What a busy day. We took in money hand over fist.*

**hands-on 1.** *Fig.* concerning a training session where novices learn by actual use of the device—such as a keyboard or control panel—that they are being taught to use. □ *Please plan to attend a hands-on seminar on the new computers next Thursday.* **2.** *Fig.* concerning an executive or manager who participates directly in operations. □ *We expect that he will be the kind of hands-on president we have been looking for.*

**Hang in there.** *Fig.* Be patient, things will work out. □ *Bob: Everything is in such a mess. I can't seem to get things done right. Jane: Hang in there, Bob. Things will work out.*

**hang on (so's) every word** *Cliché* to listen closely or with awe to what someone says. □ *The audience hung on her every word throughout the speech.*

**hang** so **out to dry** *Inf.* to defeat or punish someone. □ *The boss was really angry at Billie. He yelled at him and hung him out to dry.*

**hang tough (on** sth**)** *Sl.* to stick to one's position (on something). □ *I decided I'd hang tough on it. I tend to give in too easy.*

a **happy camper** *Inf.* a happy person. □ *The boss came in this morning and found his hard disk trashed. He was not a happy camper.*

**harp on** so/sth *Fig.* to keep talking or complaining about someone or something; to refer to someone or something again and again. □ *Stop harping on my mistakes and correct your own.*

**hatchet man** *Fig.* a man who does the cruel or difficult things for someone else; someone who does someone else's dirty work. □ *He served as the president's hatchet man and ended up doing all the dirty work.*

**haul off and** do sth **1.** *Fig. Inf.* to draw back and do something, such as strike a person. □ *Max hauled off and poked Lefty in the nose.* **2.** *Rur.* to do something without a great deal of preparation. □ *The old man hauled off and bought himself a house.*

**have a bad attitude** *Fig.* to have a negative outlook on things; to be uncooperative. □ *Perry has a bad attitude and has nothing positive to contribute to the conversation.*

**have a bone to pick (with** so**)** *Fig.* to have a disagreement to discuss with someone; to have something to argue about with someone. □ *Hey, Bill. I've got a bone to pick with you. Where is the money you owe me?*

**have a change of heart** *Fig.* to change one's attitude or decision, usually from a negative to a positive position. □ *I had a change of heart at the last minute and gave the beggar some money.*

**have a close call** Go to next.

**have a close shave** AND **have a close call** *Fig.* to have a narrow escape from something dangerous. □ *What a close shave I had! I nearly fell off the roof when I was working there.*

**have a death wish** *Fig.* to seem to be willing to take all sorts of needless risks. □ *Look at the way that guy drives. He must have some sort of a death wish.*

**have a field day** *Fig.* to experience freedom from one's usual work schedule; to have a very enjoyable time. (As with children who are released from classes to take part in sports and athletic contests.) □ *The air was fresh and clear, and everyone had a field day in the park during the lunch hour.*

**have a good thing going** *Fig.* to have something of an ongoing nature arranged for one's own benefit. □ *John inherited a fortune and doesn't have to work for a living anymore. He's got a good thing going.*

**have a green thumb** *Fig.* to have the ability to grow plants well. □ *Just look at Mr. Simpson's garden. He has a green thumb.*

**have a heart of gold** *Cliché* to be generous, sincere, and friendly. □ *Mary is such a lovely person. She has a heart of gold.*

**have a heart of stone** *Fig.* to be cold and unfriendly. □ *The villain in the play had a heart of stone. He was cruel to everyone.*

**have a hollow leg** *Fig.* to have a great capacity or need for food or drink, usually the latter. □ *Bobby can drink more beer than I can afford. I think he has a hollow leg!*

**have a roving eye** *Euph.* to be flirtatious; to be interested in having sexual relations outside of marriage. (Usually used to describe men.) □ *When they were first married, he had a roving eye.*

**have a sweet tooth** *Fig.* to desire to eat many sweet foods—especially candy and pastries. □ *I have a sweet tooth, and if I don't watch it, I'll really get fat.*

**have a thirst for** sth *Fig.* to have a craving or desire for something. □ *The tyrant had an intense thirst for power.*

**have a way with words** *Fig.* to have talent in the effective or stylish use of words. □ *Ask Perry to make the announcement. He has a way with words.*

**have a whale of a time** *Fig.* to have an exciting or fun time; to have a big time. (*Whale* = big.) □ *We had a whale of a time at Sally's birthday party.*

**have all** one's **marbles** *Inf.* to have all one's mental faculties; to be mentally sound. (Very often with a negative or said to convey doubt.) □ *I don't think he has all his marbles.*

**have all the time in the world** *Fig.* to have a very large amount of time. □ *Don't worry. I can wait. I have all the time in the world.*

**have an ax(e) to grind (with** so**)** *Fig.* to have a problem to discuss or settle with someone; to have a complaint against someone. □ *I need to talk with Chuck. I have an axe to grind with him.*

**have bats in** one's **belfry** *Inf.* to be crazy. □ *You must really have bats in your belfry if you think I'll put up with that kind of stuff.*

**have clean hands** *Fig.* to be guiltless. (As if a guilty person would have dirty or bloody hands.) □ *The police took him in, but let him go after questioning because he had clean hands.*

**have dibs on** sth *Fig.* to reserve something for oneself; to claim something for oneself. (Often said by children.) □ *John has dibs on the last piece again. It isn't fair.*

**have egg on** one's **face** *Fig.* to be embarrassed by something one has done. (As if one went out in public with a dirty face.) □ *I was completely wrong, and now I have egg on my face.*

**have eyes in the back of** one's **head** *Fig.* to seem to be able to sense what is going on behind or outside of one's field of vision. □ *My teacher has eyes in the back of her head.*

have eyes in the back of one's head

**have** one's **finger in too many pies** *Fig.* to be involved in too many things; to have too many tasks going to be able to do any of them well. □ *She never gets anything done because she has her finger in too many pies.*

**have friends in high places** *Fig.* to have influential and powerful friends. □ *You can't put me in jail! I have friends in high places! Do you know who you are dealing with?*

**have (got)** one's **mind in the gutter** *Inf.* tending to think of or say things that are obscene. □ *Why do you tell so many dirty jokes? Do you always have your mind in the gutter?*

**have** one's **head in the clouds** *Fig.* to be unaware of what is going on because of fantasies or daydreams. □ *She walks around all day with her head in the clouds. She must be in love.*

**have** one's **heart in** one's **mouth** *Fig.* to feel strongly emotional about someone or something. □ *I had my heart in my mouth when I heard the national anthem.*

**have** one's **heart stand still** *Fig.* an expression said when one's heart (figuratively) stops beating because one is shocked or feeling strong emotions. □ *I had my heart stand still once when I was overcome with joy.*

**have it both ways** *Fig.* to have both of two incompatible things. □ *John wants the security of marriage and the freedom of being single. He wants to have it both ways.*

**have kittens** to get extremely upset. □ *My mother pretty near had kittens when she found out I got fired.*

**have more luck than sense** *Fig.* to be lucky but not intelligent. □ *Jane went driving out into Death Valley without any water. She survived—she has more luck than sense.*

**have** one's **nose in a book** *Fig.* to be reading a book; to read books all the time. □ *His nose is always in a book. He never gets any exercise.*

**have one foot in the grave** *Fig.* to be almost dead. □ *I was so sick, I felt as if I had one foot in the grave.*

**have one in the oven** *Fig.* to be pregnant with a child. □ *She's got three kids now and one in the oven.*

**have seen better days** *Euph.* to be in bad condition. □ *My old car has seen better days, but at least it's still running.*

**have sticky fingers** *Fig.* to have a tendency to steal. □ *The little boy had sticky fingers and was always taking his father's small change.*

**have the shoe on the other foot** *Fig.* to experience the opposite situation (from a previous situation). □ *I used to be a student, and now I'm the teacher. Now I have the shoe on the other foot.*

**have two left feet** *Fig.* to be very awkward with one's feet. (Often refers to awkwardness at dancing.) □ *I'm sorry I can't dance better. I have two left feet.*

**have** one's **wires crossed** *Fig.* to have one's mental processes in disarray; to be confused. □ *You don't know what you are talking about. You've really got your wires crossed!*

**head for the last roundup** *Euph.* to reach the end of usefulness or of life. (Originally said of a dying cowboy.) □ *This ballpoint pen is headed for the last roundup. I have to get another one.*

**heads or tails** *Fig.* either the face of a coin or the other side of a coin. (Often used in an act of coin tossing, where one circumstance is valid if the front of a coin appears and another circumstance is valid if the other side appears.) □ *Jim looked at Jane as he flipped the coin into the air. "Heads or tails?" he asked.*

**heads will roll** *Fig.* people will get into severe trouble. (Fig. on the image of executions involving beheadings.) □ *Heads will roll when the principal sees the damaged classroom.*

a **heartbeat away from being** sth *Cliché* set to be the next ruler upon the final heartbeat of the current ruler. (The decisive heartbeat would be the current ruler's last heartbeat.) □ *The vice president is just a heartbeat away from being president.*

**hedge** one's **bets** *Fig.* to reduce one's loss on a bet or on an investment by counterbalancing the loss in some way. □ *John bought some stock and then bet Mary that the stock would go down in value in one year. He has hedged his bets perfectly. If the stock goes up, he sells it, pays off Mary, and still makes a profit. If it goes down, he reduces his loss by winning the bet he made with Mary.*

a **hell of a mess** *Inf.* a terrible mess or situation. □ *This is really a hell of a mess you've gotten us into.*

a **hell of a note** *Inf.* a surprising or amazing piece of news. □ *So you're just going to leave me like that? Well, that's a hell of a note!*

**Hell's bells (and buckets of blood)!** *Inf.* an exclamation of anger or surprise. □ *Bill: Well, Jane, looks like you just flunked calculus. Jane: Hell's bells and buckets of blood! What do I do now?*

**hem and haw (around)** *Inf.* to be uncertain about something; to be evasive; to say "ah" and "eh" when speaking—avoiding saying something meaningful. □ *Stop hemming and hawing around. I want an answer.*

a **hidden agenda** *Fig.* a secret plan; a concealed plan; a plan disguised as a plan with another purpose. □ *I am sure that the chairman has a hidden agenda. I never did trust him anyway.*

**hide** one's **light under a bushel** *Fig.* to conceal one's good ideas or talents. (A biblical theme.) □ *Jane has some good ideas, but she doesn't speak very often. She hides her light under a bushel.*

**high man on the totem pole** *Fig.* the person at the top of the hierarchy; the person in charge of an organization. □ *I don't want to talk to a vice president. I demand to talk to the high man on the totem pole.*

**highways and byways 1.** major and minor roads. □ *The city council voted to plant new trees along all the highways and byways of the town.* **2.** *Cliché* routes and pathways, both major and minor. □ *I hope I meet you again someday on life's highways and byways.*

**history in the making** *Fig.* history being made right at this moment. □ *This is a very important conference with an important vote to be taken. We are witnessing history in the making.*

**hit the (broad) side of a barn** *Fig.* to hit an easy target. (Usually negative.) □ *He can't park that car! He can't hit the broad side of a barn, let alone that parking place.*

**hit the high spots** *Fig.* to do only the important, obvious, or good things. □ *I won't discuss the entire report. I'll just hit the high spots.*

**hit the jackpot 1.** *Fig.* to win a large amount of money gambling or in a lottery. □ *I hit the jackpot in the big contest.* **2.** *Fig.* to be exactly right; to find exactly what was sought. (Fig. on ①.) □ *I hit the jackpot when I found this little cafe on Fourth Street.*

**hit the nail (right) on the head** *Fig.* to do exactly the right thing; to do something in the most effective and efficient way.

a **hive of activity** *Fig.* a location where things are very busy. □ *The hotel lobby was a hive of activity each morning.*

**hold** one's **breath** *Fig.* to wait or delay until something special happens. (Usually in the negative.) □ *I expect the mail to be delivered soon, but I'm not holding my breath. It's often late.* □ *He said he would be here by now, but don't hold your breath.*

**hold** one's **liquor** *Fig.* to be able to drink alcohol in quantity without ill effects. □ *I asked him to leave because he can't hold his liquor.*

**hold** one's **nose 1.** *Fig.* to use one's fingers to keep one's nose closed to avoid a bad smell or to keep water out. **2.** *Fig.* to attempt to ignore something unpleasant, illegal, or "rotten." (Fig. on ①.) □ *He hated doing it, but he held his nose and made the announcement everyone dreaded.*

**hold out the olive branch** *Fig.* to offer to end a dispute and be friendly; to offer reconciliation. (The olive branch is a symbol of peace and reconciliation. A biblical reference.) □ *Jill was the first to hold out the olive branch after our argument.*

**hold** one's **tongue** *Fig.* to refrain from speaking; to refrain from saying something unpleasant. □ *I felt like scolding her, but I held my tongue.*

a **hole in the wall** *Fig.* a tiny shop, room, etc. not much wider than its doorway. □ *His office is just a hole in the wall.*

**The honeymoon is over.** The early pleasant beginning (as at the start of a marriage) has ended. □ *Okay, the honeymoon is over. It's time to settle down and do some hard work.* □ *I knew the honeymoon was over at my new job when they started yelling at me to work faster.*

**hoodwink** so **into** sth *Fig.* to deceive someone into doing something. □ *She will try to hoodwink you into driving her to the airport. Watch out.*

**hoodwink** so **out of** sth *Fig.* to get something away from someone by deception. □ *Spike tried to hoodwink the old lady out of all her money.*

a **hop, skip, and a jump** *Fig.* a short distance. □ *Bill lives just a hop, skip, and a jump from here. We can be there in two minutes.*

a **horse of a different color** Go to next.

**a horse of another color** AND a **horse of a different color** *Fig.* another matter altogether. □ *I was talking about trees, not bushes. Bushes are a horse of another color.*

**hot and bothered 1.** *Fig.* excited; anxious. □ *Now don't get hot and bothered. Take it easy.* **2.** *Fig.* amorous; interested in romance or sex. □ *John gets hot and bothered whenever Mary comes into the room.*

**hot under the collar** *Fig.* very angry. □ *The boss was really hot under the collar when you told him you lost the contract.* □ *I get hot under the collar every time I think about it.*

a **house of cards** *Fig.* a fantasy; an imaginary scenario. (Fig. on the image of a structure built out of playing cards stacked on edge.) □ *That means that all my ideas for the future were nothing more than a house of cards.*

**how the other half lives** *Fig.* how poorer people live; how richer people live. □ *Now that I am bankrupt, I am beginning to understand how the other half lives.*

**hum with activity** *Fig.* [for a place] to be busy with activity. □ *Our main office was humming with activity during the busy season.*

**hunt-and-peck** *Fig.* a slow "system" of typing where one searches for a certain key and then presses it. (Fig. on the image of the movement used by fowls when feeding.) □ *I can't type. I just hunt and peck, but I get the job done—eventually.*

**hush money** *Fig.* money paid as a bribe to persuade someone to remain silent and not reveal certain information. □ *Bob gave his younger sister hush money so that she wouldn't tell Jane that he had gone to the movies with Sue.*

**hustle and bustle** *Fig.* confusion and business. □ *There is a lot of hustle and bustle in this office at the end of the fiscal year.*

**I could eat a horse!** *Fig.* I am very hungry! □ *Where's dinner? I could eat a horse!*

**I hate to eat and run.** *Cliché* an apology made by someone who must leave a social event soon after eating. □ *Bill: Well, I hate to eat and run, but it's getting late. Sue: Oh, you don't have to leave, do you? Bill: I think I really must.*

**I wouldn't touch it with a ten-foot pole.** *Cliché* I would not have anything to do with it under any circumstances. (Said about something you think is untrustworthy, as in the example, or in response to a remark that seems to invite a nasty reply. The British version is "I would not touch it with a barge-pole.") □ *Jill: This advertisement says I can buy land in Florida for a small investment. Do you think I should? Jane: I wouldn't touch it with a ten-foot pole.*

the **icing on the cake** *Fig.* an extra enhancement. □ *Oh, wow! A tank full of gas in my new car. That's icing on the cake!*

**if you get my drift** *Fig.* if you understand what I am saying or implying. □ *I've heard enough talk and seen enough inaction—if you get my drift.*

**Ignorance is bliss.** *Fig.* Not knowing is better than knowing and worrying. □ *A: I never knew that the kid who mows our lawn has been in trouble with the police. B: Ignorance is bliss!*

**I'll be a monkey's uncle!** *Fig.* I am amazed! □ *A: I just won $500,000 in the lottery! B: Well, I'll be a monkey's uncle!*

I'll eat my hat

**I'll eat my hat.** *Fig.* I will be very surprised. (Used to express strong disbelief in something.) □ *If Joe really joins the Army, I'll eat my hat.*

**I'm good. 1.** I have enough, thanks. (Said to a host or server when asked if one has enough food or drink.) □ *Q: Would you like some more cheese? A: I'm good.* **2.** I'm fine.; I'm okay. (Said in response to "How are you?" or equivalent. A few decades ago, the answer would have been "I'm well." *I'm good.* = I'm virtuous.) □ *Q: How're you? A: I'm good.*

**I'm with you.** *Fig.* I agree with you.; I will join with you in doing what you suggest. (With a stress on both *I* and *you*.) □ *Sally: I think this old bridge is sort of dangerous. Jane: I'm with you. Let's go back another way.*

**in a dead heat** *Fig.* [finishing a race] at exactly the same time; tied. □ *The two horses finished the race in a dead heat.*

***in a (pretty) pickle** *Fig.* in a mess; in trouble. (*Pickle* is used here in the sense of pickling solution or the fluid in which pickles are made. Being in a pickle of this type is viewed as unpleasant if not painful. Shakespeare referred to this kind of pickling [without the *pretty*] in *The Tempest*, Act 5, Scene 1, and *Antony and Cleopatra*, Act 2, Scene 5. The use in *Antony and Cleopatra* is almost literal. Now it is used only figuratively. *Typically: **be** ~; **get [into]** ~.) □ *John has gotten himself into a pickle. He has two dates for the party.*

***in a rut** *Fig.* in a type of boring habitual behavior. (As when the wheels of a buggy travel in the ruts worn into the ground by other buggies, making it easiest to go exactly the way all the other buggies have gone before. *Typically: **be** ~; **be stuck** ~; **get [into]** ~.) □ *My life has gotten in a rut.* □ *I'm really tired of being stuck in a rut!*

***in a stew (about** so/sth**)** *Fig.* upset or bothered about someone or something. (*Typically: **be** ~; **get [into]** ~.) □ *Now, now. Don't get in a stew. She'll be back when she gets hungry.*

***in a vicious circle** *Fig.* in a situation in which the solution of one problem leads to a second problem, and the solution of the second problem brings back the first problem, etc. (*Typically: **be** ~; **get [into]** ~.) □ *Life is so strange. I seem to be in a vicious circle most of the time.*

***in an ivory tower** *Fig.* in a place, such as a university, where one can be aloof from the realities of living. (*Typically: **be** ~; **dwell** ~; **live** ~; **work** ~.) □ *If you didn't spend so much time in your ivory tower, you'd know what people really think!*

***in apple-pie order** *Fig.* in very good order; very well organized. (*Typically: **be** ~; **get** sth ~; **put** sth ~.) □ *Please put everything in apple-pie order before you leave.*

**in bed with** so *Fig.* in close association with someone. □ *Now that John's in bed with our competitor, we are losing old clients weekly.*

*__in__ one's **birthday suit** *Fig.* naked; nude. (In the "clothes" in which one was born. *Typically: **be** ~; **get [into]** ~.) □ *We used to go down to the river and swim in our birthday suits.*

**in** one's **crosshairs** *Fig.* on one's agenda for immediate action; being studied for action at this moment. (Refers to the crosshairs of a gun sight.) □ *I recognize that the problem exists, and I have it in my crosshairs as we speak.*

**in** one's **cups** *Euph.* drunk. □ *The speaker—who was in his cups—could hardly be understood.*

**in denial** *Fig.* in a state of refusing to believe something that is true. □ *Mary was in denial about her illness and refused treatment.*

**in dribs and drabs** *Inf.* in small portions; bit by bit. □ *The whole story is being revealed in dribs and drabs.*

**in fear and trembling** *Cliché* with anxiety or fear; with dread. □ *In fear and trembling, I went into the room to take the test.*

**in fine feather 1.** *Fig.* well dressed; of an excellent appearance. (Fig. on the image of a bird that has clean, bright, and flawless feathers.) □ *Well, you are certainly in fine feather today.* **2.** *Fig.* in good form; in good spirits. (Fig. on ①.) □ *Mary was really in fine feather tonight. Her concert was great!*

*__in__ **good company** with lots of companions; in a group of people with similar experiences. (Expresses the notion that "you are not the only one." *Typically: **be** ~; **find** oneself **in** ~.) □ *So, your taxes went up this year also. Well, you're in good company. Everyone I know has the same problem.*

**in high dudgeon** *Fig.* feeling or exhibiting great resentment; taking great offense at something. □ *After the rude remarks, the person who was insulted left in high dudgeon.*

**in hog heaven** *Fig.* very happy; having a wonderful time. □ *Jane loves to quilt, so she was in hog heaven when they opened that new store for quilters.*

**in** so's **infinite wisdom** AND **in its infinite wisdom; in their infinite wisdom** *Fig.* according to some kind of knowledge of which most people are ignorant. (Usually sarcastic, referring to someone's bad or silly decision.) □ *The board, in its infinite wisdom, has decided to give us two fewer holidays this year.*

**in less than no time** *Fig.* very quickly. □ *Don't worry. This won't take long. It'll be over with in less than no time.*

**in** one's **mind's eye** *Fig.* in one's mind or imagination. (Fig. on visualizing something in one's mind.) □ *In my mind's eye, I can see trouble ahead.*

***in mint condition** *Fig.* in perfect condition. (*Typically: **be** ~; **find** sth ~.) □ *This is a fine car. It runs well and is in mint condition.*

**in my humble opinion** *Cliché* a phrase introducing the speaker's opinion. □ *"In my humble opinion," began Fred, arrogantly, "I have achieved what no one else ever could."*

**in** some **neck of the woods** *Rur.* in some vicinity or neighborhood; in some remote place. (The *some* is usually *this, that, your, their,* etc.) □ *I think that the Smiths live in your neck of the woods.*

***in on the ground floor** *Fig.* involved at the very beginning of something. (Fig. on the image of people riding in an elevator that got increasingly crowded as it ascended. You will be able to get in most easily at the lowest level. *Typically: **be** ~; **get** ~; **let** so ~.) □ *Invest now so you can get in on the ground floor.*

***in orbit 1.** [of something] circling a heavenly body. (*Typically: **be** ~; **put** sth **[into]** ~.) □ *The moon is in orbit around the earth.* □ *They put the satellite into orbit.* **2.** *Inf.* ecstatic; thrilled; emotionally high. (*Typically: **be** ~.) □ *John went into orbit when he* *got the check in the mail.* **3.** *Inf.* intoxicated. □ *After having six drinks all to herself, Julie was in orbit.*

**in point of fact** *Fig.* just to point out a fact; in fact. □ *In point of fact, I am not late. You are simply way too early.*

**in private** *Fig.* privately; without others present. □ *I enjoy spending the evening in private.*

**in rare form 1.** *Fig.* well-tuned for a good performance; at one's best. □ *The goalie is in rare form today; that's his third great save already.* **2.** *Inf.* intoxicated. □ *Gert is in rare form, but she'll have time to sleep it off.*

**in seventh heaven** *Fig.* in a very happy state. □ *Ann was really in seventh heaven when she got a car of her own.*

**in** so else's **shoes** AND **in** so else's **place** *Fig.* seeing or experiencing something from someone else's point of view. □ *You might feel different if you were in her shoes.*

**in so many words** *Fig.* exactly; explicitly; in plain, clear language. □ *I told her in so many words to leave me alone.*

**in stitches** *Fig.* laughing very hard. □ *Charlie had us in stitches with all his jokes.*

**in the ballpark** *Fig.* within prescribed limits; within the anticipated range of possibilities. (Fig. on an enclosed baseball field where a struck ball may remain in the ballpark for further play or be hit out of the park.) □ *Your figures are in the ballpark, so we can continue our negotiations.*

**\*in the boondocks** AND **\*in the boonies** *Inf.* in a rural area; far away from a city or population. (*Typically: **be** ~; **camp** ~; **live** ~; **stay** ~.) □ *Perry lives out in the boonies with his parents.*

**in the boonies** Go to previous.

**in the can** [of a finished film] completely edited and ready to be duplicated for distribution and projection. □ *I won't feel good about this film until it's in the can.*

**\*in the cards** *Fig.* in the future. (\*Typically: **be** ~; **see** sth ~.) □ *Well, what do you think is in the cards for tomorrow?* □ *I asked the boss if there was a raise in the cards for me.*

**\*in the dark (about** so/sth**)** *Fig.* uninformed about someone or something; ignorant about someone or something. (\*Typically: **be** ~; **keep** so ~; **leave** so ~; **stay** ~.) □ *I'm in the dark about who is in charge around here.* □ *I can't imagine why they are keeping me in the dark.*

**\*in the doghouse** *Fig.* in trouble; in (someone's) disfavor. (\*Typically: **be** ~; **get** ~; **find** oneself ~; **put** so [into] ~.) □ *I'm really in the doghouse with my boss. I was late for an appointment.*

**in the driver's seat** *Fig.* in control; in charge of things. (As if one were driving and controlling the vehicle.) □ *Now that Fred is in the driver's seat, there is a lot less criticism about how things are being done.*

**\*in the (home)stretch** *Fig.* in the last stage of a process. (From horse racing. \*Typically: **be** ~; **get** ~.) □ *We're in the homestretch with this project and can't change it now.* □ *We're in the stretch. Only three more days till we graduate.*

**in the lap of luxury** *Cliché* in luxurious surroundings. □ *John lives in the lap of luxury because his family is very wealthy.*

**\*in the middle of nowhere** *Fig.* in a very remote place. (\*Typically: **be (out)** ~; **drive** [into] ~; **put** so/sth [into] ~.) □ *To get to my house, you have to drive into the middle of nowhere.* □ *We found a nice place to eat, but it's out in the middle of nowhere.*

**in the money 1.** *Fig.* wealthy. □ *John is really in the money. He's worth millions.* **2.** *Fig.* in the winning position in a race or contest. (As if one had won the prize money. In horse racing the top three finishers can pay off on bets.) □ *The horses coming in first, second, and third are said to be in the money.*

**\*in the pink (of condition)** AND **\*in the pink (of health)** *Fig.* in very good health; in very good condition, physically and emotionally. (\*Typically: **be** ~**; get [into]** ~.) □ *He recovered completely from his surgery and has been in the pink ever since.* □ *She was lively and active and in the pink of condition.*

**in the pink (of health)** Go to previous.

**\*in the pipeline** *Fig.* backed up somewhere in a process; in process; in a queue. (\*Typically: **be** ~**; get** sth **[into]** ~.) □ *There's a lot of goods still in the pipeline. That means no more new orders will be shipped for a while.*

**in the prime of (**one's**) life** *Fig.* in the best and most productive and healthy period of life. □ *He was struck down by a heart attack in the prime of life.*

**in the right place at the right time** in the location where something good is to happen exactly when it happens. □ *I got a good deal on a car because I was in the right place at the right time.*

**in the same league as** so/sth AND **in the same league with** so/sth *Fig.* in the same [good] class or grouping as someone or something else. □ *You are simply not in the same league with the other players, who practice every day.* □ *This wine isn't in the same league as the domestic equivalent.*

**\*in the swim of things** *Fig.* involved in or participating in events or happenings. (\*Typically: **be** ~**; get [into]** ~.) □ *I've been ill, but soon I'll be back in the swim of things.* □ *I can't wait to settle down and get into the swim of things.*

**in the worst way 1.** *Fig.* very much. □ *Bob wants to retire in the worst way.* **2.** in a manner that is the worst possible. (This is an ambiguity that is exploited in joking.) □ *He wanted to retire in the worst way, so he got himself fired. What could be worse?*

**\*in tune with** so/sth **1.** in musical harmony with someone or something; playing or singing the exact same note as someone or something. (\*Typically: **be** ~**; get** ~.) □ *The violin is in tune with the piano.* **2.** *Fig.* in agreement with someone or something. (Fig. on

①. *Typically: **be** ~; **get** ~.) □ *Bill is just not in tune with the company's policies.*

**in two shakes of a lamb's tail** *Fig.* in a very short time; very quickly. □ *Jane returned in two shakes of a lamb's tail.*

*an **inkling (about** so/sth) *Fig.* an idea about someone or something; a hint about the nature of someone or something. (*Typically: **get** ~; **have** ~; **give** so ~.) □ *I had an inkling about the problems that you were going to run into.*

**the ins and outs (of** sth) *Fig.* the correct and successful way to do something; the special things that one needs to know to do something. □ *I don't understand the ins and outs of politics.*

**inside the box** *Fig.* **1.** as if bound by old, nonfunctional, or limiting structures, rules, or practices. (Adverbial. Compare this with **outside the box.**) □ *If you keep your discussions inside the box, you will be bound by traditional limitations.* **2.** bound by old, nonfunctional, or limiting structures, rules, or practices. (Usually **inside-the-box**; adjectival.) □ *You have some really inside-the-box ideas, Ralph. Why not be more creative?*

**in(to)** so's **clutches** *Fig.* in the control of someone who has power or authority over someone else. □ *Snow White fell into the clutches of the evil witch.*

***into overdrive** *Fig.* to pick up speed and energy. (*Typically: **go** ~; **move** ~; **shift** ~.) □ *We go into overdrive around here just before school starts. It's our busiest time.*

One **is known by the company** one **keeps.** one is thought to have the same character and qualities as the people one associates with. (Proverbial or cautionary, warning that someone is associating with bad company.) □ *Bill, who are those people? They don't look at all savory. You are known by the company you keep.*

**Is that** some quality **or what?** Isn't that something good, such as great, wonderful, yummy, super, jazzy, etc.?; That is really "some quality." □ *Is that delicious or what?* □ *Why does she say "Is that* *great or what?" when just saying "That is really great!" would sound less flighty?*

**It cuts two ways.** *Inf.* There are two sides to the situation. □ *It cuts two ways, you know. It can't always all be my fault.*

**It takes all kinds (to make a world).** *Fig.* There are many different kinds of people, and you should not condemn them for being different. □ *Child: Mommy, I saw a weird man today. He was walking down the street singing real loud. I wish they'd put weird people like that away. Mother: Now, now, honey, it takes all kinds to make a world.*

**(It) takes one to know one.** *Inf.* You are one also. □ *A: You are a stupid oaf. B: So are you. It takes one to know one.*

**It won't wash!** *Fig.* Nobody will believe it! □ *Sorry, it won't wash. Try another approach.*

**It'll all come out in the wash.** *Fig.* It does not matter.; No lasting damage has been done. □ *Tom: I feel so bad about what I said to Bill. I don't think he'll ever forgive me. Mary: Oh, don't worry. It'll all come out in the wash.*

**It'll be a cold day in hell when** sth happens. *Inf.* something will never happen or is highly unlikely. □ *It'll be a cold day in hell when the city council agrees on where to build that bridge.*

**It'll never fly.** *Fig.* It will never work!; It will never be approved! (Refers originally to an evaluation of an unlikely looking aircraft of some type.) □ *I have read your report and studied your proposal. It'll never fly.*

**It's a jungle out there.** The real world is severe.; It's hard to get by in everyday life. □ *A: Gee, people are so rude in this town. B: Yup, it's a jungle out there.*

**it's high time** *Inf.* it is about the right time for something. □ *It's high time you started thinking about saving for your old age.*

**(It's) not half bad.** *Fig.* It's not as bad as one might have thought. □ *Mary: How do you like this play? Jane: Not half bad.*

**It's six of one, half a dozen of another.** *Cliché* Two options are equivalent. □ *To get downtown, we can either take the highway or the side streets. It's six of one, half a dozen of another, since both routes take the same amount of time.*

**It's written all over** one's **face.** *Fig.* It is very evident and can easily be detected when looking at someone's face. □ *I know she's guilty. It's written all over her face.*

**It's you!** *Fig.* It suits you perfectly.; It is just your style. □ *John (trying on a jacket): How does this look? Sally: It's you!*

**It's your funeral.** *Fig.* If that is what you are going to do, you will have to endure the dire consequences. □ *Tom: I'm going to call in sick and go to the ball game instead of to work today. Mary: Go ahead. It's your funeral.*

**(I've) seen better.** *Fig.* a noncommittal and not very positive judgment about something or someone. □ *Alice: How did you like the movie? John: I've seen better.*

**(I've) seen worse.** *Fig.* a noncommittal and not totally negative judgment about something or someone. □ *Alice: How did you like the movie? John: I've seen worse.*

**jack of all trades** someone who can do several different jobs instead of specializing in one. □ *John can do plumbing, carpentry, and roofing—a real jack of all trades.*

**Jekyll and Hyde** *Fig.* someone with both an evil and a good personality. (From the novel *The Strange Case of Dr. Jekyll and Mr. Hyde* by Robert Louis Stevenson.) □ *Bill thinks Mary is so soft and gentle, but she can be very cruel—she is a real Jekyll and Hyde.*

**jockey for position 1.** to work one's horse into a desired position in a horse race. □ *Ken was behind but jockeying for position.* **2.** *Inf.* to work oneself into a desired position. (Fig. on ①.) □ *The candidates were jockeying for position, trying to get the best television exposure.*

**jog** so's **memory** *Fig.* to stimulate someone's memory to recall something. □ *Hearing the first part of the song I'd forgotten really jogged my memory.*

**Join the club!** *Inf.* an expression indicating that the person spoken to is in the same, or a similar, unfortunate state as the speaker. □ *You don't have any place to stay? Join the club! Neither do we.* □ *Did you get fired too? Join the club!*

**jump ship 1.** *Fig.* to leave one's job on a ship and fail to be aboard it when it sails; [for a sailor] to go AWOL. □ *One of the deck hands jumped ship at the last port.* **2.** *Fig.* to leave any post or position; to quit or resign, especially when there is difficulty with the job. □ *None of the editors liked the new policies, so they all jumped ship as soon as other jobs opened up.*

**jump the gun** *Fig.* to start before the starting signal. (Originally used in sports contests that are started by firing a gun.) □ *We all had to start the race again because Jane jumped the gun.*

**jump through a hoop** AND **jump through hoops** *Fig.* to do everything possible to obey or please someone. (Trained circus animals jump through hoops.) □ *What do you want me to do— jump through a hoop?*

The **jury is still out on (so/sth).** *Fig.* A decision has not been reached on someone or something.; The people making the decision on someone or something have not yet decided. □ *The jury is still out on Jane. We don't know what we are going to do about her.*

**just** one's **cup of tea** *Fig.* to be something that one prefers or desires. □ *This spy novel is just my cup of tea.*

**just fell off the turnip truck** *Rur.* ignorant; unsophisticated. □ *He stood there gawking at the buildings in town like he just fell off the turnip truck.*

**(just) taking care of business** *Fig.* doing what I am supposed to do; an answer to the question "What are you doing lately?" (Also abbreviated T.C.B.) □ *Look, officer, I'm just standing here, taking care of business, and this guy comes up and slugs me.*

**just the ticket** *Fig.* to be just the perfect thing. □ *I'm tired! A good, hot cup of coffee will be just the ticket.*

**just what the doctor ordered** *Fig.* exactly what is required, especially for health or comfort. □ *That meal was delicious, Bob. Just what the doctor ordered.*

# K

a **kangaroo court** a bogus or illegal court. □ *I've heard enough accusations! Is this a staff meeting or a kangaroo court?*

**Katie bar the door.** Prepare immediately for an advancing threat. □ *Katie bar the door, the grandchildren are here and they all look hungry.*

**keep a civil tongue (in** one's **head)** *Fig.* to speak decently and politely. □ *Please, John. Don't talk like that. Keep a civil tongue in your head.*

**keep a tight rein on** so/sth AND **keep a close rein on** so/sth *Fig.* to watch and control someone or something diligently. (Fig. on the idea of controlling a horse by a tight grip on the reins.) □ *The office manager kept a tight rein on the staff.* □ *Mary keeps a close rein on her children.*

**keep at arm's length from** so/sth AND **keep** so/sth **at arm's length** *Fig.* to retain a degree of physical or social remoteness from someone or something. □ *I try to keep at arm's length from Larry since our disagreement.*

**keep banker's hours** *Fig.* to work or be open for business for less than eight hours a day. □ *The advertising agency keeps banker's hours. They are open only until 4:00.*

**keep body and soul together** *Fig.* to manage to keep existing, especially when one has very little money. □ *I don't earn enough money to keep body and soul together.*

**keep** one's **chin up** *Fig.* to keep one's spirits high; to act brave and confident. □ *Keep your chin up, John. Things will get better.*

**keep** one's **eye on the ball 1.** *Fig.* to watch or follow the ball carefully, especially when one is playing a ball game; to follow the details of a ball game very carefully. □ *John, if you can't keep your eye on the ball, I'll have to take you out of the game.* **2.** *Fig.* to remain alert to the events occurring around oneself. (Fig. on ①.) □ *If you want to get along in this office, you're going to have to keep your eye on the ball.*

**keep in good with** so *Fig.* to remain in someone's favor. □ *I always try to keep in good with the boss's secretary.*

**Keep in there!** *Inf.* Keep trying! □ *Andy: Don't give up, Sally. Keep in there! Sally: I'm doing my best!*

**keep it down (to a dull roar)** *Fig.* to keep quiet or as quiet as possible. □ *Please try to keep it down to a dull roar, could you?*

**keep late hours** *Fig.* to stay up or stay out until very late at night. (Does not refer to arriving late to work in the morning. It refers to the *cause* of being late in the morning.) □ *I'm always tired because I keep late hours.* □ *If I didn't keep late hours, I wouldn't sleep so late in the morning and I wouldn't be late for work.*

**keep** one's **nose out of** sth *Fig.* to stay out of something, such as someone else's business. □ *Try to keep your nose out of stuff that doesn't concern you.* □ *Keep your nose out of my personal affairs.*

**keep** one's **nose to the grindstone** *Fig.* to work hard and constantly. □ *Mary kept her nose to the grindstone while her friends were out enjoying themselves.*

**keep** one's **own counsel** *Fig.* to keep one's thoughts and plans to oneself; to withhold from other people one's thoughts and plans. □ *Jane is very quiet. She tends to keep her own counsel.*

**keep** so **posted** *Fig.* to keep someone informed (of what is happening); to keep someone up-to-date. □ *If the price of corn goes up, I need to know. Please keep me posted.*

**keep** one's **powder dry** *Fig.* to save one's most powerful argument, evidence, threat, etc. [for the most opportune time]. □ *It will be a bitter divorce proceeding, and you should let her blow off steam while you keep your powder dry.*

**keep** one's **shirt on** *Fig.* to be patient. □ *Wait a minute! Keep your shirt on!* □ *Tell him to keep his shirt on.*

**keep the peace** to maintain a truce; to keep things peaceful. □ *We are doing what we can to keep the peace, but the rebels say they will attack again.*

**keep the wolf from the door** *Fig.* to maintain oneself at a minimal level; to keep from starving, freezing, etc. □ *We have a small amount of money saved, hardly enough to keep the wolf from the door.*

**Keep this to yourself.** *Fig.* a phrase introducing something that is meant to be a secret. (Notice the unique use of *but*.) □ *Andy: Keep this to yourself, but I'm going to Bora Bora on my vacation. Henry: Sounds great. Can I go too?*

**keep up appearances** *Fig.* to make things look all right whether they are or not. □ *We must keep up appearances even if it means little sacrifices here and there.*

**keep up with the Joneses** *Fig.* to try to match the lifestyle of one's neighbors. □ *I am tired of trying to keep up with the Joneses. Let's just move if we can't afford to live here.*

**keep up with the times** *Fig.* to try to appear contemporary and fashionable; to learn about contemporary ways of doing things. □ *I am too old-fashioned. I have to keep up with the times better.*

**Keep your chin up.** *Fig.* an expression of encouragement to someone who has to bear some emotional burdens. (Fixed order.) □ *Fred: I really can't take much more of this. Jane: Keep your chin up. Things will get better.*

**kick** one's **heels up**† *Fig.* to act frisky; to be lively and have fun. (Somewhat literal when said of hoofed animals.) □ *For an old man, your uncle is really kicking his heels up.*

a **kick in the guts** *Fig. Sl.* a severe blow to one's body or spirit. □ *The news was a kick in the guts, and I haven't recovered yet.*

**kill the fatted calf** *Fig.* to prepare an elaborate banquet (in someone's honor). (From the biblical story recounting the return of the prodigal son.) □ *Sorry this meal isn't much, John. We didn't have time to kill the fatted calf.*

**kill two birds with one stone** *Fig.* to solve two problems at one time with a single action. □ *I have to cash a check and make a payment on my bank loan. I'll kill two birds with one stone by doing them both in one trip to the bank.*

**kill** so **with kindness** *Fig.* to be enormously kind to someone. □ *You are just killing me with kindness. Why?*

\*a **king's ransom** *Fig.* a great deal of money. (To pay an amount as large as one might have to pay to get back a king held for ransom. \*Typically: **cost** ~; **pay** ~; **spend** ~.) □ *I would like to buy a nice watch, but I don't want to pay a king's ransom for it.*

**kiss** so's **ass** *Fig. Sl.* to fawn over someone; to flatter and curry favor with someone. □ *What does he expect me to do? Kiss his ass?*

the **kiss of death** *Fig.* an act that puts an end to someone or something. □ *The mayor's veto was the kiss of death for the new law.*

**kissing cousins** *Fig.* relatives who know one another well enough to kiss when they meet. □ *Technically, we're second cousins once removed, but I just say we're kissing cousins.*

a **knee-jerk reaction** *Fig.* an automatic or reflex reaction; an immediate reaction made without examining causes or facts. □ *With one of his typical knee-jerk reactions, he said no immediately, citing some moral argument that no one understood.*

a **knight in shining armor** *Fig.* a person, usually male, who rescues or assists a person in need of help. □ *I was stalled in the interstate for an hour until a knight in shining armor came along and gave me some help.*

**knock** one's **head (up) against a brick wall** *Fig.* to be totally frustrated. (Fig. on the image of someone banging his head against a wall in frustration.) □ *Trying to get a raise around here is like knocking your head up against a brick wall.*

**knock** sth **off**[†] **1.** *Inf.* to manufacture or make something, especially in haste. □ *I'll see if I can knock another one off before lunch.* **2.** *Fig.* to knock off some amount from the price of something, lowering its price. □ *The store manager knocked 30 percent off the price of the coat.* **3.** *Inf.* to copy or reproduce a product. □ *They are well-known for knocking off cheap versions of expensive watches.*

**knock on wood** to rap on something made of wood. (Said as a wish for good luck. Usually a phrase attached to another statement. Sometimes said while knocking or rapping on real wood.) □ *I think I am well at last—knock on wood.* □ *I knock on wood when I wish something were true.*

**knock** so **over (with a feather)** *Fig.* to leave someone stunned or surprised by something extraordinary. (Fixed order.) □ *I was so surprised that you could have knocked me over with a feather.*

**knock some heads together** *Fig.* to scold some people; to get some people to do what they are supposed to be doing. □ *If you kids don't quiet down and go to sleep, I'm going to come up there and knock some heads together.*

**knock-down-drag-out fight** a serious fight; a serious argument. □ *Stop calling each other names, or you're going to end up with a real knock-down-drag-out fight.*

**know** one's **ABCs** *Fig.* to know the alphabet; to know the most basic things (about something). □ *You can't expect to write a letter when you don't even know your ABCs.*

**know all the angles** *Inf.* to know all the tricks and artifices of dealing with someone or something. □ *Ask my accountant about taxes. He knows all the angles.*

**know no bounds** *Fig.* [for something] to seem to be boundless or endless. □ *His generosity knows no bounds. He donates to every charity.*

**know** one's **way around** *Fig.* to know how to deal with people and situations; to have had much experience at living. (Fig. on knowing distance and direction.) □ *I can get along in the world. I know my way around.*

**know when** one **is not wanted** to sense when one's presence is not welcome; to know when one is not among friends. (Usually said when someone feels hurt by being ignored by people.) □ *I'm leaving this place! I know when I'm not wanted!*

**know where all the bodies are buried** *Fig.* to know all the secrets and intrigue from the past; to know all the relevant and perhaps hidden details. □ *He is a good choice for president because he knows where all the bodies are buried.*

*a **knuckle sandwich** *Inf.* a punch in the face. (*Typically: **ask for** ~; **get** ~; **give** so ~; **want** ~.) □ *A: Ahhh! Your mother smokes cigars! B: You want a knuckle sandwich?*

a **labor of love** *Fig.* a task that is either unpaid or badly paid and that one does simply for one's own satisfaction or pleasure or to please someone whom one likes or loves. □ *Jane made no money out of the biography she wrote. She was writing about the life of a friend, and the book was a labor of love.*

**lame duck 1.** *Fig.* someone who is in the last period of a term in an elective office and cannot run for reelection. □ *As a lame duck, there's not a lot I can do.* **2.** *Fig.* having to do with someone in the last period of a term in an elective office. (Sometimes **lame-duck**.) □ *Lame-duck Congresses tend to do things they wouldn't dare do otherwise.*

**land (up)on both feet** AND **land (up)on** one's **feet 1.** to end up on both feet after a jump, dive, etc. (*Upon* is formal and less commonly used than *on*.) □ *She jumped over the bicycle and landed upon both feet.* **2.** *Fig.* to come out of something well; to survive something satisfactorily. (Fig. on ①. *Upon* is formal and less commonly used than *on*.) □ *It was a rough period in his life, but when it was over he landed on both feet.*

**land-office business** *Fig.* a large amount of business done in a short period of time. □ *We keep going. Never do land-office business—just enough to make out.*

a **landslide victory** a victory by a large margin; a very substantial victory, particularly in an election. □ *The younger candidate won a landslide victory in the presidential election.*

the **last word in** sth the most recent style, design, or trend. □ *This leather umbrella is the last word in trendy rain protection.*

a **late bloomer 1.** a plant that blooms later than similar plants or that blooms late in the season. □ *There are a few late bloomers in the garden, but by fall, we don't care much anymore about flowers.* **2.** *Fig.* a person who finally develops a useful or superior skill or talents later than expected or desired. □ *Joseph was a late bloomer, but turned out to be a formidable scholar in the long run.*

**laugh all the way to the bank** *Inf.* to be very happy about money that has been earned by doing something that other people might think is unfair or that they criticized. □ *She makes tons of money doing what no one else will do and laughs all the way to the bank.*

**laugh** one's **head off** *Fig.* to laugh very hard and loudly, as if one's head might come off. (Fixed order.) □ *The movie was so funny I almost laughed my head off.*

**laugh up** one's **sleeve** to laugh secretly; to laugh quietly to oneself. □ *I told Sally that her dress was darling, but I was laughing up my sleeve because her dress was too small.*

**lay** sth **at** so's **doorstep** AND **lay** sth **on** so's **doorstep** *Fig.* in someone's care; as someone's responsibility. □ *Why do you always have to lay your problems at my doorstep?*

**lay down** one's **arms 1.** to put one's gun, sword, club, etc. down; to stop fighting; to surrender. □ *The soldiers laid down their arms and surrendered.* **2.** *Fig.* to give up and cease being hostile. □ *I know you're upset, but please lay down your arms and try to be reasonable.*

**lay down the law (to** so**) (about** sth**)** *Fig.* to scold someone; to make something very clear to someone in a very stern manner. □ *Wow, was she mad at Ed. She really laid down the law about drinking to him.* □ *She laid down the law about drinking.*

**lay** so **low** *Fig.* to defeat, sicken, sadden, demoralize, or depress someone. □ *The sudden loss of his job laid him low for a month or two.* □ *He was laid low by unemployment.*

the **lay of the land 1.** the arrangement of features on an area of land. □ *The geologist studied the lay of the land, trying to determine if there was oil below the surface.* **2.** *Fig.* the arrangement or organization of something other than land. (Fig. on ①.) □ *As soon as I get the lay of the land in my new job, things will go better.*

**lay** so **out in lavender** *Fig.* to scold someone severely. □ *She was really mad. She laid him out in lavender and really put him in his place.*

**lay** so **to rest** *Euph.* to bury a dead person. □ *They laid her to rest by her mother and father, out in the old churchyard.*

**lead** so **on a merry chase** *Fig.* to lead someone in a purposeless pursuit. □ *What a waste of time. You really led me on a merry chase.*

**lead the life of Riley** AND **live the life of Riley** *Fig.* to live in luxury. (No one knows whom *Riley* alludes to.) □ *If I had a million dollars, I could live the life of Riley.*

**leading question** a question that suggests the kind of answer that the person who asks it wants to hear. □ *The mayor was angered by the reporter's leading questions.*

a **lead-pipe cinch** *Fig.* something very easy to do; something entirely certain to happen. □ *I knew it was a lead-pipe cinch that I would be selected to head the publication committee.*

**lean and mean** *Fig.* fit and ready for hard, efficient work. □ *The management is lean and mean and looks to turn a profit next year.*

**learn** one's **lesson** *Fig.* to receive some kind of punishment [for something]. (See also teach so a lesson.) □ *I guess I learned my lesson. I won't do it again.*

**leave a bad taste in** so's **mouth** *Fig.* [for something] to leave a bad feeling or memory with someone. □ *The whole business about the missing money left a bad taste in his mouth.*

**leave an impression (on** so) AND **leave** so **with an impression** *Fig.* to provide a lasting memory for someone after one has left. □ *Her performance was less than stunning. She didn't leave a very good impression on us.*

**leave** so **high and dry 1.** [for water] to recede and leave someone untouched. □ *The waters receded and left us high and dry.* **2.** *Fig.* to leave someone unsupported and unable to maneuver; to leave someone helpless. (Fig. on ①.) □ *All my workers quit and left me high and dry.* **3.** *Fig.* to leave someone **flat broke.** (Fig. on ①.) □ *Mrs. Franklin took all the money out of the bank and left Mr. Franklin high and dry.*

**leave** so **holding the baby** Go to next.

**leave** so **holding the bag** AND **leave** so **holding the baby** *Fig.* to allow someone to take all the blame; to leave someone appearing to be guilty. □ *They all ran off and left me holding the bag. It wasn't even my fault.*

**leave** so **in the lurch** *Fig.* to leave someone waiting for or anticipating your actions. □ *I didn't mean to leave you in the lurch. I thought we had canceled our meeting.*

**leave no stone unturned** *Fig.* to search in all possible places. (As if one might search under every rock.) □ *Don't worry. We'll find your stolen car. We'll leave no stone unturned.*

**leave** so **up in the air** *Fig.* to leave someone waiting for a decision. □ *Please don't leave me up in the air. I want to know what's going to happen to me.*

**leave** sth **up in the air** *Fig.* to leave a matter undecided. (Fig. on the image of something drifting in the air, moving neither up nor down.) □ *Let's get this settled now. I don't want to leave anything up in the air over the weekend.*

*a **leg up** *Fig.* a kind of help where someone provides a knee or crossed hand as a support for someone to place a foot on to get higher, as in mounting a horse or climbing over something. (*Typically: **get** ~; **have** ~; **give** so ~.) □ *I gave her a leg up, and soon she was on her horse.*

a **legend in** one's **own (life)time** *Fig.* someone who is very famous and widely known for doing something special.

**Less is more.** *Cliché* Fewer or smaller is better. □ *Simplicity now rules our lives. Less is more. Smaller houses and cars. The world will be a better place!*

the **lesser of two evils** *Fig.* the less bad thing of a pair of bad things. □ *I didn't like either politician, so I voted for the lesser of two evils.*

**Let bygones be bygones.** *Cliché* Forgive someone for something he or she did in the past. □ *Jill: Why don't you want to invite Ellen to your party? Jane: She was rude to me at the office picnic. Jill: But that was six months ago. Let bygones be bygones.*

**Let George do it.** *Fig.* Let someone else do it; it doesn't matter who. □ *Billie always says, "Let George do it." She is unwilling to help with things that don't interest her.*

**let grass grow under** one's **feet** *Fig.* to do nothing; to stand still. □ *Mary doesn't let the grass grow under her feet. She's always busy.*

**let** one's **guard down**† AND **lower** one's **guard; drop** one's **guard** *Fig.* to stop guarding oneself against trouble; to relax one's vigilance and become vulnerable. □ *He never let's his guard down because he trusts no one.*

**let** one's **hair down 1.** to undo one's hair and let it fall freely. □ *When she took off her glasses and let her hair down, she was incredibly beautiful.* **2.** *Fig.* to tell [someone] everything; to tell one's innermost feelings and secrets. (*Fig.* on ①.) □ *Let your hair down and tell me all about it.*

111

**let** so **have it (with both barrels)** *Fig.* to strike someone or attack someone verbally. (*With both barrels* intensifies the phrase; it alludes to firing a double-barreled shotgun.) □ *I really let Tom have it with both barrels. I told him he had better not do that again if he knows what's good for him.*

**let it all hang out** *Inf.* to be yourself, assuming that you generally are not; to become totally relaxed and unpretentious. □ *Come on. Relax! Let it all hang out.*

**let nature take its course** *Fig.* to let life progress normally as with the course of a disease, illness leading to death, or the development of sexual interests. □ *The dog was quite old and not suffering, so we decided to let nature takes its course.* □ *Well, a couple together with moonlight and soft music. They let nature take its course and were engaged by dawn.*

**let the cat out of the bag** *Fig.* to reveal a secret or a surprise by accident. □ *When Bill glanced at the door, he let the cat out of the bag. We knew then that he was expecting someone to arrive.*

**let the chips fall (where they may)** *Fig.* and do not worry about the results. □ *I have to settle this matter in my own way. I will confront her with the evidence and let the chips fall where they may.*

**let things slide** AND **let** sth **slide** *Fig.* to ignore the things that one is supposed to do; to fall behind in the doing of one's work. □ *I am afraid that I let the matter slide while I was recovering from my operation.*

**let well enough alone** AND **leave well enough alone** *Fig.* to leave things as they are (and not try to improve them). □ *There isn't much more you can accomplish here. Why don't you just let well enough alone?*

a **level playing field** *Fig.* a situation that is fair to all; a situation where everyone has the same opportunity. □ *If we started off with a level playing field, everyone would have an equal chance.*

**lick** one's **chops 1.** to show one's eagerness to eat something by licking one's lip area. (Said especially about an animal.) □ *The big bad wolf licked his chops when he saw the little pigs.* **2.** *Fig.* to show one's eagerness to do something. □ *Fred started licking his chops when he heard about the high-paying job offered at the factory.*

a **lick of work** a bit of work. (Used with a negative.) □ *I couldn't get her to do a lick of work all day long!*

**lie at death's door** *Fig.* to be close to dying. □ *I do not want to lie at death's door suffering. I hope to pass on quickly.*

**lie doggo** *Fig.* to remain unrecognized (for a long time). □ *If you don't find the typos now, they will lie doggo until the next edition.*

**lie in ruins** *Fig.* to exist in a state of ruin, such as a destroyed city, building, scheme, plan, etc. □ *My garden lay in ruins after the cows got in and trampled everything.*

**lie in state** *Fig.* [for a dead body] to be on display for public mourning. □ *The president will lie in state in the capitol rotunda.*

**life and limb** [a person's] life and body, with reference to safety and survival. □ *Your first thought when motorcycling is the protection of life and limb.*

**life in the fast lane** *Inf.* a very active or possibly risky way to live. □ *Life in the fast lane is too much for me.*

the **life of the party** *Fig.* a person who is lively and helps make a party fun and exciting. □ *Bill is always the life of the party. Be sure to invite him.*

**like a bat out of hell** *Inf.* very fast or sudden. □ *The car pulled away from the curb like a bat out of hell.*

**like a bolt out of the blue** AND **like a bolt from the blue** *Fig.* suddenly and without warning. (Refers to a bolt of lightning coming out of a clear blue sky.) □ *The news came to us like a bolt from the blue.* □ *Like a bolt out of the blue, the boss came and fired us all.*

like a fish out of water

**like a bump on a log** *Fig.* completely inert. (Derogatory.) □ *You can never tell what Julia thinks of something; she just stands there like a bump on a log.*

**like a fish out of water** *Fig.* appearing to be completely out of place; in a very awkward manner. □ *Bob stood there in his rented tuxedo, looking like a fish out of water.*

**like a three-ring circus** *Fig.* chaotic; exciting and busy. □ *Our household is like a three-ring circus on Monday mornings.*

**\*like a ton of bricks** *Inf.* like a great weight or burden. (\*Typically: **fall** ~; **hit** ~; **hit** so ~.) □ *The sudden tax increase hit like a ton of bricks. Everyone became angry.*

**like gangbusters** *Inf.* with great excitement and speed. (From the phrase "Come on like gangbusters," a radio show that "came on" with lots of noise and excitement.) □ *She works like gangbusters and gets the job done.*

**like lambs to the slaughter** AND **like a lamb to the slaughter** *Fig.* quietly and without seeming to realize the likely difficulties or dangers of a situation. □ *Our team went on the football field like lambs to the slaughter to meet the league leaders.*

**like nothing on earth 1.** *Fig.* very untidy or very unattractive. □ *Joan arrived at the office looking like nothing on earth. She had fallen in the mud.* **2.** *Fig.* very unusual; very distinctive. □ *The new car models look like nothing on earth this year.*

**like pulling teeth** *Fig.* like doing something very difficult. □ *Trying to get him to pay attention is like pulling teeth.*

**like (two) peas in a pod** *Cliché* very close or intimate. □ *Yes, they're close. Like two peas in a pod.*

**line** one's **own pocket(s)** *Fig.* to make money for oneself in a greedy or dishonest fashion. □ *They are interested in lining their pockets first and serving the people second.*

**listen to reason** to yield to a reasonable argument; to take the reasonable course. □ *She got into trouble because she wouldn't listen to reason.*

A **little bird told me.** *Fig.* a way of indicating that you do not want to reveal who told you something. (Sometimes used playfully, when you think that the person you are addressing knows or can guess who was the source of your information.) □ *Jill: Thank you for the beautiful present! How did you know I wanted a green silk scarf? Jane: A little bird told me.*

a **little white lie** *Fig.* a small, usually harmless lie; a fib. □ *Every little white lie you tell is still a lie, and it is still meant to mislead people.*

**live by** one's **wits** *Fig.* to survive by being clever. □ *When you're in the kind of business I'm in, you have to live by your wits.*

**live from hand to mouth** *Fig.* to live in poor circumstances. □ *We lived from hand to mouth during the war. Things were very difficult.*

**live off the fat of the land** *Fig.* to live on stored-up resources or abundant resources. (Similar to the following entry.) □ *If I had a million dollars, I'd invest it and live off the fat of the land.*

**live out of a suitcase** *Fig.* to stay very briefly in several places, never unpacking one's luggage. □ *I hate living out of a suitcase. For my next vacation, I want to go to just one place and stay there the whole time.*

**live out of cans** *Fig.* to eat only canned food. □ *We lived out of cans for the entire camping trip.*

**live under the same roof (with** so**)** *Fig.* to share a dwelling with someone. (Implies living in a close relationship, as a husband and wife.) □ *I don't think I can go on living under the same roof with her.*

a **living hell** *Fig.* as bad as hell would be if experienced by a living person. □ *For the two years that we were married, she made my life a living hell.*

**living large** living in luxury; spending time in grand style. □ *George loved living large, especially dining at fine French restaurants.*

**loaded for bear 1.** *Inf.* angry. (Fig. on hunting for bear, for which one needs a very powerful weapon.) □ *He left here in a rage. He was really loaded for bear.* **2.** *Sl.* drunk. (An elaboration of *loaded* = drunk.) □ *By the end of the party, Bill was loaded for bear.*

**lock horns (with** so**)** *Fig.* to get into an argument with someone. □ *Let's settle this peacefully. I don't want to lock horns with the boss.*

**lock, stock, and barrel** *Cliché* everything. (Usually thought to have meant the whole gun, lock, stock, and barrel, being parts of a rifle.) □ *We had to move everything out of the house—lock, stock, and barrel.*

the **long arm of the law** *Fig.* the police; the law. □ *The long arm of the law is going to tap you on the shoulder some day, Lefty.*

**long in the tooth** *Fig.* old. □ *That actor is getting a little long in the tooth to play the romantic lead.*

**look a gift horse in the mouth** *Fig.* to be ungrateful to someone who gives you something; to treat someone who gives you a gift badly. (Usually with a negative.) □ *Never look a gift horse in the mouth.* □ *I advise you not to look a gift horse in the mouth.*

**look as if butter wouldn't melt in** one's **mouth** *Fig.* to appear to be cold and unfeeling (despite any information to the contrary). □ *What a sour face. He looks as if butter wouldn't melt in his mouth.*

**look at** so **cross-eyed** *Fig.* to merely appear to question, threaten, or mock someone. (Often in the negative.) □ *If you so much as look at me cross-eyed, I will send you to your room.*

**look good on paper** to seem fine in theory, but not perhaps in practice; to appear to be a good plan. □ *This looks good on paper. Let's hope it works in the real world.*

**look like** sth **the cat dragged in** *Fig.* to look very shabby, worn, exhausted, or abused. (Sometimes with *drug*.) □ *Poor Dave looks like something the cat drug in. He must have been out late last night.*

**look like the cat that swallowed the canary** *Fig.* to appear as if one had just had a great success. □ *Your presentation must have gone well. You look like the cat that swallowed the canary.*

**look to** one's **laurels** *Fig.* to take care not to lower or diminish one's reputation or position, especially in relation to that of someone else potentially better; to guard one's reputation or rewards for past accomplishments. □ *With the arrival of the new member of the football team, James will have to look to his laurels and strive to remain as the highest scorer.*

**look under the hood** to examine the engine of a car; to check the oil, water, and other such routine items associated with the engine of a car. □ *I finished putting gas in. I need to look under the hood.*

a **loose cannon** *Inf.* a person whose actions are unpredictable and uncontrollable; someone who gives away secrets. □ *Some loose cannon in the State Department has been leaking stories to the press.*

**Loose lips sink ships.** Don't talk carelessly because you don't know who is listening. (From wartime. Literally, "Don't reveal even the location of a loved one on a ship, because the location could be communicated to the enemy by a spy.") □ *You never know who is going to hear what you say and how they will use what they hear. Remember, loose lips sink ships.*

**Lord knows I've tried.** *Fig.* I certainly have tried very hard. □ *Alice: Why don't you get Bill to fix this fence? Mary: Lord knows I've tried. I must have asked him a dozen times—this year alone.*

**lose** one's **appetite** *Fig.* to lose one's desire to eat. □ *After that gory movie, I'm afraid I've lost my appetite.*

**lose** one's **edge** *Fig.* to lose any advantage one had over other people; [for one's special skills] to fade and become average. □ *At the age of 28, I began to lose my edge and could no longer compete as a wrestler.*

**lose** one's **shirt** *Fig.* to lose a lot of money; to lose all of one's assets (as if one had even lost one's shirt). □ *No, I can't loan you $200. I just lost my shirt at the racetrack.*

**lose sleep over** so/sth AND **lose sleep about** so/sth *Fig.* to worry about someone or something a lot, sometimes when one should be sleeping. (Often used with *any* and the negative.) □ *Yes, Kelly is in a little bit of trouble, but I'm not going to lose any sleep over her.*

**lose touch with reality** to begin to think unrealistically; to become unrealistic. □ *I am so overworked that I am losing touch with reality.*

**lose** one's **train of thought** *Fig.* to forget what one was talking or thinking about. □ *Excuse me, I lost my train of thought. What was I talking about?*

**lost and gone forever** *Fig.* lost; permanently lost. □ *My money fell out of my pocket, and I am sure that it is lost and gone forever.*

a **lot of give-and-take 1.** *Fig.* a lot of two-way discussion. □ *It was a good meeting. There was a lot of give-and-take, and we all learned.* **2.** *Fig.* a lot of negotiating and bargaining. □ *After an afternoon of give-and-take, we were finally able to put all the details into an agreement.*

*a **lot of nerve 1.** *Fig.* great rudeness; a lot of audacity or brashness. (*Typically: **have** ~; **take** ~.) □ *He walked out on her, and that took a lot of nerve!* □ *You have a lot of nerve! You took my parking place!* **2.** *Fig.* courage. (*Typically: **have** ~; **take** ~.) □ *He climbed the mountain with a bruised foot. That took a lot of nerve.*

**loud and clear** *Fig.* clear and distinctly. (Originally said of radio reception that is heard clearly and distinctly.) □ *Tom: If I've told you once, I've told you a thousand times: Stop it! Do you hear me? Bill: Yes, loud and clear.*

a **love-hate relationship** *Fig.* a relationship of any kind that involves both devotion and hatred. □ *Tommy has a love-hate relationship with his teacher. Mostly, though, it's hate.*

**low man on the totem pole** *Fig.* the least important or lowest-ranking person of a group. □ *I was the last to find out because I'm low man on the totem pole.*

*a **low profile** *Fig.* a persona or character that does not draw attention. (*Typically: **assume** ~; **have** ~; **keep** ~; **give** oneself ~;

**maintain** ~.) □ *I try to be quiet and keep a low profile. It's hard because I just love attention.*

*the **lowdown (on** so/sth**)** *Inf.* the full story about someone or something. (*Typically: **get** ~; **have** ~; **give** so ~.) □ *Sally wants to get the low-down on the new pension plan. Please tell her all about it.*

**lower the boom on** so *Fig.* to scold or punish someone severely; to crack down on someone. □ *If Bob won't behave better, I'll have to lower the boom on him.*

**low-hanging fruit 1.** *Fig.* the easiest thing to get or achieve; an easy profit. □ *All the potential profit is just low-hanging fruit. There's no way to lose.* **2.** *Fig.* the easiest person(s) to sell something to, to convince of something, or to fool. □ *Don't be satisfied with the low-hanging fruit. Go after the hard-sell types.*

the **luck of the draw** *Inf.* the results of chance; the lack of any choice. □ *The team was assembled by chance. It was just the luck of the draw that we could work so well together.*

the **luck of the Irish** *Fig.* luck associated with the Irish people. (Also said as a catchphrase for any kind of luck.) □ *Bill: How did you manage to do it, Jeff? Jeff: It's the luck of the Irish, I guess.*

**lump** so **and** so else **together** AND **lump** sth **and** sth **else together** *Fig.* to classify people or things as members of the same category. □ *You just can't lump Bill and Ted together. They are totally different kinds of people.*

# M

**made to order** *Fig.* made to one's own measurements and on request. □ *This suit fits so well because it's made to order.* □ *His feet are so big that all his shoes have to be made to order.*

**main strength and awkwardness** *Fig.* great force; brute force. □ *They finally got the piano moved into the living room by main strength and awkwardness.*

**make a beeline for** so/sth *Fig.* to head straight toward someone or something. (Fig. on the straight flight of a bee.) □ *Billy came into the kitchen and made a beeline for the cookies.*

**make a clean breast of** sth **(to** so**)** *Fig.* to admit something to someone. □ *You should make a clean breast of the matter to someone.*

**make a dent in** sth AND **put a dent in** sth **1.** to make a depression in something. □ *I kicked the side of the car and made a dent in it.* **2.** *Fig.* to use only a little of something; to make a small amount of progress with something. (Fig. on ①.) □ *Look at what's left on your plate! You hardly made a dent in your dinner.*

**make a killing** *Fig.* to have a great success, especially in making money. □ *Bill made a killing at the racetrack yesterday.*

**make a (mental) note of** sth *Fig.* to commit something to memory for future reference. □ *You want to be considered for promotion. I'll make a note of it.*

**make a mountain out of a molehill** *Cliché* to make a major issue out of a minor one; to exaggerate the importance of something. □ *Come on, don't make a mountain out of a molehill. It's not that important.*

**make allowance(s) (for** so/sth**)** to make excuses or explanations for someone or something; to take into consideration the negative effects of someone or something. □ *We have to make allowance for the age of the house when we judge its condition.*

**make an exhibition of** oneself *Fig.* to show off; to try to get a lot of attention for oneself. □ *She is not just dancing, she is making an exhibition of herself.*

**make an impression on** so *Fig.* to produce a positive memorable effect on someone while one is present. □ *Tom made quite an impression on the banker.*

**make** so's **blood boil** *Fig.* to make someone very angry. □ *It just makes my blood boil to think of the amount of food that gets wasted around here.*

**make** so's **blood run cold** *Fig.* to shock or horrify someone. □ *I could tell you things about prisons that would make your blood run cold.*

**make good money** *Fig.* to earn a sizable amount of money. □ *I don't know what she does, but she makes good money.*

**make good time** *Fig.* to proceed at a fast or reasonable rate. □ *On our trip to Toledo, we made good time all the way.*

**make hay (while the sun shines)** *Fig.* to get work done while it's easiest to do. (It is difficult or impossible to cut and bale hay in bad weather.) □ *Come on, let's get to work before everyone else gets here and gets in our way. Let's make hay while the sun shines.*

**Make it snappy!** *Inf.* Hurry up!; Move quickly and smartly. □ *Andy: Make it snappy! I haven't got all day. Bob: Don't rush me.*

**make life miserable for** so *Fig.* to give someone misery; to be a great nuisance to someone. □ *This nagging backache is making life miserable for me.*

**make no apologies** not to apologize for something the speaker does not consider to have done wrong. □ *I make no apologies. I did it and I'm glad.*

**make no bones about** sth *Fig.* not to make a mistake (about something); no need to doubt it; absolutely. □ *Make no bones about it, Mary is a great singer.*

**make noises about** sth *Fig. Inf.* to mention or hint about something. □ *The boss has been making noises about letting some people go.*

**make or break** so [of a task, job, career choice] to bring success or ruin to someone. □ *It's a tough assignment, and it will either make or break him.*

**make (**one's**) peace with** so/sth to reconcile oneself with someone or something. □ *After many years, Frank made his peace with the Church and started participating again.*

**make the arrangements** *Euph.* to arrange a funeral. □ *A funeral services practitioner will be happy to help you make the arrangements.*

**make** so **the scapegoat for** sth to make someone take the blame for something. □ *They made Tom the scapegoat for the whole affair. It wasn't all his fault.*

**make up for lost time** *Fig.* to catch up; to go fast to balance a period of going slow or not moving. □ *We drove as fast as we could, trying to make up for lost time.*

**make waves** *Sl.* to cause difficulty. (Often in the negative.) □ *If you make waves too much around here, you won't last long.*

**makes** one's **heart sink** *Fig.* to cause one to respond to something unpleasant by developing an empty feeling inside. □ *When I heard her say those terrible things, it made my heart sink.*

the **man in the street** *Fig.* the ordinary person; ordinary people. □ *The man in the street has little interest in literature.*

a **man of few words** *Fig.* a man who speaks concisely or not at all. □ *He is a man of few words, but he usually makes a lot of sense.*

**man's inhumanity to man** *Fig.* human cruelty toward other humans. □ *It doesn't take a war to remind us of man's inhumanity to man.*

a **marvel to behold** someone or something quite exciting or wonderful to see. □ *Our new high-definition television is a marvel to behold.*

a **matter of principle** a question of following the law, guidelines, or rules. □ *I always obey the speed limit whether there's a cop around or not. It's a matter of principle.*

a **mean streak** *Fig.* a tendency for a person to do things that are mean. □ *I think that Spike has a mean streak that no one ever saw before this incident.*

**meat-and-potatoes** *Fig.* basic, sturdy, and hearty. (Often refers to a robust person, usually a man, with simple tastes in food and other things.) □ *There is no point in trying to cook up something special for the Wilsons. They are strictly meat-and-potatoes.*

a **meeting of the minds** the establishment of agreement; complete agreement. □ *We struggled to bring about a meeting of the minds on the issues.*

**melt in** one's **mouth 1.** to taste very good. (Also can be literal.) □ *This cake is so good it'll melt in your mouth.* **2.** [of meat] to be very, very tender. □ *My steak is so tender it could melt in my mouth.*

*a **mental block (against** sth) *Fig.* to have some psychological barrier that prevents one from doing something. (*Typically: **get** ~; **have** ~; **give** so ~.) □ *Perry has a mental block against speaking in public.*

a **mere trifle** *Fig.* a tiny bit; a small, unimportant matter; a small amount of money. □ *But this isn't expensive! It costs a mere trifle!*

middle-of-the-road

**mete** punishment **out**† *Fig.* to determine and deliver punishment; to deal out punishment. (Other things can be dealt out with *mete*, but punishment is the most common.) □ *The principal will decide the kind of punishment she will mete out.*

**\*method in** one's **madness** *Fig.* a purpose in what one is doing, even though it seems to be crazy. (\*Typically: **be** ~; **have** ~.) □ *Wait until she finishes; then you'll see that she has method in her madness.*

**middle-of-the-road** halfway between two extremes, especially political extremes. □ *Jane is very left-wing, but her husband is politically middle-of-the-road.*

**might and main** *Cliché* great physical strength; great force. □ *The huge warrior, with all his might and main, could not break his way through the castle gates.*

the **milk of human kindness** *Fig.* natural kindness and sympathy shown to others. (From Shakespeare's play *Macbeth*, Act 1, Scene 5.) □ *Mary is completely hard and selfish—she doesn't have the milk of human kindness in her.*

\*a **million miles away** *Fig.* lost in thought; [of someone] daydreaming and not paying attention. (Only one's mind is far away. \*Typically: **be** ~; **look to be** ~.) □ *Look at her. She is a million miles away, not paying any attention to what she is doing.*

a **millstone about** one's **neck** a continual burden or handicap. □ *This huge and expensive house is a millstone about my neck.*

**mince (**one's**) words** to soften the effect of one's words. (Often negative.) □ *A frank person never minces words.* □ *I won't mince words. You are a jerk!*

**mind** one's **Ps and Qs** AND **watch** one's **Ps and Qs** *Fig.* pay attention to details. (Older. There are numerous attempts to explain the origin of this phrase, and none is conclusive. The best of a weak set of possibilities is that the letters *p* and *q* held some difficulty for writers or typesetters. It is over 200 years old, and its origins have been a mystery for much of that time.) □ *When you go to the party, mind your Ps and Qs.*

a **miscarriage of justice** a wrong or mistaken decision, especially one made in a court of law. □ *Sentencing the old man on a charge of murder proved to be a miscarriage of justice.*

**miss (**sth**) by a mile** *Fig.* to fail to hit something by a great distance; to land **wide of the mark.** □ *Ann shot the arrow and missed the target by a mile.*

the **mists of time** *Fig.* a long time ago. □ *Those old people have lived in that house since the mists of time.*

**mix business with pleasure** to combine business discussions or transactions in a social or holiday setting. (Always spoken of negatively, even though it is widely practiced.) □ *Well, as you know,*

*I hate to mix business with pleasure, but I think we can discuss the matter on my fishing boat in the Gulf. If that's all right with you.*

**moist around the edges** *Inf.* intoxicated. □ *Charlie is more than moist around the edges. He is soused.*

**Money burns a hole in** so's **pocket.** An expression describing someone who spends money as soon as it is earned. □ *Sally can't seem to save anything. Money burns a hole in her pocket.*

**monkey suit** *Inf.* a tuxedo. (Jocular. Possibly in reference to the fancy suit worn by an organ grinder's monkey.) □ *All the men except me wore monkey suits at dinner on the cruise.*

a **mopping-up operation** a cleanup operation; the final stages in a project where the loose ends are taken care of. □ *It's all over except a small mopping-up operation.*

**more bark than bite** *Fig.* more threat than actual harm. (Alludes to the dog whose bark is more threatening than its bite is harmful.) □ *Don't worry about the boss. He's more bark than bite.*

**more dead than alive** *Fig.* exhausted; in very bad condition; near death. (Almost always an exaggeration.) □ *We arrived at the top of the mountain more dead than alive.*

**more** so/sth **than** one **can shake a stick at** *Rur.* a lot; too many to count. □ *There were more snakes than you could shake a stick at.*

the **more the merrier** *Cliché* the more people there are, the happier the situation will be. □ *The manager hired a new employee even though there's not enough work for all of us now. Oh, well, the more the merrier.*

the **morning after (the night before)** *Inf.* a hangover; the feelings associated with having drunk too much alcohol. □ *Do worries about the morning after keep you from having a good time at parties?*

a **movable feast 1.** a religious holiday that is on a different date from year to year. □ *Easter is the best-known movable feast.* **2.** *Fig.*

a meal that is served in motion or with different portions of the meal served at different locations. (Jocular or a complete misunderstanding of ① but in wide use.) □ *We enjoyed a real movable feast on the train from Washington to Miami.*

**move heaven and earth to** do sth *Fig.* to make a major effort to do something. □ *"I'll move heaven and earth to be with you, Mary," said Bill.*

**movers and shakers** *Inf.* people who get things done; organizers and managers. □ *The movers and shakers in this firm haven't exactly been working overtime.*

**Mum's the word.** *Fig.* Nothing is to be said about this.; Don't say anything about this.; I promise to say nothing. (*Mum-mum-mum* is the sound one would make while attempting to talk with the mouth closed or lips sealed. Based on Shakespeare's *King Henry VI*, Part 2, Act 1, Scene 2: "Seal up your lips, and give no words but mum.") □ *Don't repeat a word of this. Mum's the word.*

# N

**\*naked as a jaybird** *Cliché* naked; bare. (\*Also: **as** ~.) □ *Two-year-old Matilda escaped from her nurse, who was bathing her, and ran out naked as a jaybird into the dining room.*

**\*the naked eye** the human eye, unassisted by optics, such as a telescope, microscope, or spectacles. (\*Typically: **appear to** ~; **look to** ~; **see with** ~; **visible to** ~.) □ *I can't see the bird's markings with the naked eye.* □ *That's how it appears to the naked eye.*

the **naked truth** *Inf.* the complete, unembellished truth. □ *Sorry to put it to you like this, but it's the naked truth.*

**name names** to reveal the names of people who have done something wrong. (The frequently used negative is **not name any names.**) □ *Rollo went to the cops, and he's going to name names.* □ *I don't want to name any names, but somebody we both know broke the window.*

**need** sth **like a hole in the head** *Inf.* not to need something at all. □ *I need a house cat like I need a hole in the head!*

one **needs to have** one's **head examined** *Fig.* said to someone who has made a silly choice. (Psychiatrists are said to "examine" heads or brains.) □ *You did that! You need to have your head examined!*

**neither fish nor fowl** *Cliché* not any recognizable thing. □ *The car that they drove up in was neither fish nor fowl. It must have been made out of spare parts.*

**\*neither rhyme nor reason** *Cliché* without logic, order, or planning. (Describes something disorganized. \*Typically: **be** ~**; have** ~.) □ *This silly novel's plot has neither rhyme nor reason.*

a **(nervous) breakdown** *Fig.* a physical and mental collapse brought on by great anxiety over a period of time. □ *After month after month of stress and strain, Sally had a nervous breakdown.*

the **new kid on the block 1.** a child who has just moved to a certain neighborhood. □ *The new kid on the block turned out to be a really good baseball player.* **2.** *Fig.* the newest person in a group. (Fig. on ①.) □ *I'm just the new kid on the block. I've only been working here for a month.*

**\*a New York minute** *Fig.* a very short period of time. (Probably from the late 1960s. There seems to be no compelling story of origin other than that people seem to be in a hurry in New York City. \*Typically: **in** ~**; quicker than** ~.) □ *Just give me a call and I'll be there in a New York minute.*

**nickel and dime** so **(to death)** *Inf.* to make numerous small monetary charges that add up to a substantial sum. □ *Just give me the whole bill at one time. Don't nickel and dime me for days on end.*

**nine times out of ten** *Fig.* usually; almost always. □ *Nine times out of ten people will choose coffee rather than tea.*

**no end in sight** *Fig.* [with] no end anticipated or predicted. (As if one were waiting at a railroad crossing for a very long train to pass.) □ *We have been having constant troubles with our shipping department, and there's no end in sight.*

**no flies on** so *Fig.* someone is not slow; someone is not wasting time. (On the image of flies not being able to land on someone moving fast.) □ *There are no flies on Robert. He does his work very fast and very well.*

**no great shakes** *Inf.* someone or something that is not very good. (There is no affirmative version of this.) □ *Your idea is no great shakes, but we'll try it anyway.*

**no laughing matter** *Fig.* a serious issue or problem. □ *This disease is no laughing matter. It's quite deadly if not treated immediately.*

**no matter how you slice it** *Fig.* no matter what your perspective is; no matter how you try to portray something. □ *No matter how you slice it, the results of the meeting present all sorts of problems for the office staff.*

**No news is good news.** *Fig.* Not hearing any news signifies that nothing is wrong. □ *Jane: I'm worried about my sister. She hasn't called me for months. Alan: No news is good news, right?*

**no offense meant** *Fig.* I did not mean to offend [you]. (See also no offense taken.) □ *Mary: Excuse that last remark. No offense meant. Susan: It's okay. I was not offended.*

**no offense taken** *Fig.* I am not offended [by what you said]. (See also no offense meant.) □ *Pete: Excuse that last remark. I did not want to offend you. Tom: It's okay. No offense taken.*

**No pain, no gain.** *Fig.* If you want to improve, you must work so hard that it hurts. (Associated with sports and physical exercise.) □ *Player: I can't do any more push-ups. My muscles hurt. Coach: No pain, no gain.*

**No rest for the wicked.** *Fig.* It's because you are wicked that you have to work hard. (Usually jocular.) □ *A: I can't seem to ever get all my work done. B: No rest for the wicked.*

**no soap** *Inf.* no. □ *No soap, I don't lend money to anyone.*

**No such luck.** *Fig.* The luck needed for success simply was not available. □ *I'd hoped to be able to get a job in Boston, but no such luck. No one needs my skills there.*

**no thanks to you** *Fig.* I cannot thank you for what happened, because you did not cause it.; I cannot thank you for your help, because you did not give it. □ *Bob: Well, despite our previous disagreement, he seemed to agree to all our demands. Alice: Yes, no thanks to you. I wish you'd learn to keep your big mouth shut!*

no rest for the wicked

**nobody's fool** *Fig.* a sensible and wise person who is not easily deceived. □ *Anne may seem as though she's not very bright, but she's nobody's fool.*

**none of the above** none of the things named in the list of possibilities just listed or recited. □ *Q: What's wrong, Sally? Are you sick, tired, frightened, or what? A: None of the above. I have no idea what's wrong.*

**None of your lip!** *Fig.* Shut up!; I don't want to hear anything from you about anything! □ *A: You are being a real nuisance about the broken window. B: None of your lip! Just help me clean it up.*

**\*none the worse for wear** *Fig.* no worse because of use or effort. (See also the **worse for wear**. \*Typically: **be** ~; **become** ~; **look** ~.) □ *I lent my car to John. When I got it back, it was none the worse for wear.*

one's **nose is in the air** *Fig.* one is acting conceited or aloof. □ *Mary's nose is always in the air since she got into that exclusive boarding school.*

**not a dry eye (in the** place**)** *Fig.* no one in a place is free from tears or sobbing. □ *As Melinda sang, there wasn't a dry eye in the church.*

**not a kid anymore** *Fig.* no longer in one's youth. □ *You can't keep partying all weekend, every weekend. You're not a kid anymore.*

**not able to make head or tail of** sth AND **not able to make heads or tails of** sth *Fig.* not able to understand something at all. (The idioms refer to a lack of ability to tell one end from the other end—the head and the tail—but have been mixed with the notion of heads or tails as in the flipping of coins.) □ *I couldn't make heads or tails of the professor's geology lecture this morning.*

**not believe** one's **ears** *Fig.* not believe the news that one has heard. □ *I couldn't believe my ears when Mary said I won the first prize.*

**not believe** one's **eyes** *Fig.* not to believe what one is seeing; to be shocked or dumbfounded at what one is seeing. □ *When Jimmy opened his birthday present, he could hardly believe his eyes. Just what he wanted!*

**not** one's **cup of tea** *Fig.* not one's choice or preference. (Used to describe an activity you do not enjoy.) □ *You three visit the museum without me. Looking at fussy old paintings is not my cup of tea.*

**not enough room to swing a cat** not very much space. (Probably referred to swinging a cat-o-nine-tails, a complex whip of nautical origins.) □ *How can you work in a small room like this? There's not enough room to swing a cat.*

**not for all the tea in China** *Fig.* not even if you rewarded me with all the tea in China; not for anything at all. □ *No I won't do it—not for all the tea in China.*

**Not for my money.** *Fig.* Not as far as I'm concerned. (Not necessarily associated with money or finance.) □ *John: We think that Fred is the best choice for the job. Do you think he is? Mary: Not for my money, he's not.*

**not have a care in the world** *Fig.* free and casual; unworried and carefree. □ *I really feel good today—as if I didn't have a care in the world.*

**not have a leg to stand on** *Fig.* [for an argument or a case] to have no support. □ *You may think you're in the right, but you don't have a leg to stand on.*

**not hold water** *Fig.* not able to be proved; not correct or true. □ *The cop's theory will not hold water. The suspect has an ironclad alibi.*

**Not in my book.** *Fig.* Not according to my views. □ *John: Is Fred okay for the job, do you think? Mary: No, not in my book.*

**not know enough to come in out of the rain** AND **not know enough to come in from the rain** *Fig.* to be very stupid. □ *Bob is so stupid he doesn't know enough to come in out of the rain.*

**not know** so **from Adam** *Fig.* not to know someone by sight at all. □ *I wouldn't recognize John if I saw him up close. I don't know him from Adam.*

**not lay a hand on** so/sth AND **not put a hand on** so/sth not to touch or harm someone or something. □ *If you lay a hand on me, I will scream!*

**not let the grass grow under** one's **feet** *Fig.* not to stay in one place for a long time; to be always on the move. □ *He is always doing something. He never lets the grass grow under his feet.*

**not long for this world** *Fig.* about to die. □ *Our dog is nearly 12 years old and not long for this world.*

**not made of money** *Fig.* [of a person] not having a lot of money; not having an unlimited supply of money. □ *I can't afford a car like that. I'm not made of money you know.*

**not move a muscle** *Fig.* to remain perfectly motionless. □ *Be quiet. Sit there and don't move a muscle.*

**not much to look at** unattractive; ugly. (Often, a redeeming quality will be noted with this phrase.) □ *This old car is not much to look at, but it runs very well.*

**not rocket science** *Fig.* not some very complicated scientific endeavor allegedly beyond most people. □ *Come on. Taxes are easy to figure. It's not rocket science, you know!*

**not shed a tear** *Fig.* not to show any emotion even when something is very sad. □ *At his uncle's funeral, he didn't shed a tear. They never got along.*

**not show** one's **face** not to appear somewhere; not to go to some place. □ *After what she said, she had better not show her face around here again.*

**not suffer fools gladly** AND **not suffer fools lightly** not to easily endure foolish people; not to tolerate stupid or ignorant people. (Sounds a bit aloof. Biblical. From II Corinthians 11:19: "For ye suffer fools gladly, seeing ye yourselves are wise.") □ *I grow increasingly weary of people who lack the ability to reason, floss, or use apostrophes as intended. Basically, I do not suffer fools gladly, and I am weary of suffering through the results of their foolishness.*

**not suffer fools lightly** Go to previous.

**not the end of the world** *Fig.* not the worst thing that could happen. □ *Don't fret about the scratch on the side of your new car. It's not the end of the world.*

**not to judge a book by its cover 1.** to not choose to read or not to read a book because of the picture on the cover. □ *The drawings on the cover of the book didn't even match up with the story inside. I guess I will learn to not judge a book by its cover.* **2.** *Fig.*

to not make judgments or decisions based on superficial appearances. (Fig. on ①. Often applies to people.) □ *Bob turned out to be a really nice guy in spite of my first impressions. I should not judge a book by its cover.*

**Not to worry.** *Inf.* Please do not worry. □ *Sue: I think we're about to run out of money. Bill: Not to worry. I have some more traveler's checks.*

**not too shabby 1.** *Inf.* nice; well done. (With emphasis on *shabby*.) □ *Is that your car? Not too shabby!* **2.** *Inf.* very shabby; very poor indeed. (With emphasis on *too*. Sarcastic.) □ *Did you see that shot she missed? Not too shabby!*

**nothing of the kind 1.** no; absolutely not. □ *I didn't tear your jacket—nothing of the kind!* **2.** nothing like that. □ *She did nothing of the kind! She wasn't even there!*

**nothing to write home about** *Fig.* mediocre; not as good as you expected. □ *I went to that new restaurant last night. It's nothing to write home about.*

**nowhere to be found** nowhere; not able to be found; lost. □ *Her lost ring is nowhere to be found.*

**null and void** *Cliché* without legal force; having no legal effect. □ *The court declared the law to be null and void.* □ *The millionaire's will was null and void because it was unsigned.*

**nuts and bolts** *Fig.* the mundane workings of something; the basics of something. □ *She's got a lot of good, general ideas, but when it comes to the nuts and bolts of getting something done, she's no good.*

**odd man out** *Fig.* an unusual or atypical person or thing. □ *You had better learn to use the new system software unless you want to be odd man out.*

the **odds-on favorite** *Fig.* the most popular choice of a wager. □ *Fred is the odds-on favorite for president of the board of trustees.*

**of the first water 1.** *Fig.* [of a gemstone] of the finest quality. (The *water* is probably from the Arabic word for *water* also having the meaning of luster or splendor. Diamonds or pearls of the first water are of the highest quality.) □ *This is a very fine pearl—a pearl of the first water.* **2.** *Fig.* of an excellent person or thing. □ *Tom is of the first water—a true gentleman.*

**of two minds (about** so/sth**)** *Fig.* holding conflicting opinions about someone or something; being undecided about someone or something. □ *I am of two minds about whether I should go to the convention.*

**\*off on a tangent** *Fig.* to be on a somewhat related or irrelevant course while neglecting the main subject. (\*Typically: **be** ~; **go** ~; **send** so ~.) □ *Just as we started talking, Henry went off on a tangent about the high cost of living.*

**off the charts** *Fig.* record setting; beyond the expected range of measurement. (Refers especially to huge sales of a book or CD.) □ *His book was a tremendous success. It is off the charts and making heaps of money.*

**\*off the hook** *Fig.* freed from an obligation. (Fig. on the image of a fish freeing itself from a fishhook. \*Typically: **be** ~; **get** ~;

**get** so ~; **let** so ~.) □ *Thanks for getting me off the hook. I didn't want to attend that meeting.*

**off the mark** *Fig.* not quite exactly right. □ *You were off the mark when you said we would be a little late to the party. It was yesterday, in fact!*

**off the record** *Fig.* unofficial; informal. (Of comments to the press that one does not want reported.) □ *Although her comments were off the record, the newspaper published them anyway.*

**off to a running start** with a good, fast beginning, possibly a head start. □ *I got off to a running start in math this year.*

**off to the races** *Fig.* an expression characterizing the activity or excitement that is just beginning; [we are] leaving for something interesting or exciting. □ *The tour bus is out in front waiting, and we've said good-bye to everyone. Looks like we're off to the races.*

**off-the-cuff** *Fig.* spontaneous; without preparation or rehearsal. □ *Her remarks were off-the-cuff, but very sensible.*

**off-the-wall** *Fig.* odd; silly; unusual. □ *Why are you so off-the-wall today?*

***old as Methuselah** very old. (Of a person; refers to a biblical figure held to have lived to be 969. *Also: **as** ~.) □ *Old Professor Stone is as old as Methuselah but still gets around with a cane.*

one's **old stamping ground** *Fig.* the place where one was raised or where one has spent a lot of time. (There are variants with *stomping* and *grounds*.) □ *I can't wait to get back to my old stomping grounds.*

***an old warhorse** a performance piece that is performed often. (*Typically: **be** ~; **become** ~; **perform** ~; **play** ~.) □ *The symphony orchestra played a few old warhorses and then some ghastly contemporary stuff that will never again see the light of day.*

an **old wives' tale** *Fig.* a myth or superstition. □ *You really don't believe that stuff about starving a cold do you? It's just an old wives' tale.*

*__on a fool's errand__ *Fig.* involved in a useless journey or task. (*Typically: **be** ~; **go** ~.) □ *Bill went for an interview, but he was on a fool's errand. The job had already been filled.*

*__on a pedestal__ *Fig.* elevated to a position of honor or reverence. (Fig. on the image of honoring someone on display on a pedestal like a statue. *Typically: **be** ~; **place** so ~; **put** so ~.) □ *He puts his wife on a pedestal. She can do no wrong in his opinion.*

**on a shoestring** *Fig.* with a very small amount of money. □ *We lived on a shoestring for years before I got a good-paying job.*

*__on a silver platter__ *Fig.* using a presentation [of something] that is appropriate for a very formal setting. (Usually with a touch of resentment. *Typically: **give** sth **to** so ~; **present** sth ~; **serve** sth ~; **want** sth ~.) □ *Aren't paper plates good enough for you? You want dinner maybe on a silver platter?*

**on a tight leash 1.** [of an animal] on a leash, held tightly and close to its owner. □ *I keep my dog on a tight leash so it won't bother people.* **2.** *Fig.* under very careful control. (Fig. on ①.) □ *We can't do much around here. The boss has us all on a tight leash.* **3.** *Sl.* addicted to some drug. □ *Wilbur is on a tight leash. He has to have the stuff regularly.*

*__on a wing and a prayer__ *Fig.* to arrive or fly in with one's plane in very bad condition. (From a WWII song about an airplane limping home on one engine after a successful bombing run. Sometimes used figuratively of other vehicles. *Typically: **come (in)** ~; **arrive** ~.) □ *Finally we could see the plane through the smoke, coming in on a wing and a prayer.*

**on again, off again** AND **off again, on again** *Fig.* uncertain; indecisive. □ *Jane doesn't know if she's going to look for a new job. She's off again, on again about it.*

**on automatic (pilot) 1.** flying on automatic controls. □ *The pilot set the plane on automatic pilot and went to the restroom.* **2.** [of a person] functioning in a semiconscious manner. (Fig. on ①.) □ *I was out late last night, and today I'm on automatic.*

**on bended knee** *Fig.* kneeling, as in supplication. (The verb form is obsolescent and occurs now only in this phrase.) □ *Do you expect me to come to you on bended knee and ask you for forgiveness?*

**on call** *Fig.* ready to serve when called. □ *I'm sorry, but I can't go out tonight. I'm on call at the hospital.*

**\*on course** *Fig.* following the plan correctly. (Fig. on a ship or plane following the course that was plotted for it. \*Typically: **be** ~; **get** ~; **stay** ~.) □ *Is the project on course?*

**on dead center** *Fig.* exactly correct. □ *My estimate wasn't on dead center, but it was very close to the final cost.*

**on easy street** *Fig.* in a state of financial independence and comfort. □ *When I get this contract signed, I'll be on easy street.*

**on** one's **high horse** *Fig.* in a haughty manner or mood. □ *The boss is on her high horse about the cost of office supplies.*

**on ice 1.** *Fig.* stored or preserved on ice or under refrigeration. □ *I have a lot of root beer on ice for the picnic.* **2.** *Fig.* [action on someone or something] suspended or left hanging. □ *I was on ice for over a month while the matter was being debated.*

**on medication** taking medicine for a current medical problem. □ *I can't drive the car, since I am on medication.*

**on moral grounds** *Fig.* considering reasons of morality. □ *He complained about the television program on moral grounds. There was too much ridicule of his religion.*

**on pins and needles** *Fig.* anxious; in suspense. □ *I've been on pins and needles all day, waiting for you to call with the news.*

**on** so's **radar (screen)** *Fig.* being considered and thought about by someone. (Fig. on the monitoring done by air traffic controllers.) □ *The whole matter is on my radar screen, and I will have a solution soon.*

**on second thought** *Fig.* having given something more thought; having reconsidered something. □ *On second thought, maybe you should sell your house and move into an apartment.*

**on shaky ground** AND **on dangerous ground** *Fig.* [of an idea or proposal] on an unstable or questionable foundation; [of an idea or proposal] founded on a risky premise. □ *When you suggest that we are to blame, you are on shaky ground. There is no evidence that we are at fault.*

***on the back burner** *Fig.* [of something] on hold or suspended temporarily. (Fig. on the image of putting a pot that needs less active attention on a back burner of a stove, leaving space for pots that need to be stirred. Compare this with **on the front burner**. *Typically: **be** ~; **put** sth ~.) □ *The building project is on the back burner for now.*

**on the ball** *Inf.* knowledgeable; competent; attentive. □ *This guy is really on the ball.*

***on the bandwagon** *Fig.* on the popular side (of an issue); taking a popular position. (*Typically: **be** ~; **climb** ~; **get** ~; **hop** ~; **jump** ~.) □ *Jane has always had her own ideas about things. She's not the kind of person to jump on the bandwagon.*

**on the dole** *Fig.* receiving welfare money. □ *I spent six months on the dole, and believe me, it's no picnic.*

***on the edge** *Fig.* very anxious and about to become distraught; on the verge of becoming irrational. (*Typically: **be** ~; **live** ~.) □ *After the horrible events of the last week, we are all on the edge.*

**on the eve of** sth *Fig.* just before something, possibly the evening before something. □ *John decided to leave school on the eve of his graduation.*

**on the face of it** *Fig.* superficially; from the way it looks. □ *This looks like a serious problem on the face of it. It probably is minor, however.*

**on the fast track** *Fig.* following an expedited procedure; being acted upon sooner or more quickly than is typical. □ *Let's put this project on the fast track, and maybe we'll see results sooner.*

**\*on the fence (about** sth**)** *Fig.* undecided about something. (\*Typically: **be** ~; **sit** ~.) □ *Ann is on the fence about going to Mexico.*

**on the fly** *Inf.* [done] while something or someone is operating or moving. □ *I'll try to capture the data on the fly.*

**on the fringe 1.** *Fig.* at the outer boundary or edge of something. □ *He doesn't live in the city, just on the fringe.* **2.** *Fig.* at the extremes of something, typically political thought. □ *He is way out. His political ideas are really on the fringe.*

**\*on the front burner** *Fig.* receiving particular attention or consideration. (Compare this with **on the back burner**. \*Typically: **be** ~; **leave** sth ~; **put** sth ~.) □ *So, what's on the front burner for us this week?* □ *Move this project to the front burner so it will get some attention.*

**on the horizon 1.** visible where the sky meets the land or sea. □ *There are storm clouds on the horizon.* □ *Is that a ship on the horizon?* **2.** *Fig.* soon to happen. (Fig. on ①. As if what is on the horizon is heading toward one.) □ *There is some excitement on the horizon, but I can't tell you about it.*

**on the horns of a dilemma** *Fig.* having to decide between two things, people, etc. □ *Mary found herself on the horns of a dilemma. She didn't know which to choose.*

**on the job** *Fig.* working; doing what one is expected to do. □ *I can depend on my furnace to be on the job day and night.*

**on the loose** *Fig.* running around free. □ *Look out! There is a bear on the loose from the zoo.*

**\*on the market** *Fig.* openly available for sale. (\*Typically: **be** ~; **get** sth ~; **put** sth ~.) □ *We put our house on the market last year, and it still hasn't sold.*

**on the mend** *Fig.* getting better; becoming healthy again. □ *I took a leave of absence from work while I was on the mend.*

**on the off-chance** *Fig.* because of a slight possibility that something may happen or might be the case; just in case. □ *I went to the theater on the off-chance that there were tickets for the show left.*

**on (the) one hand** *Fig.* from one point of view; as one side (of an issue). □ *On one hand, I really ought to support my team. On the other hand, I don't have to time to attend all the games.*

**on the other hand** *Fig.* a phrase introducing an alternate view. □ *Mary: I like this one. On the other hand, this is nice too. Sue: Why not get both?*

**on the pill** *Inf.* taking birth control pills. □ *Is it true that Mary is on the pill?*

**on the prowl** *Inf.* looking for someone for sexual purposes. (Fig. on a prowling cat.) □ *Tom looks like he is on the prowl again tonight.*

**on the right track 1.** *Fig.* following the right track or trail; riding on the correct track, as with a train. □ *The train was on the right track when it left the station. I can't imagine how it got lost.* **2.** *Fig.* following the right set of assumptions. (Fig. on ①.) □ *You are on the right track to find the answer.*

**on the rocks 1.** *Fig.* [of an alcoholic drink] served with ice cubes. □ *I'd like mine on the rocks, please.* **2.** [of a ship] broken and marooned on rocks in the sea. □ *The ship crashed and was on the rocks until the next high tide.* **3.** *Fig.* in a state of ruin or bankruptcy. (Fig. on ②.) □ *That bank is on the rocks. Don't put your money in it.*

**\*on the safe side** *Fig.* taking the risk-free path. (\*Typically: **(just) to be** ~; **stay** ~; **keep** ~; **remain** ~.) □ *I think you should stay on the safe side and call the doctor about this fever.*

**on the same wavelength** *Fig.* thinking in the same pattern. (Fig. on tuning into a broadcast signal.) □ *We kept talking until we got on the same wavelength.*

**\*on the spot 1.** *Fig.* at exactly the right place; at exactly the right time. (\*Typically: **be** ~.) □ *It's noon, and I'm glad you're all here on the spot. Now we can begin.* **2.** *Fig.* in trouble; in a difficult situation. (\*Typically: **be** ~; **put** so ~.) □ *There is a problem in the department I manage, and I'm really on the spot.*

**on the take** *Inf.* taking bribes. (Underworld.) □ *They say that everyone in city hall is on the take.*

**on the throne 1.** *Fig.* [of royalty] currently reigning. □ *King Samuel was on the throne for two decades.* **2.** *Sl.* seated on the toilet. □ *I can't come to the phone. I'm on the throne.*

**\*on the tip of** one's **tongue** *Fig.* [of a thought or idea] about to be said or almost remembered. (\*Typically: **be** ~; **have** sth ~.) □ *I have his name right on the tip of my tongue. I'll think of it in a second.*

**on the wane** *Fig.* becoming less; fading away. □ *Her influence is on the wane, but she is still the boss.*

**on the warpath** *Inf.* very angry. □ *I am on the warpath about setting goals and standards again.*

**on the wrong side of the law** *Fig.* in the criminal culture; not abiding by the law; having to do with breaking the law and being a lawbreaker. □ *Spike has spent most his life on the wrong side of the law.*

**on the wrong track** *Fig.* going the wrong way; following the wrong set of assumptions. □ *They won't get it figured out, because they are on the wrong track.*

**on thin ice** *Fig.* in a risky situation. □ *If you don't want to find your-self on thin ice, you must be sure of your facts.*

*****on** one's **toes** *Fig.* alert. (*Typically: **be** ~; **keep** ~; **keep** one ~; **stay** ~.) □ *You have to be on your toes if you want to be in this business.*

**on** so's **watch** *Inf.* while someone is on duty; while someone is sup-posed to be in charge of a situation. □ *I am not responsible since it didn't happen on my watch.*

**one for the (record) books** *Fig.* a record-breaking or very remarkable act. □ *What a dive! That's one for the record books.* □ *I've never heard such a funny joke. That's really one for the books.*

**one sandwich short of a picnic** *Inf.* not very smart; lacking intelligence. (Jocular.) □ *Poor Bob just isn't too bright. He's one sandwich short of a picnic.*

the **one that got away** *Fig.* the big fish that got away, especially as the subject of a fisherman's story. □ *The one that got away is always bigger than the one that got caught.*

**one-night stand 1.** *Fig.* a performance lasting only one night. □ *The band did a series of one-night stands down the East Coast.* **2.** *Fig.* a romance or sexual relationship that lasts only one night. (Fig. on ①.) □ *It looked like something that would last longer than a one-night stand.*

**open a conversation** to start a conversation. □ *I tried to open a conversation with him, but he had nothing to say.*

**open for business** *Fig.* [of a shop, store, restaurant, etc.] operat-ing and ready to do business. □ *The construction will be finished in March, and we will be open for business in April.*

**open Pandora's box** *Fig.* to uncover a lot of unsuspected prob-lems. □ *When I asked Jane about her problems, I didn't know I had opened Pandora's box.*

**open** oneself **to criticism** *Fig.* to do something that makes one vulnerable to criticism. □ *By saying something so stupid in public, you really opened yourself to criticism.*

**open to question** *Fig.* [an action or opinion] inviting question, examination, or refutation. □ *Everything he told you is open to question, and you should look into it.*

**open (up)** one's **kimono** *Sl.* to reveal what one is planning. (From the computer industry, referring especially to the involvement of the Japanese in this field.) □ *Even if Tom appears to open up his kimono on this deal, don't put much stock in what he says.*

an **open-and-shut case** *Fig.* a simple and straightforward situation without complications. (Often said of criminal cases where the evidence is convincing.) □ *The murder trial was an open-and-shut case. The defendant was caught with the murder weapon.*

the **opposite sex** the other sex; [from the point of view of a female] males; [from the point of view of a male] females. (Also with *member of,* as in the example.) □ *Bill is very shy when he's introduced to a member of the opposite sex.*

**or words to that effect** *Fig.* or similar words meaning the same thing. □ *Sally: She said that I wasn't doing my job well, or words to that effect. Jane: Well, you ought to find out exactly what she means. Sally: I'm afraid I know.*

**out in left field** *Fig.* offbeat; unusual and eccentric. □ *What a strange idea. It's really out in left field.*

**out of action** *Fig.* not operating temporarily; not functioning normally. □ *The pitcher was out of action for a month because of an injury.*

**\*out of (all) proportion** *Fig.* of exaggerated importance; of an unrealistic importance or size compared to something else. (\*Typically: **be** ~; **blow** sth ~; **grow** ~.) □ *Yes, this figure is way out of proportion to the others in the painting.*

**out of character 1.** *Fig.* unlike one's usual behavior. □ *Ann's remark was quite out of character.* **2.** *Fig.* inappropriate for the character that an actor is playing. □ *Bill played the part so well that it was hard for him to get out of character after the performance.*

**out of circulation 1.** *Fig.* no longer available for use or lending. (Usually said of library materials, certain kinds of currency, etc.) □ *I'm sorry, but the book you want is temporarily out of circulation.* **2.** *Fig.* not interacting socially with other people. (Fig. on ①.) □ *I don't know what's happening, because I've been out of circulation for a while.*

**\*out of gas 1.** *Lit.* without gasoline (in a car, truck, etc.). (\*Typically: **be ~; run ~.**) □ *We can't go any farther. We're out of gas.* **2.** *Fig.* tired; exhausted; worn out. (Fig. on ①. \*Typically: **be ~; run ~.**) □ *I think the old washing machine has finally run out of gas. I'll have to get a new one.*

**\*out of harm's way** *Fig.* not liable to be harmed; away from any causes of harm. (\*Typically: **be ~; get ~; get** so **~.**) □ *We should try to get all the civilians out of harm's way.*

**out of hock 1.** *Inf.* [of something] bought back from a pawn shop. □ *When I get my watch out of hock, I will always be on time.* **2.** *Inf.* out of debt; having one's debts paid. □ *When I pay off my credit cards, I'll be out of hock for the first time in years.*

**out of order 1.** [of something or things] out of the proper sequence. □ *All these cards were alphabetized, and now they're out of order.* **2.** *Fig.* [of something] incapable of operating; [of something] broken. □ *The elevator is out of order again.* **3.** *Fig.* not following correct parliamentary procedure. □ *Anne inquired, "Isn't a motion to table the question out of order at this time?"*

**\*out of practice** *Fig.* performing poorly due to a lack of practice. (\*Typically: **be ~; get ~; go ~.**) □ *I used to be able to play the piano extremely well, but now I'm out of practice.*

**out of print** *Fig.* [for a book] to be no longer available from the publisher. □ *The book you want just went out of print, but perhaps I can find a used copy for you.*

**\*out of** one's **shell** *Fig.* to make a person become more open and friendly. (Fig. on the image of a shy turtle being coaxed to put its head out of its shell. \*Typically: **bring** one ~; **come** ~; **get** one ~.) □ *We tried to bring Greg out of his shell, but he is very shy.* □ *He's quiet, and it's hard to get him out of his shell.*

**\*out of sight 1.** not visible; too far away to be seen. (\*Typically: **be** ~; **get** ~; **go** ~; **keep** ~; **stay** ~.) □ *The cat kept out of sight until the mouse came out.* **2.** *Inf.* figuratively stunning, unbelievable, or awesome. (Older. \*Typically: **be** ~; **get** ~.) □ *Wow, this music is out of sight!* **3.** *Inf.* very expensive; high in price; [of a price] so high that it cannot "be seen" in the distance. (\*Typically: **be** ~; **get** ~; **go** ~.) □ *The cost of medical care has gone out of sight.* **4.** *Sl.* heavily intoxicated. (\*Typically: **be** ~.) □ *They've been drinking since noon, and they're out of sight.*

**out of the ballpark** *Fig.* greater than the amount of money suggested or available. □ *Your estimate is completely out of the ballpark. Just forget it.*

**\*out of the closet 1.** *Fig.* revealing that one is homosexual. (\*Typically: **be** ~; **come** ~; **bring** so ~.) □ *Tom surprised his parents when he came out of the closet.* **2.** *Fig.* revealing one's secret interests. (\*Typically: **be** ~; **come** ~; **get** ~.) □ *It's time that all of you lovers of chamber music came out of the closet and attended our concerts.*

**out of the hole** *Fig.* out of debt. □ *I can't seem to get out of the hole. I keep spending more money than I earn.*

**out of the ordinary** *Fig.* unusual. □ *It was a good meal, but not out of the ordinary.*

**out of the picture** *Fig.* no longer relevant to a situation; departed; dead. □ *Now that Tom is out of the picture, we needn't concern ourselves about his objections.*

**out of the public eye** *Fig.* not visible or conspicuous. □ *The mayor tends to keep out of the public eye unless she's running for office.*

**out of the woods** *Fig.* past a critical phase; out of the unknown. □ *When the patient got out of the woods, everyone relaxed.*

**\*out of the woodwork** *Fig.* out into the open from other places or a place of concealment. (\*Typically: **bring** so/sth ~; **come** ~; **creep** ~.) □ *When the cake appeared, all the office people suddenly came out of the woodwork.*

**\*out on a limb** *Fig.* in a dangerous position to do something; at risk. (\*Typically: **be** ~; **go** ~; **put** so ~.) □ *I don't want to go out on a limb, but I think we can afford to do it.*

**out the window** *Inf.* gone; wasted. □ *All that work gone out the window because my computer crashed.*

**outside the box 1.** *Fig.* as if not bound by old, nonfunctional, or limiting structures, rules, or practices. (An adverb. Compare this with **inside the box**.) □ *Nothing can be done outside the box in such a rigid intellectual environment.* **2.** not bound by old, nonfunctional, or limiting structures, rules, or practices. (Usually **outside-the-box**. An adjective.) □ *You have some really outside-the-box ideas, Ralph.*

**\*over a barrel** *Fig.* out of one's control; in a dilemma. (\*Typically: **get** so ~; **have** so ~; **put** so ~.) □ *He got me over a barrel, and I had to do what he said.*

**Over my dead body!** *Inf.* a defiant phrase indicating the strength of one's opposition to something. (A joking response is "That can be arranged.") □ *Bill: I think I'll rent out our spare bedroom. Sue: Over my dead body! Bill (smiling): That can be arranged.*

**over the hump** *Fig.* over the hard part; past the midpoint. □ *Things should be easy from now on. We finally got over the hump.*

**over the moon** *Fig.* delighted; amazingly happy. □ *When I got the news, I was just over the moon!*

**owe** so **a debt of gratitude** *Fig.* a large amount of thanks owed to someone who deserves gratitude. (Actually payment of the debt is owed.) □ *We owe you a debt of gratitude for all you have done for us.*

\***one's own worst enemy** *Fig.* consistently causing oneself to fail; more harmful to oneself than other people are. (\*Typically: **be** ~; **become** ~.) □ *Ellen: My boss is my enemy. He never says anything good about me. Jane: Ellen, you're your own worst enemy. If you did your job responsibly, your boss would be nicer.*

# P

**pack** so/sth **(in**†**) like sardines** *Fig.* to squeeze in as many people or things as possible. (From the way that many sardines are packed into a can.) □ *The bus was full. The passengers were packed like sardines.*

a **pack of lies** a series of lies. □ *The thief told a pack of lies to cover up the crime.* □ *John listened to Bill's pack of lies about the fight and became very angry.*

**paddle** one's **own canoe** *Fig.* to do something by oneself; to be alone. □ *Sally isn't with us. She's off paddling her own canoe.*

**paint the town (red)** *Sl.* to go out and celebrate; to go on a drinking bout; to get drunk. □ *I feel like celebrating my promotion. Let's go out and paint the town.*

*a **paper trail** *Fig.* a series of records that is possible to examine to find out the sequence of things that happen. (*Typically: **have** ~; **leave** ~; **make** ~.) □ *The legal department requires all these forms so that there is a paper trail of all activity.*

**par for the course** *Fig.* typical; about what one could expect. (This refers to golf courses, not school courses.) □ *So he went off and left you? Well that's about par for the course. He's no friend.*

**Pardon me for living!** *Inf.* a very indignant response to a criticism or rebuke. □ *Fred: Oh, I thought you had already taken yourself out of here! Sue: Well, pardon me for living!*

**part** so's **hair** *Fig.* to come very close to someone. (Usually an exaggeration.) □ *That plane flew so low that it nearly parted my hair.*

**partners in crime** persons who cooperate in some legal task. □ *The legal department and payroll are partners in crime as far as the average worker is concerned.*

**pass judgment (on** so/sth**)** *Fig.* to make a judgment about someone or something. □ *I should not pass judgment on you, but I certainly could give you some good advice about how to be more pleasant.*

**pass muster** *Fig.* to measure up to the required standards. □ *If you don't wear a jacket and tie, you won't pass muster at that fancy restaurant. They won't let you in.*

**pass the hat (around**†**) (to** so**)** *Fig.* to collect donations of money from people. □ *Jerry passed the hat around to all the other workers.*

**pass the time of day** *Fig.* to chat with someone casually. □ *Fred likes to stop and pass the time of day with old Walter.*

**passport to** sth *Fig.* something that allows something good to happen. □ *Anne's new job is a passport to financial security.*

*a **past master at** sth *Fig.* someone proven extremely good or skillful at an activity. (*Typically: **be** ~; **become** ~.) □ *Pam is a past master at the art of complaining.*

**patch a quarrel up**† *Fig.* to put an end to a quarrel; to reconcile quarreling parties. □ *Tom and Fred were able to patch their quarrel up.*

*__patient as Job__ very patient. (Refers to the biblical figure Job. *Also: **as** ~.) □ *If you want to teach young children, you must be as patient as Job.*

the **patter of tiny feet** *Inf.* the sound of young children; having children in the household. □ *I really liked having the patter of tiny feet in the house.*

**pay dividends** *Fig.* to give someone an added bonus of some type. (Fig. on the dividends paid by stocks and some other financial assets.) □ *I think that your investment in time at the boys club will pay dividends for you for a long time.*

**pay homage to** so/sth *Fig.* to openly honor or worship someone or something. □ *I refuse to pay homage to your principles.*

**pay the penalty 1.** *Fig.* to pay a fine for doing something wrong. □ *You ran the red light, and now you will have to pay the penalty.* **2.** *Fig.* to suffer the consequences for doing something wrong. (Fig. on ①.) □ *My head really hurts. I am paying the penalty for getting drunk last night.*

**pay the piper** *Fig.* to face the results of one's actions; to receive punishment for something. □ *You can put off paying your debts only so long. Eventually you'll have to pay the piper.*

a **penny-pincher** *Fig.* someone who objects to the spending of every single penny. □ *If you weren't such a penny-pincher, you'd have some decent clothes.*

**Perish the thought.** *Fig.* Do not even consider thinking of such a (negative) thing. □ *If you should become ill—perish the thought—I'd take care of you.*

**pet hate** *Fig.* something that is disliked intensely and is a constant or repeated annoyance. □ *Another pet hate of mine is having to stand in line.*

**pet peeve** *Fig.* a frequent annoyance; one's "favorite" or most often encountered annoyance. □ *My pet peeve is someone who always comes into the theater after the show has started.*

a **photo op(portunity)** *Fig.* a time or event designed for taking pictures of a celebrity. □ *All the photographers raced toward a photo op with the president.*

**pick and choose** *Fig.* to choose very carefully from a number of possibilities; to be selective. □ *You must take what you are given. You cannot pick and choose.*

**pick** so's **brain(s)** *Fig.* to talk with someone to find out information about something. □ *I spent the afternoon with Donna, picking her brain for ideas to use in our celebration.*

**pick** so's **pocket 1.** to secretly steal something from someone's pocket. □ *Somebody picked my pocket downtown, and now my credit cards are maxed out.* **2.** *Fig.* to take someone's assets legally, as through taxation. (Jocular or cynical.) □ *The governor's been picking our pockets for every little project his friends can dream up!*

**pick** sth **to pieces 1.** to pick at something until it falls apart. □ *Eat your sandwich, child! Don't just pick it to pieces.* **2.** *Fig.* to destroy an argument or performance by attacking and criticizing every detail.

the **picture of (good) health** in a very healthy condition. □ *The doctor says I am the picture of good health.*

**pie in the sky 1.** *Fig.* a future reward after death, considered as a replacement for a reward not received on earth. □ *Don't hold out for pie in the sky. Get realistic.* **2.** *Fig.* having to do with a hope for a special reward. (This is hyphenated before a nominal.) □ *Get rid of your pie-in-the-sky ideas!* □ *What these pie-in-the-sky people really want is money.*

a **pipe dream** *Fig.* a wish or an idea that is impossible to achieve or carry out. (From the dreams or visions induced by the smoking of an opium pipe.) □ *Going to the West Indies is a pipe dream. We'll never have enough money.*

the **pit of** one's **stomach** *Fig.* the middle of one's stomach; the location of a "visceral response." □ *I got a strange feeling in the pit of my stomach when they told me the bad news.*

**place** so **in an awkward position** *Fig.* to put someone in an embarrassing or delicate situation. □ *Your decision places me in an awkward position.*

a **place to call** one's **own** *Fig.* a home of one's very own. □ *I am tired of living with my parents. I want a place to call my own.*

pie in the sky (sense 1)

**plaster** one's **hair down**[†] *Fig.* to use water, oil, or cream to dress the hair for combing. (The result looks plastered to the head.) ☐ *Tony used some strange substance to plaster his hair down.*

**play cat and mouse with** so *Fig.* to be coy and evasive with someone. ☐ *I know what you are up to. Don't play cat and mouse with me!*

**play first chair 1.** *Fig.* to be the leader of a section of instruments in an orchestra or a band. ☐ *Sally learned to play the violin so well that she now plays first chair in the orchestra.* **2.** *Fig.* to act as a leader. (Fig. on ①.) ☐ *I need someone to make sure this job gets done. Who plays first chair around here?*

**play footsie with** so **1.** *Inf.* to get romantically or sexually involved with someone. (Refers literally to secretly pushing or rubbing feet with someone under the table.) □ *Someone said that Ruth is playing footsie with Henry even though they are both married to someone else.* **2.** *Inf.* to get involved in a scheme with someone; to cooperate with someone. (Fig. on ①.) □ *The guy who runs the butcher shop was playing footsie with the city meat inspector.*

**play hardball (with so)** *Inf.* to act strong and aggressive about an issue with someone. □ *Things are getting a little tough. The president has decided to play hardball on this issue.*

**play in the big leagues** *Fig.* to be involved in something of large or important proportions. (Refers originally to playing a professional sport at the highest level.) □ *The conductor shouted at the oboist, "You're playing in the big leagues now! Tune up or ship out!"*

**play it for all it's worth** *Fig.* to exploit a problem, disability, or injury to get as much sympathy or compensation as possible. □ *He injured his hand before the examination, and he played it for all it was worth in order to get the exam delayed.*

**play politics 1.** *Fig.* to negotiate politically. □ *Everybody at city hall is playing politics as usual.* **2.** to allow politics to dominate in matters where principle should prevail. □ *They're not making reasonable decisions. They're just playing politics.*

**play possum** *Fig.* to pretend to be inactive, unobservant, asleep, or dead. (The *possum* refers to an opossum.) □ *I knew that Bob wasn't asleep. He was just playing possum.* □ *I can't tell if this animal is dead or just playing possum.*

**play (the) devil's advocate** *Fig.* to put forward arguments against or objections to a proposition—which one may actually agree with—purely to test the validity of the proposition. (The devil's advocate challenges the evidence presented for the canonization of a saint to make sure that the grounds for canonization are sound.) □ *Mary offered to play devil's advocate and argue against our case so that we would find out any flaws in it.*

**play the (stock) market** *Fig.* to invest in the stock market. (As if it were a game or as if it were gambling.) □ *I've learned my lesson playing the market. I lost a fortune.*

**play** one's **trump card 1.** [in certain card games] to play a card that, according to the rules of the game, outranks certain other cards and is thus able to take any card of another suit. □ *Bob played his trump card and ended the game as the winner.* **2.** *Fig.* to use a special trick; to use one's most powerful or effective strategy or device. (Fig. on ①.) □ *I thought that the whole situation was hopeless until Mary played her trump card and solved the whole problem.*

**play with a full deck** *Fig.* to operate as if one were mentally sound. (Usually in the negative. One cannot play cards properly with a partial deck.) □ *Look sharp, you dummies! Pretend you are playing with a full deck.*

**play with fire** *Fig.* to do something dangerous or risky. (Usually *playing with fire.*) □ *Be careful with that knife! You are playing with fire!*

**plight** one's **troth to** so *Fig.* to become engaged to be married to someone. (Literary or jocular.) □ *I chose not to plight my troth to anyone who acts so unpleasant to my dear aunt.*

The **plot thickens.** Things are becoming more complicated or interesting. □ *John is supposed to be going out with Mary, but I saw him last night with Sally. The plot thickens.*

a **pocket of resistance** *Fig.* a small group of people who resist change or domination. □ *The accounting department seems to be a pocket of resistance when it comes to automating.*

**point the finger at** so *Fig.* to blame someone; to identify someone as the guilty person. □ *Don't point the finger at me! I didn't take the money.*

**poison** so **against** so/sth *Fig.* to cause someone to have negative or hateful thoughts about someone, a group, or something. □ *Your negative comments poisoned everyone against the proposal.*

**poke fun at** so/sth to make fun of someone or something. □ *You shouldn't poke fun at me for my mistakes.*

**\*poles apart** *Fig.* very different; far from coming to an agreement. (Refers to the distance between the north and south poles. \*Typically: **be** ~; **become** ~; **grow** ~.) □ *They'll never sign the contract because they are poles apart.*

a **political football** *Fig.* an issue that becomes politically divisive; a problem that doesn't get solved because the politics of the issue get in the way. □ *The question of campaign contributions has become a political football. All the politicians who accept questionable money are pointing fingers at each other.*

**\*poor as a church mouse** AND **\*poor as church mice** very poor. (\*Also: **as** ~.) □ *My aunt is as poor as a church mouse.*

**pose a challenge** to represent a challenge; to be a challenge [for someone]. □ *Finding places to seat all the guests in this small room really poses a challenge.*

**pose a question** *Fig.* to ask a question; to imply the need for asking a question. □ *Genetic research poses many ethical questions.*

a **poster child (for** sth**)** *Fig.* someone who is a classic example of a state or type of person. (From mid-20th-century *poster boy*, the term for a specific child stricken with polio who appeared on posters encouraging contributions to The March of Dimes. Later *poster girls* brought on the *child.*) □ *She is a poster child for soccer moms.*

a **pot of gold 1.** a container filled with gold, as in the myth where it is guarded by a leprechaun. □ *I was hoping to find a pot of gold in the cellar, but there were only cobwebs.* **2.** *Fig.* an imaginary reward. □ *Whoever gets to the porch first wins a pot of gold.*

*a **pound of flesh** *Fig.* a payment or punishment that involves suffering and sacrifice on the part of the person being punished. (*Typically: **give** so ~; **owe** so ~; **pay** so ~; **take** ~.) □ *He wants revenge. He won't be satisfied until he takes his pound of flesh.*

**pour** one's **heart out to** so AND **pour** one's **heart out**† *Fig.* to tell one's personal feelings to someone else. □ *I didn't mean to pour my heart out to you, but I guess I just had to talk to someone.*

**pour oil on troubled water(s)** *Fig.* to calm someone or something down. (A thin layer of oil will actually calm a small area of a rough sea.) □ *Don can calm things down. He's good at pouring oil on troubled waters.*

the **power behind the throne** *Fig.* the person who actually controls the person who is apparently in charge. □ *Mr. Smith appears to run the shop, but his brother is the power behind the throne.*

a **power play** *Fig.* a strategy using one's power or authority to carry out a plan or to get one's way. □ *In a blatant power play, the manager claimed he had initiated the sales campaign.*

**preach to the choir** AND **preach to the converted** *Fig.* to make one's case primarily to one's supporters; to make one's case only to those people who are present or who are already friendly to the issues. □ *There is no need to convince us of the value of hard work. We already know that. You are just preaching to the choir.* □ *Bob found himself preaching to the converted when he was telling Jane the advantages of living in the suburbs. She already hates city life.*

**preach to the converted** Go to previous.

**press** so/sth **into service** to force someone or something to serve or function. □ *I don't think you can press him into service just yet. He isn't trained.* □ *I think that in an emergency, we could press this machine into service.*

the **price** one **has to pay** *Fig.* the sacrifice that one has to make; the unpleasantness that one has to suffer. □ *Being away from home a lot is the price one has to pay for success.*

*a **price on** one's **head** *Fig.* a reward for one's capture. (*Typically: **get** ~; **have** ~; **put** ~; **place** ~.) □ *We captured a thief who had a price on his head, and the sheriff gave us the reward.*

**pride and joy** *Fig.* something or someone that one is very proud of. (Often in reference to a baby, a car, a house, etc. Fixed order.) □ *And this is Roger, our little pride and joy.*

the **primrose path** *Fig.* invitingly appealing prospects that soon evaporate. □ *She led him down the primrose path until she got tired of him.*

**publish or perish** *Fig.* [for a professor] to try to publish scholarly books or articles to prevent getting released from a university or falling into disfavor in a university. (Also occurs as other parts of speech. See the example.) □ *This is a major research university, and publish or perish is the order of the day.*

**pull all the stops out**† *Fig.* to use everything available; to not hold back. (Fig. on the image of pulling out all of the stops on an organ so that it will sound as loud and full as possible.) □ *Todd pulled all the stops out for his exhibition and impressed everyone with his painting artistry.*

**pull in** one's **ears** *Fig.* to stop listening in on someone or something. □ *Now, pull in your ears. This is none of your business.*

**pull** sth **out of the fire** AND **pull** sth **from the fire** *Fig.* to rescue something; to save something just before it's too late. □ *Can we rescue this project? Is there time to pull it out of the fire?*

**pull** one's **punches 1.** *Fig.* [for a boxer] to strike with light blows to enable the other boxer to win. □ *Bill has been barred from the boxing ring for pulling his punches.* **2.** *Fig.* to hold back in one's criticism. (Fig. on ①. Usually in the negative. The *one's* can be replaced with *any* in the negative.) □ *I didn't pull any punches. I told her exactly what I thought of her.*

**pull rank on** so *Fig.* to use one's higher position, office, or rank to pressure someone into doing something. (Fig. on military usage.) □ *I hate to pull rank on you, but I'll take the lower bunk.*

**pull the plug (on** sth**)** *Fig.* to reduce the power or effectiveness of something; to disable something. □ *Jane pulled the plug on the whole project.*

**pull the rug out**† **(from under** so**)** *Fig.* to make someone or someone's plans fall through; to upset someone's plans. (Fig. on the image of upsetting someone by jerking the rug that they are standing on.) □ *Don pulled the rug out from under me in my deal with Bill Franklin.*

**pull the wool over** so's **eyes** *Fig.* to deceive someone. □ *Don't try to pull the wool over her eyes. She's too smart.*

**pull** oneself **up by** one's **(own) bootstraps** *Fig.* to improve or become a success by one's own efforts. □ *If Sam had a little encouragement, he could pull himself up by his bootstraps.*

**punch a clock** *Fig.* to punch or register one's arrival or departure on a workplace time clock or other similar record-keeping device on a daily basis. □ *Now that I am my own boss, I don't have to punch a clock every day.*

**push** so's **buttons** *Fig.* to arouse or anger a person by bringing up things that are sure to draw a lively response or to use a manner that will draw a lively response. (The response is usually negative.) □ *You always know how to get me mad! Why do you always push my buttons when you know it makes me so upset?*

**pushing the envelope** *Fig.* attempting to expand the definition, categorization, dimensions, or perimeters of something farther than is usual. □ *The engineers wanted to completely redesign the product but were pushing the envelope when it came to public acceptance.*

**pushing up (the) daisies** *Fig.* dead and buried. (Usually in the future tense.) □ *If you talk to me like that again, you'll be pushing up the daisies!*

**put a plug in**† **(for** so/sth**)** *Fig.* to say something favoring someone or something; to advertise someone or something. □ *I hope that when you are in talking to the manager, you put a plug in for me.*

**put a smile on** so's **face** *Fig.* to please someone; to make someone happy. □ *We are going to give Andy a pretty good raise, and I know that'll put a smile on his face.*

**put all** one's **eggs in one basket** *Fig.* to make everything dependent on only one thing; to place all one's resources in one place, account, etc. (If the basket is dropped, all is lost.) □ *Don't invest all your money in one company. Never put all your eggs in one basket.*

**put** one's **best foot forward** *Fig.* to act or appear at one's best; to try to make a good impression. □ *When you apply for a job, you should always put your best foot forward.*

**put** one's **dibs on** sth *Fig.* to lay a claim to something; to announce one's claim to something. □ *She put her dibs on the last piece of cake.*

**put** so's **eye out**† to puncture or harm someone's eye and destroy its ability to see. □ *Careful with that stick or you'll put your eye out.*

**put** one's **face on** *Fig.* [for a woman] to apply cosmetics. □ *We'll be on our way once my wife has put her face on.*

**put** one's **finger on** sth *Fig.* to identify and state the essence of something. □ *That is correct! You have certainly put your finger on the problem.*

**put** one's **hand to the plow** *Fig.* to get busy; to help out; to start working. (Fig. on the image of grasping a plow, ready to work the fields.) □ *You should start work now. It's time to put your hand to the plow.*

**put** one's **head on the block (for** so/sth**)** *Fig.* to take great risks for someone or something; to go to a lot of trouble or difficulty for someone or something; to attempt to gain favor for someone or something. (Fig. on the notion of sacrificing one's life by decapitation for the sake of someone else.) □ *I don't know why I should put my head on the block for Joan. What has she ever done for me?*

**put** people's **heads together** *Fig.* to join together with someone to confer. □ *Let's put our heads together and come up with a solution to this problem.*

**put ideas into** so's **head** *Fig.* to suggest something—usually something bad—to someone (who would not have thought of it otherwise). □ *Bill keeps getting into trouble. Please don't put ideas into his head.*

**put** sth **in a nutshell** *Fig.* to state something very concisely. (Fig. on the small size of a nutshell and the amount that it would hold.) □ *The entire explanation is long and involved, but let me put it in a nutshell for you.*

**put** one's **nose to the grindstone** *Fig.* to get busy doing one's work. □ *The boss told me to put my nose to the grindstone.*

**put** one **on** one's **honor** *Fig.* to inform one that one is trusted to act honorably, legally, and fairly without supervision. □ *I'll put you on your honor when I have to leave the room during the test.*

**put** sth **on the street** *Sl.* to tell something openly; to spread news. □ *There is no need to put all this gossip on the street. Keep it to yourself.*

**put one foot in front of the other 1.** *Fig.* to walk deliberately. □ *I was so tired that I could hardly even put one foot in front of the other.* **2.** *Fig.* to do things carefully and in their proper order. (Fig. on ①.) □ *Let's do it right now. Just put one foot in front of the other. One thing at a time.*

**put** some creature **out of its misery** *Fig.* to kill an animal in a humane manner. □ *The vet put that dog with cancer out of its misery.*

**put out (some) feelers (on** so/sth**)** to arrange to find out about something in an indirect manner. □ *I put out some feelers on Betty to try to find out what is going on.*

**put paid to** sth *Fig.* to consider something closed or completed; to mark or indicate that something is no longer important or pending. (As if one were stamping a bill "paid.") □ *At last, we were able to put paid to the matter of who is to manage the accounts.*

**put some teeth into** sth *Fig.* to increase the power or efficacy of something. □ *The mayor tried to put some teeth into the new law.*

**Put that in your pipe and smoke it!** *Inf.* See how you like that!; It is final, and you have to live with it. □ *Well, I'm not going to do what you want, so put that in your pipe and smoke it!*

**put the arm on** so *Fig.* to apply pressure to someone. □ *John's been putting the arm on Mary to get her to go out with him.*

**put the fear of God in(to)** so *Fig.* to frighten someone severely; [for something] to shock someone into contrite behavior. □ *A near miss like that really puts the fear of God into you.*

**put the pedal to the metal** *Sl.* to press a car's accelerator to the floor; to drive very fast. □ *Put the pedal to the metal, and we'll make up some lost time.*

**put** so **through the wringer** *Fig.* to give someone a difficult time; to interrogate someone thoroughly. (Fig. on putting something through an old-fashioned clothes wringer.) □ *The lawyer really put the witness through the wringer!*

**put to bed with a shovel** *Sl.* dead and buried. (Fig. on the image of digging a grave.) □ *You wanna be put to bed with a shovel? Just keep talking that way.*

**put** so/sth **to the test** *Fig.* to see what someone or something can achieve. □ *I'm going to put my car to the test right now, and see how fast it will go.*

**put two and two together** *Fig.* to figure something out from the information available. □ *Don't worry. John won't figure it out. He can't put two and two together.*

**put** sth **under the microscope** AND **put** sth **under a microscope** *Fig.* to examine, analyze, or study something in great detail. (Can also be used literally, of course.) □ *I'll have to study your proposition. Let me put it under the microscope for a while and see what it will cost us in time and money, and I'll get back to you.*

**Put up or shut up! 1.** *Inf.* Do something or stop promising to do it! □ *I'm tired of your telling everyone how fast you can run. Now, do it! Put up or shut up!* **2.** *Inf.* a command that a person bet money in support of what the person advocates. □ *You think you can beat me at cards? Twenty bucks says you're wrong. Put up or shut up!*

**put words in(to)** so's **mouth** *Fig.* to interpret what someone said so that the words mean what you want and not what the speaker wanted. □ *I didn't say that! You are putting words into my mouth.*

**Put your money where your mouth is!** *Inf.* Stop just talking and stake your own money! (From gambling. Can also be said to someone giving investment advice.) □ *You want me to bet on that horse? Did you? Why don't you put your money where your mouth is?* □ *If this is such a good stock, you buy it. Put your money where your mouth is!*

**quality time** *Fig.* time spent with someone allowing interaction and closeness. □ *He was able to spend a few minutes of quality time with his son, Buxton, at least once every two weeks.*

**quick and dirty** *Fig.* [done] fast and carelessly; [done] fast and cheaply. □ *The contractor made a lot of money on quick and dirty projects that would never last very long.*

**quick as a flash** Go to next.

**\*quick as a wink** AND **\*quick as a flash; \*quick as (greased) lightning; \*swift as lightning** very quickly. (\*Also: **as** ~.) □ *As quick as a wink, the thief took the lady's purse.* □ *Quick as greased lightning, the thief stole my wallet.*

**quick as (greased) lightning** Go to previous.

**quick on the draw** Go to next.

**quick on the trigger** AND **quick on the draw 1.** *Fig.* quick to draw a gun and shoot. □ *Some of the old cowboys were known to be quick on the trigger.* **2.** *Fig.* quick to respond to anything. (Fig. on ①.) □ *John gets the right answer before anyone else. He's really quick on the trigger.*

**quit while** one **is ahead** *Fig.* to stop doing something while one is still successful. □ *Get into the market. Make some money and get out. Quit while you're ahead.*

**quote, unquote** *Fig.* a parenthetical expression said before a word or short phrase indicating that the word or phrase would be in quotation marks if used in writing. □ *So I said to her, quote, unquote, it's time we had a little talk.*

the **race card** *Cliché* the issue of race magnified and injected into a situation that might otherwise be nonracial. (*Typically: **deal** ~; **play** ~; **use** ~.) □ *At the last minute, the opposition candidate played the race card and lost the election for himself.*

**rack** one's **brain(s)** *Fig.* to try very hard to think of something. □ *Don't waste any more time racking your brain for the answer. Just go look it up online.*

**rain cats and dogs** *Fig.* to rain very hard. □ *I'm not going out in that storm. It's raining cats and dogs.*

*a **rain check (on** sth**) 1.** *Fig.* a piece of paper allowing one to see an event—which has been canceled—at a later time. (Originally said of sporting events that had to be canceled because of rain. *Typically: **get** ~; **have** ~; **take** ~; **give** so ~.) □ *The game was canceled because of the storm, but we all got rain checks on it.* **2.** *Fig.* a reissuing of an invitation at a later date. (Said to someone who has invited you to something that you cannot attend now but would like to attend at a later time. *Typically: **get** ~; **have** ~; **take** ~; **give** so ~.) □ *We would love to come to your house, but we are busy next Saturday. Could we take a rain check on your kind invitation?* **3.** *Fig.* a piece of paper that allows one to purchase an item on sale at a later date. (Stores issue these pieces of paper when they run out of specially priced sale merchandise. *Typically: **get** ~; **have** ~; **take** ~; **give** so ~.) □ *The store was all out of the shampoo they advertised, but I got a rain check.* □ *Yes, you should always take a rain check so you can get it at the sale price later when they have more.*

**rain on** so's **parade** AND **rain on** so/sth *Fig.* to spoil something for someone; to cause someone distress in the same way that unwelcome rain would cause distress. □ *I hate to rain on your parade, but your plans are all wrong.* □ *She really rained on our plans.*

**raise Cain** *Fig.* to make a lot of trouble; to raise hell. (A biblical reference, from Genesis 4. Probably a punning mincing of *raise hell.*) □ *Fred was really raising Cain about the whole matter.*

**raise** one's **sights** *Fig.* to set higher goals for oneself. (Fig. on the image of someone lifting the sights of a gun in order to fire farther.) □ *When you're young, you tend to raise your sights too high.* □ *On the other hand, some people need to raise their sights.*

**raise the bar** *Fig.* to make a task a little more difficult. (As with raising the bar in high jumping or pole vaulting.) □ *Just as I was getting accustomed to my job, the manager raised the bar and I had to perform even better.*

**rank and file 1.** *Fig.* the regular soldiers, not the officers. □ *I think there is low morale among the rank and file, sir.* **2.** *Fig.* the ordinary members of a group, not the leaders. (Fig. on ①.) □ *The last contract was turned down by the rank and file last year.*

**rant and rave (about** so/sth**)** to shout angrily and wildly about someone or something. □ *Barbara rants and raves when her children don't obey her.*

the **rat race** *Fig.* a fierce struggle for success, especially in one's career or business. □ *Bob got tired of the rat race. He's retired and moved to the country.*

**rattle** so's **cage** *Fig.* to alert or annoy someone in a way that sets him or her into action. (As if one were trying to excite or stimulate an animal by rattling its cage.) □ *The plumber didn't show up again. I guess I'll have to call and rattle his cage.*

a **ray of sunshine** *Fig.* a bit of good or happy news in an unhappy situation; a person or thing whose presence makes an unhappy situation a little happier. □ *When you came in, you were a ray of sunshine for our little group of homeless children.*

**reach first base (with** so/sth**)** Go to get to first base (with so/sth).

**read between the lines** *Fig.* to infer something (from something else); to try to understand what is meant by something that is not written explicitly or openly. □ *After listening to what she said, if you read between the lines, you can begin to see what she really means.*

**read it and weep** *Inf. Fig.* read the bad news; hear the bad news. □ *I'm sorry to bring you the bad news, but read it and weep.*

**read** so **like a book** *Fig.* to understand someone very well. □ *I've got John figured out. I can read him like a book.*

**read** so's **lips** *Fig.* to manage to understand speech by watching and interpreting the movements of the speaker's lips. □ *I couldn't hear her but I could read her lips.*

**read** so's **mind** *Fig.* to guess what someone is thinking. □ *You'll have to tell me what you want. I can't read your mind, you know.* □ *If I could read your mind, I'd know what you expect of me.*

**ready to roll** *Fig. Lit.* ready to start something. (Specifically, of a journey where wheels will be rolling or of filming where film spools or videotape will be rolling—even when digital storage is used.) □ *Everything is set up and we're ready to roll.*

**ready, willing, and able** *Cliché* eager or at least willing [to do something]. □ *If you need someone to help you move furniture, I'm ready, willing, and able.*

the **real McCoy** *Fig.* an authentic thing or person. (There are many clever tales devised as origins for this expression. There is absolutely no evidence for any of them, however. There is evidence in the U.K. for metaphoric uses of "the Real MacKay" [referring to authentic MacKay Whiskey], but no evidence of how MacKay became McCoy in the U.S.) □ *Of course it's authentic! It's the real McCoy!*

**rear its ugly head** *Fig.* [for something unpleasant] to appear or become obvious after lying hidden. □ *The question of money always rears its ugly head in matters of business.*

**recharge** one's **batteries** *Fig.* to get some refreshing rest. (Alludes to recharging electrical storage batteries.) □ *I need to get home and recharge my batteries. I'll be back on the job early tomorrow morning.*

a **red herring** a piece of information or suggestion introduced to draw attention away from the real facts of a situation. (A smoked [and therefore red] herring is a strong-smelling fish that could be drawn across a trail of scent to mislead hunting dogs and put them off the scent.) □ *The detectives were following a red herring, but they're on the right track now.* □ *The mystery novel has a couple of red herrings that keep readers off-guard.*

**red tape** *Fig.* over-strict attention to the wording and details of rules and regulations, especially by government workers. (From the color of the tape used by government departments in England to tie up bundles of documents.) □ *Because of red tape, Frank took weeks to get a visa.*

*the **red-carpet treatment** *Fig.* very special treatment; royal treatment. (*Typically: **get** ~; **have** ~; **give** so ~.) □ *I love to go to fancy stores where I get the red-carpet treatment.*

*regular as clockwork** *Cliché* very regular; completely predictable. (*Also: **as** ~.) □ *George goes down to the bus stop at 7:45 every morning, as regular as clockwork.*

a **regular fixture** *Fig.* someone who is found so frequently in a place as to be considered a fixture of, or part of, the place. □ *The manager attached himself to the luncheon club and became a regular fixture there.*

**reinvent the wheel** *Fig.* to make unnecessary or redundant preparations. □ *You don't need to reinvent the wheel. Read up on what others have done.*

**religious about** doing sth *Fig.* strict about something; conscientious about something. □ *Bob is religious about paying his bills on time.*

**remember** so **to** so to carry the greetings of someone to someone else. □ *I will remember you to my brother, who asks of you often.*

**resonate with** so *Fig.* [for an idea, issue, or concept] to appeal to someone or cause someone to relate to it. (Very close to a *Cliché.*) □ *The concept of wearing worn-looking clothing seems to resonate with young people.* □ *Your notion just doesn't resonate with the public in general.*

**rest in peace** *Fig.* to lie dead peacefully for eternity. (A solemn entreaty used in funeral prayers, eulogies, etc.) □ *We prayed that the deceased would rest in peace.*

The **rest is history.** *Fig.* Everyone knows the rest of the story that I am referring to. □ *Bill: Then they arrested all the officers of the corporation, and the rest is history.* □ *Bob: Hey, what happened between you and Sue? Bill: Finally we realized that we could never get along, and the rest is history.*

**rest on** one's **laurels** *Fig.* to stop trying because one is satisfied with one's past achievements. □ *We rested on our laurels too long. Our competitors took away a lot of our business.*

**return the favor** *Fig.* to do a good deed for someone who has done a good deed for you. (Sometimes used ironically for the return of a bad deed.) □ *You helped me last week, so I'll return the favor and help you this week.*

**ride off in all directions** *Fig.* to behave in a totally confused manner; to try to do everything at once. □ *Bill has a tendency to ride off in all directions. He's not organized enough.*

**ride the gravy train** *Fig.* to live in ease or luxury. □ *I wouldn't like loafing if I were rich. I don't want to ride the gravy train.*

**riding for a fall** *Fig.* risking failure or an accident, usually due to overconfidence. □ *Tom drives too fast, and he seems too sure of himself. He's riding for a fall.*

rest on one's laurels

**right in the kisser** *Inf.* right in the mouth or face. □ *Wilbur poked the cop right in the kisser.*

**(right) off the top of** one's **head** *Fig.* without giving it too much thought or without precise knowledge. □ *Mary: How much do you think this car would be worth on a trade? Fred: Well, right off the top of my head, I'd say about a thousand.*

the **right stuff** *Fig.* the right or correct character or set of skills to do something well. □ *She's got the right stuff to be a winner.*

**ring a bell** *Fig.* [for something] to cause someone to remember something or for it to seem familiar. (Fig. on a bell serving as a reminder or alarm.) □ *I've never met John Franklin, but his name rings a bell.*

**ring in the new year** *Fig.* to celebrate the beginning of the new year at midnight on December 31. □ *We are planning a big party to ring in the new year.*

**ring out the old (year)** *Fig.* to celebrate the end of a year while celebrating the beginning of a new one. □ *I don't plan to ring out the old this year. I'm just going to go to bed.*

**ring true** *Fig.* to sound or seem true or likely. (From testing the quality of metal or glass by striking it and evaluating the sound made.) □ *The student's excuse for being late doesn't ring true.*

a **riot of color** *Cliché* a selection of many bright colors. □ *The landscape was a riot of color each autumn.*

a **ripe old age** *Fig.* a very old age. □ *Mr. Smith died last night, but he lived to the ripe old age of 99.* □ *All the Smiths seem to reach a ripe old age.*

**ripple through** sth *Fig.* to move through something or a group of people in a ripple or wave motion. □ *A murmur of excitement rippled through the crowd.*

**Rise and shine!** *Fig.* Get out of bed and be lively and energetic! (Often a command.) □ *Father always calls "Rise and shine!" in the morning when we want to go on sleeping.*

**rise from the ashes** *Fig.* [for a structure] to be rebuilt after destruction. □ *The entire west section of the city was destroyed, and a group of new buildings rose from the ashes in only a few months.*

**riveted to the ground** *Fig.* [of someone or someone's feet] unable to move. □ *My feet were riveted to the ground, and I could not move an inch.*

**road hog** *Fig.* someone who drives carelessly and selfishly. □ *Look at that road hog driving in the middle of the road and stopping other drivers from passing him.*

**rob Peter to pay Paul** *Fig.* to take or borrow from one in order to give or pay something owed to another. □ *Why borrow money to pay your bills? That's just robbing Peter to pay Paul.*

**rob the cradle** *Fig.* to marry or date someone who is much younger than oneself. □ *Uncle Bill—who is nearly 80—married a 30-year-old woman. That is really robbing the cradle.*

**rock the boat** *Fig.* to cause trouble where none is welcome; to disturb a situation that is otherwise stable and satisfactory. (Often negative.) □ *Look, Tom, everything is going fine here. Don't rock the boat!* □ *You can depend on Tom to mess things up by rocking the boat.*

a **rocky road** *Fig.* a difficult period of time. □ *Bob's been going down quite a rocky road since his divorce.* □ *Life is a rocky road.*

**roll over and play dead** *Fig.* to just give up and be unable to cope with life or a problem. □ *Why can't I complain about this? Am I supposed to roll over and play dead?*

**romp through** sth *Fig.* to perform something fast and playfully. □ *The conductor romped through the slow movement of the symphony as if it were a march.*

**room and board** *Fig.* food to eat and a place to live; the cost of food and lodging. □ *That college charges too much for room and board.*

a **rotten apple** *Inf.* a single bad person or thing. (Sometimes there is the implication that the "rot" will spread to others, as with the one rotten apple that spoils the rest in the barrel.) □ *There always is a rotten apple to spoil it for the rest of us.* □ *Leave it to one rotten apple to bring down the conversation to the basest level.*

**rotten to the core** *Fig.* really bad; corrupt. □ *That lousy punk is rotten to the core.*

a **rounding error** *Fig.* a large amount of money that is relatively small in comparison to a much larger sum. □ *To a large company* *like Smith & Co., a few thousand dollars is just a rounding error. It's not a lot at all.*

a **royal pain** *Fig.* a great annoyance. □ *This guy's a royal pain, but we have to put up with him because he's the boss.*

the **royal treatment** very good treatment; very good and thoughtful care of a person. □ *I really got the royal treatment when I stayed at that expensive hotel.*

**rub elbows (with** so**)** AND **rub shoulders with** so *Fig.* to associate with someone; to work closely with someone. (No physical contact is involved.) □ *I don't care to rub elbows with someone who acts like that!*

**rub salt in a wound** *Fig.* to deliberately make someone's unhappiness, shame, or misfortune worse. □ *Don't rub salt in the wound by telling me how enjoyable the party was.*

**rub shoulders with** so Go to rub elbows (with so).

**ruffle** so's **feathers** *Fig.* to irritate or annoy someone. (As a bird might expand its feathers out.) □ *I didn't mean to ruffle his feathers. I just thought that I would remind him of what he promised us.*

a **rule of thumb** *Fig.* a general principle developed through experiential rather than scientific means. □ *As a rule of thumb, I move my houseplants outside in May.*

**rule the roost** *Fig.* to be the boss or manager, especially at home. □ *Who rules the roost at your house?*

**rule with a velvet glove** *Fig.* to rule in a very gentle way. □ *She rules with a velvet glove, but she gets things done, nonetheless.*

**rule with an iron fist** *Fig.* to rule in a very stern manner. □ *The dictator ruled with an iron fist and terrified the citizens.*

**run a taut ship** Go to run a tight ship.

**run a tight ship** AND **run a taut ship** *Fig.* to run a ship or an organization in an orderly and disciplined manner. (*Taut* and *tight* mean the same thing. *Taut* is correct nautical use. Whereas *taut* may well refer to a sailing ship's rigging being pulled tightly, it usually characterizes the discipline and cooperation among the crew.) □ *The new office manager really runs a tight ship.* □ *Captain Jones is known for running a taut ship.*

**run (around) in circles** Go to next.

**run around like a chicken with its head cut off** AND **run (around) in circles** *Fig.* to run around frantically and aimlessly; to be in a state of chaos. (Fig. on a chicken that continues to run around aimlessly after its head has been chopped off.) □ *I spent all afternoon running around like a chicken with its head cut off.*

**run in the family** *Fig.* [for a characteristic] to appear in many (or all) members of a family. □ *My grandparents lived well into their 90s, and it runs in the family.*

**run like clockwork** *Fig.* to run very well; to progress very well. □ *I want this office to run like clockwork—with everything on time and everything done right.*

**run on all cylinders 1.** *Fig.* [for an engine] to run well and smoothly. □ *This car is now running on all cylinders, thanks to the tune-up.* **2.** *Fig.* to function well or energetically. (Fig. on ①.) □ *Our department seems to be running on all cylinders. Congratulations.*

**run rampant** *Fig.* to run, develop, or grow out of control. □ *Weeds have run rampant around the abandoned house.*

**Run that by (me) again.** AND **Run it by (me) again.** *Inf.* Please repeat what you just said.; Please go over that one more time. □ *Alice: Do you understand? Sue: No. I really didn't understand what you said. Run that by me again, if you don't mind.*

**run the gamut** to cover a wide range [from one thing to another]. □ *She wants to buy the house, but her requests run the gamut from* *expensive new carpeting to completely new landscaping.* □ *His hobbies run the gamut from piano repair to portrait painting.*

**run the gauntlet 1.** to race, as a punishment, between parallel lines of men who thrash one as one runs. (Also spelled *gantlet.*) □ *The knight was forced to doff his clothes and run the gauntlet.* **2.** AND **run the gauntlet of** sth *Fig.* to endure a series of problems, threats, or criticism. (Fig. on ①.) □ *After the play, the director found himself running the gauntlet of questions and doubts about his ability.*

# S

a **sacred cow** *Fig.* something that is regarded by some people with such respect and veneration that they do not like it being criticized by anyone in any way. (From the fact that the cow is regarded as sacred in India and is not eaten or mistreated.) □ *A university education is a sacred cow in the Smith family. Fred is regarded as a failure because he quit school at 16.*

**sadder but wiser** *Cliché* unhappy but knowledgeable [about someone or something—after an unpleasant event]. □ *After the accident, I was sadder but wiser and would never make the same mistake again.*

**saddled with** so/sth *Fig.* burdened with someone or something. □ *I've been saddled with the children all day. Let's go out tonight.*

**safe and sound** *Fig.* unharmed and whole or healthy. □ *It was a rough trip, but we got there safe and sound.*

**sage advice** *Fig.* very good and wise advice. □ *My parents gave me some sage advice when I turned 18.*

the **salt of the earth** *Fig.* the most worthy of people; a very good or worthy person. (A biblical reference, Matthew 5:13.) □ *Mrs. Jones is the salt of the earth. She is the first to help anyone in trouble.*

**same difference** *Inf.* the same; no difference at all. □ *Pink, fuchsia, what does it matter? Same difference.*

the **same old story** something that occurs or has occurred in the same way often. □ *The company is getting rid of workers. It's the same old story—a shortage of orders.*

the **sands of time** *Fig.* the accumulated tiny amounts of time; time represented by the sand in an hourglass. □ *The sands of time will make you grow old like everyone else.*

**save** one's **breath** *Fig.* to refrain from talking, explaining, or arguing. □ *There is no sense in trying to convince her. Save your breath.*

**school** so **in** sth *Fig.* to train, discipline, or coach someone in something. □ *The voice coach schooled the singer in excellent breathing techniques.*

the **school of hard knocks** *Fig.* the school of life's experiences, as opposed to a formal, classroom education. □ *I didn't go to college, but I went to the school of hard knocks. I learned everything by experience.*

**school of thought** *Fig.* a particular philosophy or way of thinking about something. □ *One school of thought holds that cats cause allergic reactions.*

**scrape the bottom of the barrel** to select from among the worst; to choose from what is left over. □ *The worker you sent over was the worst I've ever seen. Send me another—and don't scrape the bottom of the barrel.*

**scratch** so's **back** *Fig.* to do a favor for someone in return for a favor done for you. □ *You scratch my back, and I'll scratch yours.*

**scratch the surface** *Fig.* to just begin to find out about something; to examine only the superficial aspects of something. □ *We don't know how bad the problem is. We've only scratched the surface.*

a **sea change** *Fig.* a major change or transformation. □ *This is not the time for a sea change in our manufacturing division. There are too many orders at the moment.*

**seal** so's **fate** AND **seal the fate of** so *Fig.* to determine finally the fate of someone. □ *His lying and cheating sealed his fate. He was convicted and sent to prison.*

the **seamy side of life** *Fig.* the most unpleasant or roughest aspect of life. (A reference to the inside of a garment where the seams show.) □ *Mary saw the seamy side of life when she worked as a volunteer in the homeless shelter.*

**\*second thoughts (about** so/sth) *Fig.* new doubts about someone or something. (\*Typically: **get** ~; **have** ~; **give** so ~.) □ *I'm beginning to get second thoughts about Tom.* □ *You're giving me second thoughts about going there.*

**see (right) through** so/sth *Fig.* to understand or detect the true nature of someone or something. □ *You can't fool me anymore. I can see through you and all your tricks.*

**see stars** *Fig.* to seem to see flashing lights after receiving a blow to the head. □ *I saw stars when I bumped my head on the attic ceiling.*

**see the color of** so's **money** *Fig.* to verify that someone has money or has enough money. □ *So, you want to make a bet? Not until I see the color of your money.*

**see the error of** one's **ways** *Fig.* to understand that one has done something wrong. □ *I thought you would see the error of your ways if I kept pointing it out to you.* □ *I saw the error of my ways and reformed my behavior.*

**see the light (of day)** *Fig.* to come to the end of a very busy time. □ *Finally, when the holiday season was over, we could see the light of day. We had been so busy!*

**seek professional help** *Euph.* to get psychiatric or psychological treatment. □ *If you are seriously thinking of suicide, now is the time to seek professional help.*

**sell** sth **for a song** *Fig.* to sell something for very little money. (As in trading something of value for the singing of a song.) □ *I had to sell my car for a song because I needed the money in a hurry.*

**sell like hotcakes** *Fig.* [for something] to be sold very fast. □ *The new gas and electric hybrid cars are selling like hotcakes.*

**sell** one's **soul (to the devil)** *Fig.* to do something very extreme [in order to obtain or accomplish something]. □ *I would sell my soul for a good steak about now.* □ *Tom would sell his soul to the devil to go out with Tiffany.*

**send** so **on a wild-goose chase** *Fig.* to send someone on a pointless or futile search. □ *Fred was sent on a wild-goose chase while his friends prepared a surprise party for him.*

**send out the wrong signals** AND **send** so **the wrong signals** *Fig.* to signify something that is not true; to imply something that is not true. □ *I hope I haven't been sending out the wrong signals, but I do not really care to extend this relationship.*

**send up a trial balloon** *Inf.* to suggest something and see how people respond to it; to test public opinion. □ *Mary had an excellent idea, but when we sent up a trial balloon, the response was very negative.*

**serve as a guinea pig** *Fig.* [for someone] to be experimented on; to allow some sort of test to be performed on one. (Fig. on the use of guinea pigs for biological experiments.) □ *Jane agreed to serve as a guinea pig. She'll be the one to try out the new flavor of ice cream.*

**serve notice (on** so**)** *Fig.* to formally or clearly state or announce something to someone. □ *John served notice that he wouldn't prepare the coffee anymore.* □ *I'm serving notice that I'll resign as secretary next month.*

**set great store by** so/sth *Fig.* to have positive expectations for someone or something; to have high hopes for someone or something. □ *I set great store by my computer and its ability to help me in my work.*

**set** one's **heart against** sth *Fig.* to turn against something; to become totally against something. □ *Jane set her heart against going to Australia.*

**set** one's **heart on** so/sth *Fig.* to be determined to get or do someone or something. □ *Jane set her heart on going to London.*

a **set of pipes** *Fig.* a very loud voice; a good singing voice. □ *With a set of pipes like that, she's a winner.*

a **set of wheels** *Fig.* a car. □ *Man, look at that set of wheels that chick has!*

**set** some place **on its ear** AND **turn** sth **on its ear** *Fig.* to excite, impress, or scandalize the people living in a place. (Typical places are: the world, the whole town, the campus, the office, etc.) □ *Her rowdy behavior set the whole town on its ear.*

**set** so **straight** to make certain that someone understands something exactly. (Often said in anger or domination.) □ *Please set me straight on this matter. Do you or do you not accept the responsibility for the accident?*

**set** so's **teeth on edge 1.** *Fig.* [for a scraping sound] to irritate someone's nerves. (Fig. on the facial expression someone might assume when enduring such a sound.) □ *That noise sets my teeth on edge!* □ *Tom's teeth were set on edge by the incessant screaming of the children.* **2.** *Fig.* [for a person or an idea] to upset someone very much. (Fig. as in ①.) □ *Her overbearing manner usually sets my teeth on edge.*

**set the world on fire** *Fig.* to do exciting things that bring fame and glory. (Frequently with the negative.) □ *You don't have to set the world on fire. Just do a good job.*

**set tongues (a)wagging** *Fig.* to cause people to start gossiping. □ *If you don't get the lawn mowed soon, you will set tongues wagging in the neighborhood.*

**set up housekeeping** to furnish a house and provide kitchen equipment to make a house livable; to settle down and prepare to live in a house, perhaps with someone else. □ *My brother and I bought a house and set up housekeeping. Then he got married and left me with the mess.*

**settle a score with** so AND **settle the score (with** so**)** *Fig.* to clear up a problem with someone; to get even with someone. □ *John wants to settle a score with his neighbor.*

**settle** so's **affairs** *Fig.* to deal with one's business matters; to manage the business affairs of someone who can't. □ *When my uncle died, I had to settle his affairs.* □ *I have to settle my affairs before going to Mexico for a year.*

a **seven-day wonder** *Fig.* a person or a process supposedly perfected in only seven days. (Sarcastic.) □ *Tommy is no seven-day wonder. It took him six years to get through high school!*

**sever ties with** so *Fig.* to end a relationship or agreement suddenly or completely. □ *The company severed its ties with the dishonest employee.*

*a **shadow of** oneself AND *a **shadow of itself;** *a **shadow of** one's **former self** *Fig.* someone or something that is not as strong, healthy, full, or lively as before. (*Typically: **be** ~; **become** ~.) □ *The sick man was a shadow of his former self.* □ *The abandoned mansion was merely a shadow of itself.*

a **shady character** AND a **suspicious character** *Fig.* an untrustworthy person; a person who makes people suspicious. □ *There is a suspicious character lurking about in the hallway. Please call the police.*

a **shady deal** *Fig.* a questionable and possibly dishonest deal or transaction. □ *The lawyer got caught making a shady deal with a convicted felon.*

a **shaggy-dog story** a kind of funny story that relies for its humor on its length and its sudden ridiculous ending. □ *Don't let John tell his favorite shaggy-dog story. It'll go on for hours.*

**shake a leg 1.** *Inf.* to hurry; to move faster. (Often as a command. Older.) □ *Let's shake a leg, you guys. We gotta be there in 20 minutes.* **2.** *Inf.* to dance. (Older.) □ *Hey, Jill! You wanna shake a leg with me?*

**shake the foundations of** sth *Fig.* to disturb or question the essence or underlying principles of something. □ *The death of his father shook the very foundations of his religious beliefs.*

**shank it** *Sl.* to use one's legs to get somewhere; to walk. □ *My car needs fixing, so I had to shank it to work today.*

**shank's mare** *Fig.* travel on foot. □ *You'll find that shank's mare is the quickest way to get across town.*

**Shape up or ship out.** *Fig.* Either improve one's performance or behavior or leave. (Used as a command.) □ *John was late again, so I told him to shape up or ship out.*

**share and share alike** *Cliché* having or taking equal shares. (*Share* may be interpreted as either a noun or a verb.) □ *The two roommates agreed that they would divide expenses—share and share alike.*

**a sharp tongue** *Fig.* an outspoken or harsh manner; a critical manner of speaking. □ *He has quite a sharp tongue. Don't be totally unnerved by what he says or the way he says it.*

a **sharp wit** *Fig.* a good and fast ability to make jokes and funny comments. □ *Terry has a sharp wit and often makes cracks that force people to laugh aloud at inappropriate times.*

**ships that pass in the night** *Cliché* people who meet each other briefly by chance, sometimes having a sexual liaison, and who are unlikely to meet again or have an ongoing relationship. □ *Mary wanted to see Jim again, but to him, they were ships that passed in the night.* □ *We will never be friends. We are just ships that passed in the night.*

**shoot** so **down in flames** *Inf.* to ruin someone; to bring about someone's downfall. □ *It was a bad idea, okay, but you didn't have to shoot me down in flames at the meeting.*

**shoot from the hip** *Fig.* to speak directly and frankly. (Alluding to the rapidness of firing a gun from the hip.) □ *John has a tendency to shoot from the hip, but he generally speaks the truth.*

**shoot** oneself **in the foot** *Fig.* to cause oneself difficulty; to be the cause of one's own misfortune. □ *Again, he shot himself in the foot by saying too much to the press.*

**shoot (some) hoops** *Fig.* to attempt to score baskets (in basketball) as entertainment. □ *Hey, Wilbur! Let's go shoot some hoops.*

**short and sweet** *Cliché* brief (and pleasant because of briefness). □ *That was a good sermon—short and sweet.* □ *I don't care what you say, as long as you make it short and sweet.*

a **shot in the arm 1.** an injection of medicine. □ *The doctor administered the antidote to the poison by a shot in the arm.* **2.** *Inf.* a boost or act of encouragement. (Fig. on ①.) □ *The pep talk was a real shot in the arm for all the guys.* **3.** *Inf.* a drink of liquor. □ *How about a little shot in the arm, bartender?*

**should have stood in bed** *Fig.* an expression used on a bad day, when one should have stayed in one's bed. □ *The minute I got up and heard the news this morning, I knew I should have stood in bed.*

**show** one's **mettle** AND **prove** one's **mettle** to demonstrate one's skill, courage, and ability. □ *The contest will be an opportunity for you to prove your mettle.*

a **show of hands** *Fig.* a display of raised hands [in a group of people] that can be counted for the purpose of votes or surveys. □ *Jack wanted us to vote on paper, not by a show of hands, so that we could have a secret ballot.*

**show** one's **(true) colors** *Fig.* to show what one is really like or what one is really thinking. □ *Whose side are you on, John? Come on. Show your colors.*

a **shrinking violet** *Fig.* someone who is very shy and not assertive. □ *I am not exactly a shrinking violet, but I don't have the guts to say what you said to her.*

**shuffle off this mortal coil** *Euph.* to die. (Often jocular or formal euphemism. Not often used in consoling someone.) □ *When*

*I shuffle off this mortal coil, I want to go out in style—bells, flowers, and a long, boring funeral.*

**\*sick (and tired) of** so/sth *Fig.* tired of someone or something, especially something that one must do again and again or someone or something that one must deal with repeatedly. (\*Typically: **be** ~; **become** ~; **get** ~; **grow** ~.) □ *I am sick and tired of cleaning up after you.* □ *Mary was sick of being stuck in traffic.*

**sick to death (of** so/sth**)** *Inf.* totally disgusted with someone or something. □ *This reporting about the scandals in the government just has me sick to death.*

a **sight for sore eyes** *Fig.* a welcome sight. □ *Oh, am I glad to see you here! You're a sight for sore eyes.*

**sign** one's **life away** *Fig.* to sign a document, usually a mortgage loan, that requires many years of payments and obligations. □ *Well, I signed my life away, but at least we have a house with wood floors and granite counters!*

a **sign of the times** *Fig.* something that signifies the situation evident in the current times. □ *Your neighbor's unmowed grass is just a sign of the times. Nobody really cares any longer.*

**sign on the dotted line** *Fig.* to indicate one's agreement to something. □ *He is thinking favorably about going with us to Canada, but he hasn't signed on the dotted line.*

**sign** one's **own death warrant** *Fig.* to do something (knowingly) that will most likely result in severe trouble. (As if one were ordering one's own execution.) □ *The killer signed his own death warrant when he walked into the police station and gave himself up.*

**signed, sealed, and delivered** *Fig.* formally and officially signed; [for a formal document to be] executed. (*Sealed* refers to the use of a special seal that indicates the official nature of the document.) □ *I can't begin work on this project until I have the contract signed, sealed, and delivered.*

**since time immemorial** *Fig.* since a very long time ago. (Literally, since time before recorded history.) □ *My hometown has had a big parade on the Fourth of July since time immemorial.*

**singing the blues** *Fig.* expressing one's sadness or regret. (Fig. on how one feels when singing a style of balladry associated with lost love and unfaithful lovers.) □ *I failed to get the contract from the client, and that left me singing the blues.*

**sink or swim** *Fig.* to fail or succeed. (Fig. on the choices available to someone who has fallen into the water.) □ *After I've studied and learned all I can, I have to take the test and sink or swim.*

**sink** one's **teeth into** sth Go to **get** one's **teeth into** sth.

**sit at the feet of** so *Fig.* to pay homage to someone; to pay worshipful attention to someone. □ *The graduate student sat at the feet of the famous professor for years.*

**sit in judgment (up)on** so/sth to make a judgment about someone or something. □ *I don't want to sit in judgment upon you or anyone else, but I do have some suggestions.*

**sit on** one's **hands** *Fig.* to do nothing; to fail to help. □ *We need the cooperation of everyone. You can't sit on your hands!*

**sit on its hands** AND **sit on their hands** *Fig.* [for an audience] to refuse to applaud. □ *The performance was really quite good, but the audience sat on its hands.*

**sit on the fence** *Fig.* not to take sides in a dispute; not to make a clear choice between two possibilities. (Fig. on the image of someone straddling a fence, representing indecision.) □ *When Jane and Tom argue, it is best to sit on the fence and not make either of them angry.*

**sitting on a gold mine** *Fig.* in control of something very valuable; in control of something potentially very valuable. □ *When I found out how much the old book was worth, I realized that I was sitting on a gold mine.*

**sitting on a powder keg** *Fig.* in a risky or explosive situation; in a situation where something serious or dangerous may happen at any time. (A powder keg is a keg of gunpowder.) □ *Things are very tense at work. The whole office is sitting on a powder keg.*

**sitting on top of the world** *Fig.* being successful and feeling pleased about it. □ *Wow, I'm sitting on top of the world.*

**\*sitting pretty** *Fig.* living in comfort or luxury; living in a good situation. (\*Typically: **be** ~; **leave** so ~.) □ *My uncle died and left enough money for me to be sitting pretty for the rest of my life.*

**six feet under** *Fig.* dead and buried. □ *They put him six feet under two days after he died.*

the **sixty-four-dollar question** *Fig.* the most important question; the question that everyone wants to know the answer to. □ *Now for the sixty-four-dollar question. What's the stock market going to do this year?*

**skate on thin ice** *Fig.* to be in a risky situation. (Fig. on the image of someone taking the risk of ice skating on thin ice.) □ *I try to stay well informed so I don't end up skating on thin ice when the teacher asks me a question.*

**skeleton(s) in the closet** a hidden and shocking secret. □ *You can ask anyone about how reliable I am. I don't mind. I don't have any skeletons in the closet.*

**skinny dip** *Fig.* to swim naked. □ *The boys were skinny dipping in the creek when Bob's mother drove up.*

**slam dunk 1.** [in basketball] a goal scored by shooting the ball down from above the rim. □ *He was wide open and scored on an easy slam dunk.* **2.** *Fig.* an action or accomplishment that is easily done. (Fig. on ①.) □ *Finishing that project with all his experience should be a slam dunk for George.*

**slam the brakes on**† *Fig.* to push on a vehicle's brakes suddenly and hard. (Informal. *The* can be replaced by a possessive pro-

sitting on top of the world

noun.) □ *The driver in front of me slammed her brakes on, and I nearly ran into her.*

a **slap in the face** *Fig.* an insult; an act that causes disappointment or discouragement. □ *Failing to get into a good college was a slap in the face to Tim after his years of study.*

**slash and burn 1.** of a farming technique where vegetation is cut down and burned before crops are planted. (Hyphenated before nominals.) □ *The small farmers' slash-and-burn technique destroyed thousands of acres of forest.* **2.** *Fig.* of a crude and brash way of doing something. (Hyphenated before nominals.) □ *The new manager's method was strictly slash and burn. He looks decisive to his boss and merciless to the people he fires.*

**sleep around the clock** *Fig.* to sleep for a full 24 hours; to sleep for a very long time. □ *I was so tired I could have slept around the clock.*

a **sleeping giant** *Fig.* a great power that is still and waiting. □ *The huge country to the south is a sleeping giant, waiting for its chance to become sufficiently industrialized to have real prosperity.*

a **slip of the tongue** *Fig.* an error in speaking in which a word is pronounced incorrectly, or in which the speaker says something unintentionally. □ *I failed to understand the instructions because the speaker made a slip of the tongue at an important point.*

**slip** one's **trolley** *Sl.* to become a little crazy; to lose one's composure. (Fig. on the old-fashioned U.S. streetcar, which got its electric power via spring-loaded poles that pushed upward into contact with overhead electric wires. If the wheels that rode on the wires slipped off, the streetcar came to a stop.) □ *He slipped his trolley and went totally bonkers.*

a **slippery customer 1.** a slimy or slippery creature. □ *This little fish is a slippery customer. Get me something to scoop it back into its bowl.* **2.** *Fig.* a clever and deceitful customer. (Fig. on ①.) □ *Watch out for that guy with the big padded coat. He may snatch something. He's a real slippery customer.*

a **slippery slope** *Fig.* a dangerous pathway or route to follow; a route that leads to trouble. □ *The matter of euthanasia is a slippery slope with both legal and moral considerations.*

**slow going** *Fig.* the rate of speed when one is making slow progress. □ *It was slow going at first, but I was able to finish the project by the weekend.*

**smack (dab) in the middle** *Fig.* exactly in the middle. □ *I want a piece that is not too big and not too small—just smack in the middle.*

a **smack in the face** *Inf.* something that will humiliate someone, often when it is considered deserved; an insult. □ *Being rejected* *by Jane was a real smack in the face for Tom, who thought she was fond of him.*

**small change** *Fig.* an insignificant person. (Also a rude term of address.) □ *Don't worry about him. He's just small change.* □ *Look, small change, why don't you just move along?*

a **small fortune** *Inf.* a rather sizable amount of money. □ *I've got a small fortune tied up in home theater equipment.*

**small fry 1.** newly hatched fish; small, juvenile fish. □ *The catch was bad today. Nothing but small fry.* **2.** *Fig.* unimportant people. (Fig. on ①.) □ *The police have only caught the small fry. The leader of the gang is still free.* **3.** *Fig.* children. (Fig. on ①.) □ *Wallace is taking the small fry to the zoo for the afternoon.*

**small potatoes** *Fig.* something or someone insignificant; **small fry.** □ *This contract is small potatoes, but it keeps us in business till we get into the real money.*

a **smear campaign (against** so**)** a campaign aimed at damaging someone's reputation by making accusations and spreading rumors. □ *The politician's opponents are engaging in a smear campaign against him.*

**smell a rat** *Fig. Inf.* to suspect that something is wrong; to sense that someone has caused something wrong. □ *I don't think this was an accident. I smell a rat. Bob had something to do with this.*

**smell blood** *Fig. Inf.* to be ready for a fight; to be ready to attack; to be ready to act. (Fig. on the behavior of sharks, which are sent into a frenzy by the smell of blood.) □ *Lefty was surrounded, and you could tell that the guys from the other gang smelled blood.*

**smell fishy** *Fig. Inf.* to seem suspicious. □ *Barlowe squinted a bit. Something smells fishy here, he thought.*

**smell like a rose** *Inf.* to seem innocent. □ *I came out of the whole mess smelling like a rose, even though I caused all the trouble.*

**Smile when you say that.** *Inf.* I will interpret that remark as a joke or as kidding. □ *John: You're a real pain in the neck. Bob: Smile when you say that.*

**smoke and mirrors** *Fig.* deception and confusion. (Said of statements or more complicated rhetoric used to mislead people rather than inform them. Refers to the way a magician uses optical illusion to create believability while performing a trick. Fixed order.) □ *Most people know that the politician was just using smoke and mirrors to make things look better than they really were.*

**smoke-filled room** *Fig.* a room where a small group of people make important decisions. (Usually used in reference to political parties.) □ *The smoke-filled rooms are still producing the candidates for most offices, despite all the political reforms.*

the **smoking gun** *Inf.* the indisputable sign of guilt. (Fig. on a murderer being caught just after shooting the victim.) □ *The chief of staff decided that the aide should be found with the smoking gun.*

**smooth (so's) ruffled feathers** *Fig.* to attempt to calm or placate someone who is upset. (As a bird tries to align and neaten ruffled feathers.) □ *Crystal looks a little upset. Do you think I should try to smooth her ruffled feathers?*

**snake in the grass** *Fig.* a sneaky and despised person. □ *How could I ever have trusted that snake in the grass?*

**snap so's head off** *Fig.* to speak very sharply to someone. □ *How rude! Don't snap my head off!*

**snatch victory from the jaws of defeat** *Cliché* to win at the last moment. □ *At the last moment, the team snatched victory from the jaws of defeat with a last-second full-court basket.*

a **snow job** *Inf.* a systematic deception; a deceptive story that tries to hide the truth. □ *You can generally tell when a student is trying to do a snow job.*

**So much for that.** *Inf.* That is the end of that.; We will not be dealing with that anymore. □ *John tossed the stub of a pencil into the* *trash. "So much for that," he muttered, fishing through his drawer for another.*

**so much so that . . .** to such a great degree that. . . . □ *We are very tired. So much so that we have decided to retire for the night.*

**(So) what else is new?** *Inf.* This isn't new. It has happened before.; Not this again. □ *Mary: Taxes are going up again. Bob: So what else is new?*

**soft in the head** *Inf.* stupid; witless. □ *George is just soft in the head. He'll never get away with his little plan.*

**soft sell** *Inf.* a polite attempt to sell something; a very gentle sales pitch. □ *Some people won't bother listening to a soft sell. You gotta let them know you believe in what you are selling.*

**soft soap 1.** *Inf.* flattering but insincere talk; sweet talk. □ *Don't waste my time with soft soap. I know you don't mean it.* **2.** *Inf.* to attempt to convince someone (of something) by gentle persuasion. (Usually **soft-soap**.) □ *Don't try to soft-soap her. She's an old battle-ax.*

**soft touch 1.** *Fig.* a gentle way of handling someone or something. □ *Kelly lacks the kind of soft touch needed for this kind of negotiation.* **2.** *Inf.* a gullible person; a likely victim of a scheme. □ *Here comes the perfect soft touch—a nerd with a gleam in his eye.*

**\*some elbow room** *Fig.* room to move about in; extra space to move about in. (\*Typically: **allow** ~; **get** ~; **have** ~; **give** so ~; **need** ~.) □ *This table is too crowded. We all need some elbow room.*

**\*some loose ends** *Fig.* some things that are not yet finished; some problems not yet solved. (\*Typically: **have** ~; **leave**~; **tie** ~ **up**†; **take care of** ~.) □ *I have to stay in town this weekend and tie up some loose ends.*

**(some) new blood** AND **fresh blood** *Fig.* new personnel; new members brought into a group to revive it. □ *We're trying to get some new blood in the club. Our membership is falling.*

**\*some shut-eye** *Fig.* some sleep. (\*Typically: **get** ~**; have** ~**; use** ~**; need** ~.) □ *I need to get home and get some shut-eye before I do anything else.*

**\*sound as a dollar 1.** *Cliché* very secure and dependable. (\*Also: **as** ~.) □ *I wouldn't put my money in a bank that isn't sound as a dollar.* **2.** *Cliché* sturdy and well-constructed. (\*Also: **as** ~.) □ *The garage is still sound as a dollar. Why tear it down?*

**sound the death knell 1.** [for a bell] to ring slowly signaling a funeral or a death. □ *The old bell sounded the death knell many times during the plague.* **2.** *Fig.* to signal the end of something. □ *The elimination of the funding for the project sounded the death knell for Paul's pet project.*

**sour grapes** *Fig.* something that one cannot have and so disparages as if it were never desirable. □ *Of course you want to buy this expensive jacket. Criticizing it is just sour grapes, but you still really want it.*

**sow** one's **wild oats** to do wild and foolish things in one's youth. (Extended from a sexual meaning originally having to do with early male copulatory experiences.) □ *Jack was out sowing his wild oats last night, and he's in jail this morning.* □ *Mrs. Smith told Mr. Smith that he was too old to be sowing his wild oats and that he would hear from her lawyer.*

**spare no expense** to spend liberally or as much as needed. □ *Please go out and buy the biggest turkey you can find, and spare no expense.*

**spare tire 1.** *Inf.* a thickness in the waist; a roll of fat around one's waist. □ *I've got to get rid of this spare tire.* **2.** *Inf.* an unneeded person; an unproductive person. □ *You spare tires over there! Get to work.*

**speak down to** so to address someone in simpler terms than necessary; to speak condescendingly to someone. □ *There is no need to speak down to me. I can understand anything you are likely to say.*

**speak** so's **language** *Fig.* to say something that one agrees with or understands. □ *I gotcha. Now you're speaking my language.*

**speak** one's **mind** *Fig.* to say frankly what one thinks (about something). □ *You can always depend on John to speak his mind. He'll let you know what he really thinks.*

**speak the same language** *Fig.* [for people] to have similar ideas, tastes, etc. □ *Jane and Jack get along very well. They really speak the same language about almost everything.*

**speak volumes** *Fig.* [for something that is seen] to reveal a great deal of information. □ *The unsightly yard and unpainted house speak volumes about what kind of people live there.*

**speak with one voice** *Fig.* [for members of a group] to think and mean the same thing; [for a group of people] to advocate a single position. □ *I'm sure we all speak with one voice in this matter. There will be no tree harvest in the forest!*

**spell disaster** *Fig.* to indicate or predict disaster. □ *What a horrible plan! It would spell disaster for all of us!*

**spell trouble** *Fig.* to signify future trouble; to mean trouble. □ *The sky looks angry and dark. That spells trouble.*

**spending money** *Inf.* cash, as opposed to money in the bank. □ *I'm a little short of spending money at the present. Could I borrow 10 dollars?*

**spick-and-span** *Fig.* very clean. □ *I have to clean up the house and get it spick-and-span for the party Friday night.*

**spin a yarn** *Fig.* to tell a tale. □ *My uncle is always spinning yarns about his childhood.*

**spin doctor** *Fig.* someone who gives a twisted or deviously deceptive version of an event. (Usually in the context of manipulating the news for political reasons.) □ *Things were going bad for the candidate, so he got himself a new spin doctor.*

**spin** one's **wheels** *Inf.* to waste time; to remain in a neutral position, neither advancing nor falling back. (Fig. on a car that is running but is not moving because its wheels are spinning in mud, etc.) □ *I'm just spinning my wheels in this job. I need more training to get ahead.*

**spit and polish** *Fig.* orderliness; ceremonial precision and orderliness. □ *I like spit and polish. It comes from being in the military.*

**split hairs** *Fig.* to quibble; to try to make petty distinctions. □ *They don't have any serious differences. They are just splitting hairs.*

**split** one's **sides (with laughter)** *Fig.* to laugh so hard that one's sides almost split. (Always an exaggeration.) □ *The members of the audience almost split their sides with laughter.*

**split the difference** *Fig.* to divide the difference evenly (with someone else). □ *You want to sell for $120, and I want to buy for $100. Let's split the difference and close the deal at $110.*

**spoiled rotten** *Fig.* indulged in; greatly spoiled. □ *I was spoiled rotten when I was a child, so I'm used to this kind of wasteful luxury.*

**spoon-feed** so *Fig.* to treat someone with too much care or help; to teach someone with methods that are too easy and do not stimulate the learner to independent thinking. □ *You mustn't spoon-feed the new recruits by telling them what to do all the time. They must learn to use their initiative.*

**spread like wildfire** *Fig.* [for something] to spread rapidly. □ *Rumors spread like wildfire when people are angry.*

**spread the word** *Fig.* to tell many people some kind of information. □ *I need to spread the word that the meeting is canceled for this afternoon.*

**spread** oneself **too thin** *Fig.* to do so many things at one time that you can do none of them well. □ *It's a good idea to get involved in a lot of activities, but don't spread yourself too thin.*

a **square peg (in a round hole)** *Fig.* someone who is uncomfortable or who does not belong in a particular situation. (Also the *Cliché: trying to fit a square peg into a round hole* = trying to combine two things that do not belong or fit together.) □ *I feel like a square peg in a round hole at my office. Everyone else there seems so ambitious, competitive, and dedicated to the work, but I just want to make a living.*

**squawk about** sth *Fig.* to complain about something. □ *Stop squawking about how much money you lost. I lost twice as much.*

**squeak through (**sth**)** *Fig.* to manage just to get past a barrier, such as an examination or interview. □ *Sally just barely squeaked through the interview, but she got the job.*

**squeak** sth **through** *Fig.* to manage just to get something accepted or approved. □ *Tom squeaked the application through at the last minute.*

**squirrel** sth **away**† *Fig.* to hide something or store something in the way that a squirrel stores nuts for use in the winter. □ *I squirreled a little money away for an occasion such as this.*

**stain** sth **with** sth *Fig.* to injure or blemish someone's reputation. □ *They stained his reputation with their charges.*

**stand corrected** *Fig.* to admit that one has been wrong. □ *We appreciate now that our conclusions were wrong. We stand corrected.*

**stand on ceremony** *Fig.* to hold rigidly to protocol or formal manners. (Often in the negative.) □ *We are very informal around here. Hardly anyone stands on ceremony.*

**stand on** one's **head** *Fig.* to attempt to impress someone by hard work or difficult feats. □ *You don't have to stand on your head to succeed in this office. Just do your assigned work on time.*

**stand on** one's **(own) two feet** *Fig.* to act in an independent and forthright manner. □ *Dave will be better off when he gets a job and can stand on his own feet.*

**stand to reason** *Fig.* to seem reasonable. □ *It stands to reason that it'll be colder in January than it is in November.*

**stand up and be counted** *Fig.* to state one's support (for someone or something). □ *If you believe in more government help for farmers, write your representative—stand up and be counted.*

**stand up in court** *Fig.* [for a case] to survive a test in a court of law. □ *These charges will never stand up in court. They are too vague.*

a **standing joke** *Fig.* a subject that regularly and over a period of time causes amusement whenever it is mentioned. □ *Their mother's inability to make a decision was a standing joke in the Smith family all their lives.*

**stark raving mad** *Cliché* totally insane; completely crazy; out of control. (Often an exaggeration.) □ *When she heard about what happened at the office, she went stark raving mad.*

**start from scratch** *Fig.* to start from the very beginning; to start from nothing. □ *Whenever I bake a cake, I start from scratch. I never use a cake mix in a box.*

**state of mind** *Fig.* basic attitude or outlook at a point in time. □ *She was in a terrible state of mind when she was interviewed for a job.*

**state of the art** *Fig.* using the most recent technology. (Hyphenated before nouns.) □ *This state-of-the-art radio is capable of filling the whole room with sound.*

**stay the course** *Fig.* to keep going the way things are even though things are difficult. (This is the current usage, but *stay* can also mean stop. Both nautical and equestrian origins have been proposed. Currently, it seems to be used a lot by politicians.) □ *Don't be panicked by the market into selling your assets. Stay the course and you will be better off.*

**steal a base** *Fig.* to sneak from one base to another in baseball. □ *The runner stole second base, but he nearly got put out on the way.*

**steal** so's **thunder** *Fig.* to lessen someone's force or authority. □ *What do you mean by coming in here and stealing my thunder? I'm in charge here!*

**steaming (mad)** *Fig.* very angry; very mad; very upset. □ *The principal was steaming mad when he found that his office had been vandalized.*

**step in(to the breach)** *Fig.* [for someone] to assume a position or take on a responsibility when there is a need or an opportunity to do so. □ *The person who was supposed to help didn't show up, so I stepped into the breach.*

**step out of line** *Fig.* to misbehave; to deviate from normal, expected, or demanded behavior. □ *Tom stepped out of line once too often and got yelled at.*

**step up to the plate 1.** *Fig.* [for a batter in baseball] to move near home plate in preparation for striking the ball when it is pitched. □ *The batter stepped up to the plate and glared at the pitcher.* **2.** *Fig.* to move into a position where one is ready to do a task. □ *It's time for Tom to step up to the plate and take on his share of work.*

**stew in** one's **own juice** *Fig.* to be left alone to suffer one's anger or disappointment. □ *John has such a terrible temper. When he got mad at us, we just let him go away and stew in his own juice.*

**stick in the mud** *Fig.* a dull and old-fashioned person. □ *Some stick in the mud objected to the kind of music we wanted to play in church.*

**stick out a mile** *Fig.* to project outward very obviously. □ *His stomach sticks out a mile. What do you suppose is in there?*

**stick to** one's **ribs** *Fig.* [for food] to last long and fortify one well; [for food] to sustain one even in the coldest weather. □ *This oat-*

*meal ought to stick to your ribs. You need something hearty on a cold day like this.*

**stinking rich** *Inf.* very rich. □ *I'd like to be stinking rich for the rest of my life.*

**stir up a hornet's nest** *Fig.* to create a lot of trouble. □ *If you say that to her, you will be stirring up a hornet's nest.*

a **stone's throw away** *Fig.* a short distance; a relatively short distance. □ *John saw Mary across the street, just a stone's throw away.*

**stop (dead) in** one's **tracks** *Fig.* to stop completely still suddenly because of fear, a noise, etc. □ *The deer stopped dead in its tracks when it heard the hunter step on a fallen branch.*

**stop on a dime** *Inf.* to come to a stop in a very short distance. □ *This thing will stop on a dime.*

**straddle the fence** *Fig.* to support both sides of an issue. (As if one were partly on either side of a fence.) □ *The mayor is straddling the fence on this issue, hoping the public will forget it.*

*****straight as an arrow 1.** *Cliché* [of something] very straight. (*Also: **as** ~.) □ *The road to my house is as straight as an arrow, so it should be very easy to follow.* **2.** *Cliché* [of someone] honest or forthright. (*Straight* here means honest. *Also: **as** ~.) □ *Tom is straight as an arrow. I'd trust him with anything.*

*****a **straight face** *Fig.* a face free from smiles or laughter. (*Typically: **have** ~; **keep** ~.) □ *It's hard to keep a straight face when someone tells a funny joke.*

*****(straight) from the horse's mouth** *Fig.* from an authoritative or dependable source. (Alludes to the authenticity of a tip about the winner of a horse race. A tip that came straight from the horse could be assumed to be true. An exaggeration in any case. *Typically: **be** ~; **come** ~; **get** sth ~; **hear** sth ~.) □ *I know it's true! I heard it straight from the horse's mouth!* □ *This comes straight from the horse's mouth, so it has to be believed.*

**straight from the shoulder** *Fig.* very direct, without attenuation or embellishment. (The allusion is not clear, but it could refer to a straight shot from a rifle.) □ *Okay, I'll give it to you straight from the shoulder. You're broke.*

**strain at the leash** *Fig.* [for a person] to want to move ahead with things, aggressively and independently. (Fig. on the image of an eager or poorly disciplined dog pulling on its leash, trying to hurry its owner along.) □ *She wants to fix things right away. She is straining at the leash to get started.*

a **straw man** *Fig.* a weak proposition posited only to be demolished by a simple countering argument. □ *So you can knock down your own straw man! Big deal. The question is how can you deal with real problems.*

**stretch a point** AND **stretch the point** *Fig.* to interpret a point flexibly and with great latitude. □ *Would it be stretching a point to suggest that everyone is invited to your picnic?*

**stretch** one's **legs** *Fig. Lit.* to walk around, stretch, and loosen one's leg muscles after sitting down or lying down for a time. (This means, of course, to stretch or exercise only the muscles of the legs.) □ *After sitting in the car all day, the travelers decided to stretch their legs.*

**strictly business 1.** *Fig.* a matter or issue that is all business and no pleasure. □ *This meeting is strictly business. We don't have time for any leisure activity.* **2.** *Fig.* a person who is very businesslike and does not waste time with nonbusiness matters. □ *Joe is strictly business. I don't think he has a sense of humor. At least I have never seen it.*

**strike a match** *Fig.* to light a match by rubbing it on a rough surface. □ *When Sally struck a match to light a cigarette, Jane said quickly, "No smoking, please."*

**strike it rich** *Fig.* to acquire wealth suddenly. □ *Sally ordered a dozen oysters and found a huge pearl in one of them. She struck it rich!*

**strike up the band 1.** *Fig.* to cause a (dance) band to start playing. □ *Strike up the band, maestro, so we all can dance the night away.* **2.** *Fig.* to cause something to start. □ *Strike up the band! Let's get moving or we'll be late.*

**\*strings attached** *Fig.* having conditions or obligations associated. (\*Typically: **with some** ~; **without any** ~; **with no** ~; **with a few** ~.) □ *My parents gave me use of their car without any strings attached.*

a **stroke of genius** *Fig.* an act of genius; a very clever and innovative idea or task. □ *Your idea of painting the rock wall red was a stroke of genius.*

**strong-arm tactics** *Fig.* the use of force. □ *Strong-arm tactics are out. The boss says be gentle and don't hurt anybody.*

**strut** one's **stuff** *Sl.* to walk proudly and show off one's best features or talents. □ *Get out there on that stage and strut your stuff!*

**stuff and nonsense** *Fig.* foolishness; foolish talk. □ *I don't understand this book. It's all stuff and nonsense as far as I am concerned.*

**stuff the ballot box** *Fig.* to fill a ballot box with illegal votes or with more votes than the number of actual voters. □ *The politician was charged with stuffing the ballot box.*

a **sucker for punishment** *Fig.* someone who seems to do things frequently that result in punishment or being put at a disadvantage. □ *I don't know why I volunteered for this job. I'm a sucker for punishment I guess.*

**suit** one's **actions to** one's **words** *Fig.* to behave in accordance with what one has said; to do what one has promised or threatened to do. □ *Mr. Smith suited his actions to his words and punished the children.*

**sum and substance** *Fig.* a summary; the gist. □ *In trying to explain the sum and substance of the essay, Thomas failed to mention the middle name of the hero.*

surf the Net

**Sunday driver** *Fig.* a slow and leisurely driver who appears to be sightseeing and enjoying the view, holding up traffic in the process. (Also a term of address.) □ *I'm a Sunday driver, and I'm sorry. I just can't bear to go faster.*

**surf and turf** *Fig.* fish and beef; lobster and beef. (A meal incorporating both expensive seafood and an expensive cut of beef. Refers to the sea and to the pasture. Fixed order.) □ *Walter ordered the surf and turf, but Alice ordered only a tiny salad.*

**surf the Net** *Fig.* to browse around in the contents of the Internet. □ *I spend an hour a day or more surfing the Net.*

the **survival of the fittest** *Fig.* the idea that the most able or fit will survive (while the less able and less fit will perish). (This is used literally as a principle of the process of evolution.) □ *In col-*

*lege, it's the survival of the fittest. You have to keep working in order to survive and graduate.*

**swallow** one's **pride** *Fig.* to forget one's pride and accept something humiliating. □ *When you're trying to master a new skill, you find yourself swallowing your pride quite often.*

**swear like a trooper** *Inf.* to curse and swear with great facility. (The *trooper* here refers to a soldier.) □ *The clerk started swearing like a trooper, and the customer started crying.*

**sweet nothings** *Fig.* affectionate but unimportant or meaningless words spoken to a loved one. □ *Jack was whispering sweet nothings in Joan's ear when they were dancing.*

**sweeten the pot** *Fig.* to increase the amount of money bet in a card game with hopes of encouraging other players to bet more enthusiastically. □ *John sweetened the pot hoping others would follow.*

**swimming in** sth *Fig.* to experience an overabundance of something. □ *We are just swimming in orders right now. Business is good.*

**swing into high gear** *Inf.* to begin operating at a fast pace; to increase the rate of activity. □ *The chef swings into high gear around six o'clock in preparation for the theater crowd.*

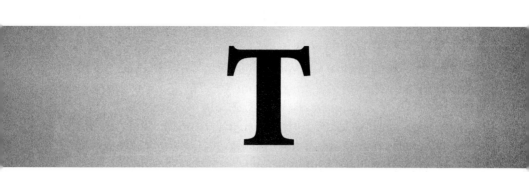

**table a motion** *Fig.* to postpone the discussion of something during a meeting. □ *The motion for a new policy was tabled until the next meeting.*

the **tail wagging the dog** a situation where a small part is controlling the whole of something. □ *John was just hired yesterday, and today he's bossing everyone around. It's a case of the tail wagging the dog.*

**take a backseat (to** so/sth**)** *Fig.* to become less important than someone or something else. □ *My homework had to take a backseat to football during the play-offs.*

**take a bath (on** sth**)** *Sl.* to accumulate large losses on a business transaction or an investment. (Refers to *getting soaked* = being heavily charged for something.) □ *Sally took a bath on that stock that she bought. Its price went down to nothing.*

**Take a deep breath.** *Fig. Lit.* Take a breath and relax instead of getting stressed or angry. □ *A: I am so mad, I could scream. B: Now, take a deep breath and just relax.*

**take a firm grip on** so/sth *Fig.* to gain control of someone or something. □ *You will have to take a firm grip on Andrew. He has a mind of his own.*

**take a gander (at** so/sth**)** *Fig.* to look at someone or something. □ *I wanted to take a gander at the new computer before they started using it.*

**take a potshot at** so/sth **1.** *Fig.* to shoot at someone or something, as with a shotgun. (A *potshot* refers to the type of shooting done to provide meat for the cooking pot.) □ *The hunters were taking potshots at each other in the woods.* **2.** *Fig.* to criticize or censure someone or something, often just to be mean. (Fig. on ①.) □ *Everyone in the audience was taking potshots at the comedian's toupee.*

**take a powder** *Sl.* to leave; to leave town. (Underworld.) □ *Willie took a powder and will lie low for a while.*

**take a turn for the better** *Fig.* to start to improve; to start to get well. □ *Things are taking a turn for the better at my store. I may make a profit this year.*

**take a turn for the worse** *Fig.* to start to get worse. □ *It appeared that she was going to get well; then, unfortunately, she took a turn for the worse.*

**take an oath** *Fig.* to make an oath; to swear to something. □ *You must take an oath that you will never tell anyone about this.*

**take** so's **blood pressure** *Fig.* to measure a person's blood pressure. □ *The doctor takes my blood pressure every time I am in the office.*

**take** so's **breath away** *Fig.* to overwhelm someone with beauty or grandeur; to surprise or astound someone. □ *The magnificent painting took my breath away.*

**take care of number one** AND **take care of numero uno** *Inf.* to take care of oneself. □ *Mike, like everybody else, is most concerned with taking care of number one.*

**take center stage** *Fig.* [for someone or something] to manage to become the central attraction. □ *The new arthritis drug took center stage at the medical convention.*

**take** one's **cue from** so to use someone else's behavior or reactions as a guide to one's own. (From the theatrical cue = a signal to speak, enter, exit, etc.) □ *If you don't know which spoons to use at the dinner, just take your cue from John.*

**take** so **for a ride 1.** *Fig.* to deceive someone. □ *You really took those people for a ride. They really believed you.* **2.** *Fig.* to take away and murder a person. (Underworld.) □ *Mr. Big told Mike to take Fred for a ride.*

**take** so **for dead** *Fig.* to assume that someone who is still alive is dead. □ *When we found her, we took her for dead, but the paramedics were able to revive her.*

**take** one's **gloves off**† AND **take the gloves off**† *Fig.* to stop being calm or civil and show an intention of winning a dispute by any means. (As if boxers were to remove their gloves in order to inflict more damage.) □ *Both of them took their gloves off and really began arguing.*

**take** one's **hat off**† **to** so *Fig.* to salute or pay an honor to someone. □ *Good work. I take my hat off to you.*

**take issue with** so *Fig.* to argue with someone. □ *I heard your last statement, and I have to take issue with you.*

**take issue with** sth *Fig.* to disagree with or argue about something. □ *I want to take issue with the last statement you made.*

**Take it away!** *Inf.* Start up the performance!; Let the show begin! (Typically a public announcement of the beginning of a musical performance.) □ *And now, here is the band playing "Song of Songs." Take it away!*

**take it from the top** *Fig.* to begin [again] at the beginning, especially the beginning of a piece of music. (Originally in reference to the top of a sheet of music.) □ *The conductor stopped the band and had the players take it from the top again.*

**take it on the lam** *Sl.* to get out of town; to run away. (Underworld.) □ *Both crooks took it on the lam when things got hot.*

**take it to** one's **grave** to carry a secret with one until one dies. □ *I will never tell anyone. I'll take your secret to my grave.*

**take its course** *Fig.* to continue along its way; [for a disease] to progress the way it normally progresses until it is cured naturally. □ *There is really no good medicine for this. This disease simply has to take its course.*

**take** one's **life into** one's **(own) hands** *Fig.* to risk one's life; to do something that puts one's life at risk. □ *If you choose to swim in that rushing river, you are taking your life into your hands.*

**take** one's **medicine** *Fig.* to accept the consequences or the bad fortune that one deserves. (Fig. on the image of having to take unpleasant-tasting medicine.) □ *Billy knew he was going to get spanked, and he didn't want to take his medicine.*

**take office** *Fig.* to begin serving as an elected or appointed official. □ *All the elected officials took office just after the election.*

**take** sth **on faith** *Fig.* to accept or believe something on the basis of little or no evidence. □ *Please try to believe what I'm telling you. Just take it on faith.*

**take** sth **on the chin 1.** *Fig.* to absorb a blow on the chin. □ *The boxer tried to duck, but took the blow on the chin.* **2.** *Fig.* to experience and endure bad news or other trouble. (Fig. on ①.) □ *The worst luck comes my way, and I always end up taking it on the chin.*

**take out a loan** *Fig.* to get a loan of money, especially from a bank. □ *Mary took out a loan to buy a car.*

**take over the reins (of** sth**)** *Fig.* to take control. □ *I'm ready to retire and will do so when they find someone else to take over the reins of the company.*

**take pains with** so/sth *Fig.* to deal with someone or something with great care. □ *He really took pains with me to make sure I understood it all.*

**take shape** *Fig.* [for something, such as plans, writing, ideas, arguments, etc.] to begin to be organized and specific. □ *As my manuscript took shape, I started showing it to publishers.*

**take solace (in** sth**)** *Fig.* to console oneself with some fact. □ *I am inordinately impoverished, but I take solace in the fact that I have a splendiferous vocabulary.*

**take (some) names** *Sl.* to make a list of wrongdoers. (Often figuratively, referring to a schoolteacher making a list of the names of misbehaving students to be sent to the principal.) □ *Gary is coming by to talk about the little riot last night, and I think he's taking names.*

**take steps (to prevent** sth**)** *Fig.* to do what is necessary to prevent something. □ *I took steps to prevent John from learning what we were talking about.*

**take** so's **temperature** *Fig.* to measure a person's body temperature with a thermometer. □ *The nurse took my temperature and said I was okay.*

**take the bull by the horns** *Fig.* to confront a problem head-on and deal with it openly. □ *It's time to take the bull by the horns and get this job done.*

**take the coward's way out** *Euph.* to kill oneself. □ *I can't believe that Bill would take the coward's way out. His death must have been an accident.*

**take the fall** *Sl.* to get arrested for a particular crime. (Especially when others are going unpunished for the same crime.) □ *Walt and Tony pulled the job off together, but Tony took the fall.*

**take the Fifth (Amendment)** *Fig.* to claim that telling someone something would get the teller in trouble. (Fig. on the use of the Fifth Amendment to the U.S. Constitution. This amendment is sometimes cited by persons testifying to Congress because it allows a person to decline to answer a question that will result in

take the coward's way out

self-incrimination or the admission of guilt.) □ *She asked me where I'd been last night, but I took the Fifth.*

**take the floor** *Fig.* to stand up and address the audience. □ *When I take the floor, I'll make a short speech.* □ *The last time you had the floor, you talked for an hour.*

**take the law into** one's **own hands** *Fig.* to attempt to administer the law; to pass judgment on someone who has done something wrong. □ *The shopkeeper took the law into his own hands when he tried to arrest the thief.*

**take the liberty of** doing sth *Fig.* to do something for someone voluntarily; to do something slightly personal for someone that would be more appropriate if one knew the person better. (Often used as an overly polite exaggeration in a request.) □ *I took the liberty of ordering an entree for you. I hope you don't mind.*

**take the pledge** *Fig.* to promise to abstain from drinking alcohol. (Refers to the temperance pledge of T-Totalism [teetotalism] = total abstinence.) □ *I'm not ready to take the pledge yet, but I will cut down.*

**take the plunge** *Inf.* to marry someone. □ *I'm not ready to take the plunge yet.*

**take the rap (for** sth**)** *Inf.* to take the blame for (doing) something; to receive the criminal charge for committing a crime. □ *I won't take the rap for the crime. I wasn't even in town.* □ *Who'll take the rap for it? Who did it?*

**take the stage** *Fig.* to become the center of attention; to become the focus of everyone's attention. □ *Later in the day, the problems in the warehouse took the stage, and we discussed them until dinner time.*

**take the stand** *Fig.* to go to and sit in the witness chair in a courtroom. □ *I was in court all day, waiting to take the stand.*

**take the words out of** so's **mouth** *Fig.* to say something just before someone else was going to say the same thing; to say something that someone who agrees with you might have said. □ *When you said "expensive," you took the words right out of my mouth!*

**take things easy 1.** *Fig.* to live well and comfortably. □ *I'll be glad when I can make enough money to take things easy.* **2.** *Fig.* to relax temporarily and recuperate. □ *The doctor says I'm supposed to take things easy for a while.*

**take** so **to the cleaners 1.** *Sl.* to take a lot of someone's money; to swindle someone. □ *The lawyers took the insurance company to the cleaners, but I still didn't get enough to pay for my losses.* **2.** *Sl.* to defeat or best someone. □ *Look at the height they've got! They'll take us to the cleaners!*

**take umbrage at** sth *Fig.* to feel that one has been insulted by something. □ *Mary took umbrage at the suggestion that she was being unreasonable.*

**take** sth **with a grain of salt** Go to next.

**take** sth **with a pinch of salt** AND **take** sth **with a grain of salt** *Fig.* to listen to a story or an explanation with considerable doubt. □ *You must take anything she says with a grain of salt. She doesn't always tell the truth.*

**tale of woe** *Fig.* a sad story; a list of personal problems; an excuse for failing to do something. □ *This tale of woe that we have all been getting from Kelly is just too much.*

**talk a blue streak** *Fig.* to talk very much and very rapidly. □ *Billy didn't talk until he was two, and then he started talking a blue streak.*

**talk around** sth *Fig.* to talk but avoid talking directly about the subject. □ *You are just talking around the matter! I want a straight answer!*

**talk in circles** *Fig.* to talk in a confusing or roundabout manner. □ *I couldn't understand a thing he said. All he did was talk in circles.*

**talk shop** *Fig.* to talk about business or work matters at a social event where such talk is out of place. □ *All right, everyone, we're not here to talk shop. Let's have a good time.*

**talk the talk and walk the walk** AND **talk the talk; walk the walk** *Cliché* to behave as one is expected to behave in looks and manner of speech. □ *Listen to him wow the boss. He can sure talk the talk, but can he walk the walk?*

**talk turkey** *Fig.* to talk business; to talk frankly. □ *John wanted to talk turkey, but Jane just wanted to joke around.*

**tan** so's **hide** *Fig. Rur.* to spank someone. □ *Billy's mother said she'd tan Billy's hide if he ever did that again.*

**tap dance like mad** *Sl.* to appear busy continuously; to have to move fast or talk cleverly to distract someone. □ *Any public official knows how to tap dance like mad when the press gets too nosy.*

**tar and feather** so to punish or humiliate someone by coating them with tar and feathers. □ *The people of the village tarred and feathered the bank robber and chased him out of town.*

**tax-and-spend** *Fig.* spending freely and taxing heavily. (Referring to a legislative body that repeatedly passes expensive new laws and keeps raising taxes to pay for the cost. Fixed order.) □ *The only thing worse than a tax-and-spend legislature is one that spends and runs up a worsening deficit.*

**teach** so **a lesson** *Fig.* to get even with someone for bad behavior. □ *John tripped me, so I punched him. That ought to teach him a lesson.*

**teach** one's **grandmother to suck eggs** *Fig.* to try to tell or show someone more knowledgeable or experienced than oneself how to do something. □ *Don't suggest showing Mary how to knit. It will be like teaching your grandmother to suck eggs.*

a **team player** *Fig.* someone who works well with the group; someone who is loyal to the group. □ *Ted is a team player. I am sure that he will cooperate with us.*

**tear** so/animal **limb from limb** to rip someone or an animal to bits. □ *The crocodiles attacked the wading zebras and tore them limb from limb.*

**teething troubles 1.** pain and crying on the part of a baby whose teeth are growing in. □ *Billy has been whining because of teething troubles.* **2.** *Fig.* difficulties and problems experienced in the early stages of a project, activity, etc. (Fig. on ①.) □ *There have been a lot of teething troubles with the new computer system.*

**telegraph** one's **punches 1.** *Fig.* to signal, unintentionally, what blows one is about to strike. (Boxing.) □ *Don't telegraph your punches, kid! You'll be flat on your back in three seconds.* **2.** *Fig.* to signal, unintentionally, one's intentions. (Fig. on ①.) □ *When you go in there to negotiate, don't telegraph your punches. Don't let them see that we're in need of this contract.*

a **tempest in a teacup** AND a **tempest in a teapot** an argument or disagreement over a very minor matter. □ *The entire issue of who was to present the report was just a tempest in a teapot.*

a **tempest in a teapot** Go to previous.

**test the water(s)** *Fig.* to try something; to see what something is like before getting involved too deeply with it. (Fig. on finding out the temperature of water before swimming or bathing in it.) □ *I attended a meeting of the club once just to test the water before I joined as a dues-paying member.*

**Thank God for small favors.** Be thankful that something good has happened in a bad situation. □ *He had a heart attack, but it was right there in the doctor's office, so they could take care of him right away. Thank God for small favors.*

**Thank goodness!** AND **Thank heavens!; Thank God!** *Fig.* Oh, I am so thankful! □ *John: Well, we finally got here. Sorry we're so late. Mother: Thank goodness! We were all so worried.*

**Thank you for sharing.** *Inf.* a sarcastic remark made when someone tells something that is unpleasant, overly personal, disgusting, or otherwise annoying. □ *Thank you for sharing. I really needed to hear about your operation.*

**thanks a bunch** *Inf.* thanks. □ *Thanks a bunch for your help.* □ *He said, "Thanks a bunch," and walked out.*

**Thanks, but no thanks.** *Inf.* Thank you, but I am not interested. (A way of turning down something that is not very desirable.) □ *Alice: How would you like to buy my old car? Jane: Thanks, but no thanks.* □ *John: What do you think about a trip over to see the Wilsons? Sally: Thanks, but no thanks. We don't get along.*

**That makes two of us.** *Inf.* The same is true for me. □ *Bill: I just passed my biology test. Bob: That makes two of us!*

**That'll be the day!** *Inf.* It will be an unusually amazing day when that happens! □ *Sue: I'm going to get this place organized once and for all! Alice: That'll be the day!*

**That's all folks!** That is everything.; It's over. (The formulaic announcement of the end of a Warner Brothers color cartoon in movie theaters. Usually stuttered by Porky Pig.) □ *We're finished playing for the evening. That's all folks!*

**That's easy for you to say.** *Inf.* You can say that easily because it really does not affect you the way it affects others. □ *Waiter: Here's your check. Mary: Thanks. (turning to others) I'm willing to just split the check evenly. Bob: That's easy for you to say. You had lobster!*

**That's not the half of it!** *Fig.* It is much worse than you think!; There is much more to this than you think! □ *Yes, the window broke, but that's not the half of it. The rain came in and ruined the carpet!*

**That's the story of my life.** *Fig.* This recent failure is just typical of the way everything in my life has been. □ *A: Sorry, but it looks like another year for you in the eighth grade. B: That's the story of my life.*

**Them's fighting words!** *Rur.* What you just said will lead to a fight. (Said as a threat.) □ *I heard what you said about my brother, and them's fighting words.*

**There are plenty of (other) fish in the sea.** *Fig.* There are other choices. (Used to refer to persons.) □ *When John broke up with Ann, I told her not to worry. There are plenty of other fish in the sea.* □ *It's too bad that your secretary quit, but there are plenty of other fish in the sea.*

**thereby hangs a tale** *Fig.* there is an interesting story connected with this matter. □ *Yes, she comes in late most mornings, and thereby hangs a tale. She has a drinking problem.*

**There's a time and place for everything.** This is not the appropriate time or place [for doing what you are doing or going to do]. □ *Stop that Jimmy! There's a time and place for everything.*

**There's no time like the present.** Do it now. □ *Ask her to marry you before another day goes by. There's no time like the present.*

**There's the rub.** *Fig.* That's the problem. (From Shakespeare's *Hamlet*, Act 3, Scene 1, in the famous line "To sleep: perchance to dream: ay, there's the rub . . .".) □ *It's available online, but they require a credit card and I don't have one. There's the rub.*

**They must have seen you coming.** *Inf.* You were really cheated. They saw you coming and decided they could cheat you easily. □ *Andy: It cost $200 dollars. Rachel: You paid $200 for that thing? Boy, they must have seen you coming.*

a **thing of the past** something that is old-fashioned or obsolete. □ *Taking off hats in elevators is a thing of the past.*

**think inside the box** *Fig.* to think in traditional fashion, bound by old, nonfunctional, or limiting structures, rules, or practices. (As if thinking or creativity were confined or limited by a figurative box. See also **inside the box.** Compare this with **think outside the box.**) □ *You guys only think inside the box and will never find a better solution.*

**think on** one's **feet** *Fig.* to be able to speak and reason well while (standing and talking) in front of an audience, especially extemporaneously. □ *I am not able to think on my feet too well before a bunch of people.*

**think out loud** *Fig.* to say one's thoughts aloud. □ *Excuse me. I didn't really mean to say that. I was just thinking out loud.*

**think outside the box** *Fig.* to think freely, not bound by old, nonfunctional, or limiting structures, rules, or practices. (As if thinking or creativity were confined in or limited by a figurative box. See also **outside the box.** Compare this with **think inside the box.**)

□ *Let's think outside the box for a minute and try to find a better solution.*

**think twice about** so/sth *Fig.* to give careful consideration to someone or something. □ *Ed may be a good choice, but I suggest that you think twice about him.*

**think twice (before** doing sth**)** *Fig.* to consider carefully whether one should do something; to be cautious about doing something. (Often negative, showing a lack of caution.) □ *You should think twice before quitting your job.* □ *I don't think twice about driving through Chicago at rush hour.*

**This is where I came in.** *Fig.* I have heard all this before. (Said when a situation begins to seem repetitive, as when a film one has seen part of before reaches familiar scenes.) □ *John sat through a few minutes of the argument, and when Tom and Alice kept saying the same thing over and over, John said, "This is where I came in," and left the room.*

**three squares (a day)** *Inf.* three nourishing meals a day. (With breakfast, lunch, and dinner considered the usual three meals. *Square* is clearly from *square meal*, which means, strangely, well-rounded meal. The *square* is the same as that found in *square deal*. Tales about sailors eating off of square plates or military academy cadets eating while sitting squarely in their chairs, while enticing, are not linked by any evidence to this term.) □ *If I could limit myself to three squares, I could lose some weight.*

**\*through the cracks** *Fig.* [moving] past the elements that are intended to catch or detect such things. (\*Typically: **fall** ~**; go** ~**; slip** ~.) □ *I am afraid that some of these issues will slip through the cracks unless we make a note about each one.*

**through thick and thin** *Cliché* through good times and bad times. □ *We've been together through thick and thin, and we won't desert each other now.*

**throw a (monkey) wrench in the works** *Inf.* to cause problems for someone's plans. (*Monkey wrench* = a type of flat-jawed adjustable wrench. □ *I don't want to throw a wrench in the works, but have you checked your plans with a lawyer?*

**throw caution to the wind** *Cliché* to become very careless. □ *Jane, who is usually cautious, threw caution to the wind and went swimming in the ocean.*

**throw down the gauntlet** *Fig.* to challenge someone to an argument or to (figurative) combat. (This *gauntlet* was a glove.) □ *When Bob challenged my conclusions, he threw down the gauntlet. I was ready for an argument.*

**throw** sth **in(to) the pot** *Fig.* to add an idea or suggestion to the discussion. (Fig. on making a pot of soup or stew.) □ *Let me throw something in the pot. Let's think about selling stock in the company.*

**throw the book at** so *Fig.* to charge or convict someone with as many crimes as is possible. □ *I made the police officer angry, so he took me to the station and threw the book at me.*

**throw** so **to the dogs** *Fig.* to abandon someone to enemies or evil. □ *The spy served the evil empire well, but in the end, they threw him to the dogs.*

**throw** so **to the wolves** *Fig.* to sacrifice someone to save the rest; to abandon someone to harm. (Fig. on the image of giving one person to the wolves to eat so the rest can get away.) □ *The investigation was going to be rigorous and unpleasant, and I could see they were going to throw someone to the wolves.*

**thrust and parry** *Fig.* to enter into verbal combat [with someone]; to compete actively [with someone]. (Fig. on the sport of fencing.) □ *I spent the entire afternoon thrusting and parrying with a committee of so-called experts in the field of insurance.*

a **thumbnail sketch** *Fig.* a brief or small picture or description. □ *The manager gave a thumbnail sketch of her plans.*

**thunder** sth **out**[†] *Fig.* to respond with words spoken in a voice like thunder. □ *He thundered the words out so everyone could hear them.*

**tickle the ivories** *Inf.* to play the piano. □ *I used to be able to tickle the ivories real nice.*

**tie the knot 1.** *Fig.* to marry a mate. □ *We tied the knot in a little chapel on the Arkansas border.* **2.** *Fig.* [for a cleric or other authorized person] to unite a couple in marriage. □ *It only took a few minutes for the ship's captain to tie the knot.*

a **tight race** *Fig.* a close race. □ *It was a tight race right up to the final turn when my horse pulled ahead and won easily.*

**tighten** one's **belt** *Fig.* to manage to spend less money; to use less of something. □ *Things are beginning to cost more and more. It looks like we'll all have to tighten our belts.*

**till kingdom come** *Fig.* until the end of the world; forever. □ *Do I have to keep assembling these units till kingdom come?*

**tilt at windmills** *Fig.* to fight battles with imaginary enemies; to fight against unimportant enemies or issues. (As with the fictional character Don Quixote, who attacked windmills. *Tilt = joust with.*) □ *I'm not going to fight this issue. I've wasted too much of my life tilting at windmills.*

**time flies (when you're having fun)** *Fig.* time passes very quickly. (From the Latin *tempus fugit.*) □ *I didn't really think it was so late when the party ended. Doesn't time fly?*

**time hangs heavy (on** so's **hands)** *Fig.* there is too much time and not enough to do. □ *I'm bored and nervous. Time hangs heavy on my hands.*

the **tip of the iceberg** *Fig.* only the part of something that can be easily observed, but not the rest of it, which is hidden. (Referring to the fact that the major bulk of an iceberg is below the surface of the water.) □ *The problems that you see here now are just the tip of the iceberg. There are numerous disasters waiting to happen.*

**to beat the band** *Inf.* very briskly; very fast; in an extreme way. (Possibly originally meaning to make more noise than the band or to march faster than a marching band.) □ *He's selling computers to beat the band since he started advertising.*

**to boot** *Inf.* in addition; to complement or complete. □ *She got an F on her term paper and flunked the final to boot.*

**to put it mildly** *Fig.* to understate something; to say something politely. □ *She was angry at almost everyone—to put it mildly.*

**to the ends of the earth** *Fig.* to the remotest and most inaccessible points on the earth. □ *I'll pursue him to the ends of the earth.*

**to the letter** *Fig.* exactly as instructed; exactly as written. □ *We didn't prepare the recipe to the letter, but the cake still turned out very well.*

**to the manner born** AND **to the manor born 1.** *Fig.* expected to behave in a particular manner that comes naturally. (This sense is close to Shakespeare's original in *Hamlet* and is meant to be the *manner* version and should be spelled that way.) □ *Everyone in the valley is in the habit of drinking heavily, and since I was born here, I am legitimately to the manner born.* **2.** *Fig.* privileged; acting as if one had been born in a manor house and were used to the privileges and pleasures thereof. (This originated as a misunderstanding or mishearing of the *Hamlet* line and has then acquired a meaning more appropriate to the spelling *manor*. The punning potential was further developed in the BBC television series *To the Manor Born* starring Penelope Keith, whose manner was definitely appropriate to the manor house she was forced to sell.) □ *I'm not exactly to the manor born, but I can hold my own among those with wealth and station.*

**to the nth degree** *Fig.* to the maximum amount. □ *Jane is a perfectionist and tries to be careful to the nth degree.*

**to the tune of** some amount of money *Fig.* to a certain amount of money. □ *My checking account is overdrawn to the tune of $340.*

the **toast of** some place *Fig.* a notably famous and sought-after person in a particular place. (This suggests that this person would frequently be the subject of toasts. One of the most popular places is *the town*.) □ *Since she became the American Idol, she is the toast of every town in the U.S.* □ *Tony, the city's favorite weather man, is the toast of St. Louis.*

**toe the mark** AND **toe the line** *Fig.* to do what one is expected to do; to follow the rules. (Sometimes spelled incorrectly as *tow the line*. The *mark* and *line* refer to a line on the ground that must act either as a barrier or a line that one must stand behind to show readiness. The link between the alleged origins and the current use is not comfortably clear.) □ *You'll get ahead, Sally. Don't worry. Just toe the mark, and everything will be okay.*

**too big for** one's **britches** *Rur.* too haughty for one's status or age. □ *Bill's getting a little too big for his britches, and somebody's going to straighten him out.*

**too close for comfort** *Cliché* [for a misfortune or a threat] to be dangerously close or threatening. (Usually in the past tense.) □ *When I was in the hospital, I nearly died from pneumonia. Believe me, that was too close for comfort.*

**too much too soon** too much responsibility too early; too much money too soon in one's career. □ *Sarah got too much too soon and became lazy because there was no longer any motivation for her to work.*

**tools of the trade 1.** the special hand tools one needs to do one's physical labor. □ *Chisels and knives are the tools of the trade for a woodcarver.* **2.** *Fig.* the equipment, supplies, books, computers, telephones, etc. people need to work in the professions and allied support groups. □ *We have to have computers! Computers are the tools of the trade for writers!*

**top brass** *Fig.* the highest leader(s); the boss(es). (Originally military.) □ *You'll have to check it out with the top brass. She'll be home around five.*

**toss a salad** *Fig.* to mix the various ingredients of a salad together. (The components of the salad are lifted and dropped in the bowl repeatedly in order to coat everything with dressing.) □ *I tossed the salad just before my guests arrived.*

**toss** one's **cookies** *Sl.* to vomit. □ *Don't run too fast after you eat or you'll toss your cookies.*

**touch and go** *Fig.* very uncertain or critical. □ *Jane had a serious operation, and everything was touch and go for two days after her surgery.*

a **tough break** *Fig.* a bit of bad fortune. □ *John had a lot of tough breaks when he was a kid, but he's doing okay now.*

a **tough call** *Fig.* a difficult judgment to make. □ *We're still undecided on whether to buy a place or rent—it's a tough call.*

a **tough cookie** *Fig.* a person who is difficult to deal with. □ *There was a tough cookie in here this morning who demanded to see the manager.*

**Tout suite!** *Fig.* right away; with all haste. (Older. Pronounced "toot sweet." From French *toute de suite.*) □ *"I want this mess cleaned up, tout suite!" shouted Sally, hands on her hips and steaming with rage.*

**town-and-gown** *Fig.* the relations between a town and the university located within the town; the relations between university students and the nonstudents who live in a university town. (Usually in reference to a disagreement. Fixed order.) □ *There is another town-and-gown dispute in Adamsville over the amount the university costs the city for police services.*

so's **train of thought** *Fig.* someone's pattern of thinking or sequence of ideas; what a person was just thinking about. □ *I cannot seem to follow your train of thought on this matter. Will you explain it a little more carefully, please?*

a **travesty of justice** *Fig.* a miscarriage of justice; an act of the legal system that is an insult to the system of justice. □ *The lawyer complained that the judge's ruling was a travesty of justice.*

**tread water** *Fig.* to make no progress. (Fig. on the idea of just staying afloat.) □ *I'm not getting anywhere in my career. I'm just treading water, hoping something good will happen.*

**trial balloon** *Inf.* a test of someone's or the public's reaction. □ *It was just a trial balloon, and it didn't work.*

**trials and tribulations** *Cliché* problems and tests of one's courage or perseverance. □ *I promise not to tell you of the trials and tribulations of my day if you promise not to tell me yours!*

**\*tricks of the trade** *Fig.* special skills and knowledge associated with any trade or profession. (*Typically: **know the** ~; **learn the** ~; **know a few** ~; **show** so **the** ~; **teach** so **a few**~.) □ *I know a few tricks of the trade that make things easier.*

**trip the light fantastic** *Fig.* to dance. (Jocular.) □ *Shall we go trip the light fantastic?*

**true to form** *Fig.* exactly as expected; following the usual pattern. □ *And true to form, Mary left before the meeting was adjourned.*

**try** so's **patience** *Fig.* to strain someone's patience; to bother someone as if testing the person's patience. (*Try* means *test* here.) □ *You really try my patience with all your questions!*

**tub of lard** *Inf.* a fat person. (Insulting.) □ *That tub of lard can hardly get through the door.*

**tunnel vision 1.** *Fig.* a visual impairment wherein one can only see what is directly ahead of oneself. □ *I have tunnel vision, so I have to keep looking from side to side.* **2.** *Fig.* an inability to recognize other ways of doing things or thinking about things. □ *The boss really has tunnel vision about sales and marketing. He sees no reason to change anything.*

**turn a blind eye (to** so/sth**)** *Fig.* to ignore something and pretend you do not see it. □ *The usher turned a blind eye to the little boy who sneaked into the theater.*

**turn a deaf ear (to** so/sth**)** to ignore what someone says; to ignore a cry for help. □ *How can you just turn a deaf ear to their cries for food and shelter?*

**turn a profit** *Fig.* to earn a profit. □ *The company plans to turn a profit two years from now.*

**turn back the clock** *Fig.* to try to make things the way they were before; to reverse some change. □ *Jill: I wish I was back in college. I had so much fun then. Jane: You can't turn back the clock. Even if you went back to school, it wouldn't be the same.*

the **turn of the century** the time when the year changes to one with two final zeros, such as from 1899 to 1900. (Although technically incorrect—a new century begins with the year ending in 01—most people ignore this.) □ *My family moved to America at the turn of the century.*

**turn on a dime** *Fig.* [for a vehicle] to turn in a very tight turn. □ *I need a vehicle that can turn on a dime.*

**turn on the waterworks** *Fig.* to begin to cry. □ *Every time Billy got homesick, he turned on the waterworks.*

**turn some heads** *Fig.* to cause people to look (at someone or something); to get attention (from people). □ *That new bikini of yours is sure to turn some heads.*

**turn the clock back**† *Fig.* to try to return to the past. □ *You are not facing up to the future. You are trying to turn the clock back to a time when you were more comfortable.*

**turn the other cheek** *Fig.* to ignore abuse or an insult. □ *When Bob got mad at Mary and yelled at her, she just turned the other cheek.*

**turn the tide** *Fig.* to cause a reversal in the direction of events; to cause a reversal in public opinion. □ *It looked as if the team was going to lose, but near the end of the game, our star player turned the tide.*

**turn turtle** *Fig.* to turn upside down. □ *The sailboat turned turtle, but the sailors only got wet.*

**turn** so's **water off**† *Sl.* to deflate someone; to silence someone. □ *He said you were stupid, huh? Well, I guess that turns your water off!*

**twelve good men and true** *Fig.* a jury composed of trustworthy men. □ *He was convicted by a jury of twelve good men and true. Not a wino in the lot.*

**twiddle** one's **thumbs** *Fig.* to pass the time by twirling one's thumbs. □ *What am I supposed to do while waiting for you? Sit here and twiddle my thumbs?*

**twilight years** *Fig.* the last years before death. □ *In his twilight years, he became more mellow and stopped yelling at people.*

**two shakes of a lamb's tail** *Inf.* quickly; rapidly. □ *I'll be there in two shakes of a lamb's tail.*

**\*two strikes against** one *Fig.* a critical number of things against one; a position wherein success is unlikely or where the success of the next move is crucial. (*Typically: **get** ~; **have** ~.) □ *Poor Bob had two strikes against him when he tried to explain where he was last night.*

a **two-time loser** *Inf.* a confirmed loser; a person who has already failed at a previous attempt at some task. □ *Martin is a two-time loser, or at least he looks like one.*

a **two-way street** *Inf.* a reciprocal situation. □ *This is a two-way street, you know. You will have to help me someday in return.*

**under a cloud (of suspicion)** *Fig.* suspected of something. □ *Someone stole some money at work, and now everyone is under a cloud of suspicion.*

**\*under a spell** *Fig.* enchanted; under the control of magic. (*Typically: **be** ~; **have** so ~; **put** so ~.) □ *Her soft voice and faint perfume put Buxton under a spell. Then the enchantment was broken when he found his wallet missing.*

**\*under arrest** arrested and in the custody of the police in preparation for the filing of a charge. (*Typically: **be** ~; **put** so ~.) □ *Am I under arrest, officer? What did I do?*

**\*under fire** *Fig.* during an attack; being attacked. (*Typically: **be** ~; **resign** ~; **think** ~.) □ *There was a scandal in city hall, and the mayor was forced to resign under fire.*

**under oath** *Fig.* bound by an oath; having taken an oath. □ *I was placed under oath before I could testify in the trial.*

**under** one's **own steam** *Fig.* by one's own power or effort. □ *I missed my ride to class, so I had to get there under my own steam.*

**under the sun** *Fig.* anywhere on earth at all. □ *Isn't there anyone under the sun who can help me with this problem?*

**under the table 1.** *Sl.* intoxicated. □ *Jed was under the table by midnight.* **2.** *Fig.* secret; clandestine. (Hyphenated before a nominal.) □ *It was strictly an under-the-table deal.*

**under the weather 1.** *Inf.* ill. □ *I feel sort of under the weather today.* □ *Whatever I ate for lunch is making me feel a bit under the*

(un)til the cows come home

*weather.* **2.** *Inf.* intoxicated. ☐ *Daddy's had a few beers and is under the weather again.*

**unsung hero** *Fig.* a hero who has gotten no praise or recognition. ☐ *The time has come to recognize all the unsung heroes of the battle for low-cost housing.*

**(un)til hell freezes over** *Inf.* forever. ☐ *That's all right, boss; I can wait till hell freezes over for your answer.*

**(un)til the cows come home** *Rur.* until the last; until very late. (Referring to the end of the day, when the cows come home to be fed and milked.) ☐ *Where've you been? Who said you could stay out till the cows come home?*

***(up and) about** AND ***up and around** out of bed and moving about. (*Typically: **be** ~**; get** ~.) ☐ *The flu put Alice into bed for three days, but she was up and around on the fourth.*

**up and around** Go to previous.

**up and running** *Fig.* [of a machine] functioning. □ *As soon as we can get the tractor up and running, we will plant the corn crop.*

**up for grabs 1.** *Fig.* available for anyone; not yet claimed. (As if something, such as a handful of money, had been thrown up into the air, and people were to grab at as many bills as they could get.) □ *The election is up for grabs. Everything is still very chancy.* **2.** *Fig.* in total chaos. □ *This is a madhouse. The whole place is up for grabs.*

**up in the air (about** so/sth) *Fig.* undecided about someone or something; uncertain about someone or something. □ *I don't know what Sally plans to do. Things were sort of up in the air the last time we talked.*

**up North** to or at the northern part of the country or the world. □ *When you say "up North," do you mean where the polar bears live, or just in the northern states?*

**up stakes** *Inf.* to prepare for leaving and then leave. (*Up* has the force of a verb here. The phrase suggests pulling up tent stakes in preparation for departure.) □ *It's that time of the year when I feel like upping stakes and moving to the country.*

**up the creek (without a paddle)** AND **up a creek; up shit creek** *Inf.* in an awkward position with no easy way out. (Caution with *shit*.) □ *You are up a creek! You got yourself into it, so get yourself out.*

**up to no good** *Fig.* doing something bad. □ *There are three boys in the front yard. I don't know what they are doing, but I think they are up to no good.*

**\*up to speed 1.** *Fig.* moving, operating, or functioning at a normal or desired rate. (\*Typically: **be** ~; **bring** sth ~; **get** ~; **get** sth ~.) □ *Terri did everything she could to bring her workers up to speed, but couldn't.* **2.** AND **\*up to speed on** so/sth *Fig.* fully apprised about someone or something; up-to-date on the state of someone or something. (*Typically: **be** ~; **bring** so ~; **get** ~; **get** so ~.) □ *I'll feel better about it when I get up to speed on what's going on.*

**upon impact** *Fig.* at the place or time of an impact. □ *The car crumpled upon impact with the brick wall.*

**upper crust** *Fig.* the higher levels of society; the upper class. (From the top, as opposed to the bottom, crust of a pie.) □ *Jane speaks like that because she pretends to be part of the upper crust, but her father was a miner.*

**upset the apple cart** *Fig.* to mess up or ruin something. □ *Tom really upset the apple cart by telling Mary the truth about Jane.*

**use some elbow grease** *Fig.* use some effort, as in scrubbing something. (As if lubricating one's elbow would make one more efficient. Note the variation in the example.) □ *I tried elbow grease, but it doesn't help get the job done.*

**user friendly** *Fig.* easy to use. (Hyphenated before nominals.) □ *The setup instructions for the printer were not user friendly.* □ *I have a user-friendly computer that listens to my voice and does what I tell it.*

**usher** so **in**† to lead or guide someone into a place. □ *Four policemen ushered a sad-faced Wallace Travelian into the station house.*

**usher** sth **in**† *Fig.* to introduce or welcome something; to signal the beginning of something, such as spring, colder weather, the New Year, the shopping season, etc. □ *Warm temperatures ushered spring in early this year.*

**vale of tears** *Fig.* the earth; mortal life on earth. (*Vale* is a literary word for *valley*.) □ *When it comes time for me to leave this vale of tears, I hope I can leave some worthwhile memories behind.*

**vent** one's **spleen** *Fig.* to get rid of one's feelings of anger caused by someone or something by attacking someone or something else. □ *Jack vented his spleen at his wife whenever things went badly at work.*

the **(very) picture of** sth *Fig.* the perfect example of something; an exact image of something. □ *The young newlyweds were the picture of happiness.* □ *My doctor told me that I was the very picture of good health.*

*a **vested interest in** sth *Fig.* a personal or biased interest, often financial, in something. (*Typically: **have** ~; **give** so ~.) □ *Margaret has a vested interest in wanting her father to sell the family firm. She has shares in it and would make a large profit.*

the **villain of the piece** *Fig.* someone or something that is responsible for something bad or wrong. (Fig. on the role of the villain in a drama or other literary work.) □ *We couldn't think who had stolen the meat. The dog next door turned out to be the villain of the piece.*

**vim and vigor** *Cliché* energy; enthusiasm. □ *Show more vim and vigor! Let us know you're alive.*

a **visit from the stork** *Fig.* a birth. (According to legend, babies are brought to their parents by a stork.) □ *I hear that Maria is expecting a visit from the stork.*

**vote a split ticket** *Fig.* to cast a ballot on which one's votes are divided between two or more parties. □ *I always vote a split ticket since I detest both parties.*

**vote a straight ticket** *Fig.* to cast a ballot on which all one's votes are for members of the same political party. □ *I'm not a member of any political party, so I never vote a straight ticket.*

a **vote of confidence 1.** a specific act of voting that signifies whether a governing body still has the majority's support. □ *The government easily won the vote of confidence called for by the opposition.* **2.** *Fig.* a statement of confidence in a person or a group. □ *The little talk that his father gave him before the game served as a great vote of confidence for Billy.*

a **vote of thanks** *Fig.* a speech expressing appreciation and thanks to a speaker, lecturer, organizer, etc. and inviting the audience to applaud. □ *Mary was given a vote of thanks for organizing the dance.*

**vote with** one's **feet** *Fig.* to express one's dissatisfaction with something by leaving, especially by walking away. □ *I think that the play is a total flop. Most of the audience voted with its feet during the second act.*

**vote with** one's **wallet** *Fig.* to show one's displeasure at a business establishment's goods or pricing by spending one's money elsewhere. (Probably derived from **vote with** one's **feet**.) □ *If you didn't like it, you should have complained to the manager and voted with your wallet.*

# W

**wade through** sth *Fig.* to struggle through something with difficulty. (Fig. on the image of slogging through something such as water or mud.) □ *I have to wade through 40 term papers in the next two days.*

**wait for the other shoe to drop** *Fig.* to wait for the inevitable next step or the final conclusion. □ *He just opened his mail and moaned. Now, I'm waiting for the other shoe to drop when he finds the subpoena.*

**wait on** so **hand and foot** *Fig.* to serve someone very well, attending to all personal needs. □ *I don't mind bringing you your coffee, but I don't intend to wait on you hand and foot.*

**wait-and-see attitude** *Fig.* a skeptical attitude; an uncertain attitude in which someone will just wait to see what happens before reacting. □ *His wait-and-see attitude seemed to indicate that he didn't really care what happened.*

**wake the dead** *Fig.* to be so loud as to wake those who are "sleeping" the most soundly: the dead. □ *You are making enough noise to wake the dead.*

**wake up and smell the coffee** *Fig.* to become aware and sense what is going on around oneself. □ *You are so without a clue. Wake up and smell the coffee! Life is passing you by.*

**walk off the job 1.** *Fig.* to abandon a job abruptly. □ *Fred almost walked off the job when he saw how bad things were.* **2.** *Fig.* to go on strike at a workplace. □ *The workers walked off the job and refused to negotiate.*

**walk on eggshells 1.** *Fig.* to walk very carefully; to take steps gingerly. □ *Since he stumbled and fell against the china cabinet, Bill has been walking on eggshells.* **2.** *Fig.* to be very diplomatic and inoffensive. □ *I was walking on eggshells trying to explain the remark to her without offending her further.*

**walk on thin ice** *Fig.* to be in a very precarious position. □ *Careful with radical ideas like that. You're walking on thin ice.*

**walk the plank** *Fig.* to suffer punishment at the hand of someone. (Fig. on the image of pirates making their blindfolded captives die by walking off the end of a plank jutting out over the open sea.) □ *Fred may think he can make the members of my department walk the plank, but we will fight back.*

**walk through** sth *Fig.* to rehearse something in a casual way; to go through a play or other performed piece, showing where each person is to be located during each speech or musical number. □ *Let's walk through this scene one more time.*

**waltz around** sth *Fig.* to move around or through a place happily or proudly. □ *Who is that person waltzing around, trying to look important?*

**warm body** *Inf.* a person; just any person (who can be counted on to be present). □ *See if you can get a couple of warm bodies to stand at the door and hand out programs.*

**warm the cockles of** so's **heart** *Fig.* to make someone feel warm and happy. □ *Hearing that old song again warmed the cockles of her heart.*

**warts and all** *Cliché* in spite of the flaws. □ *It's a great performance—warts and all.*

**wash** one's **hands of** so/sth *Fig.* to end one's association with someone or something. (Fig. on the notion of getting rid of a problem by removing it as if it were dirt on the hands.) □ *I washed my hands of Tom. I wanted no more to do with him.*

**wash over** so *Fig.* [for a powerful feeling] to flood over a person. □ *A feeling of nausea washed over me.*

**waste** one's **breath** *Fig.* to waste one's time talking; to talk in vain. □ *Don't waste your breath talking to her. She won't listen.*

a **waste of space** something that is completely without value. □ *The wrecked furniture in here is just a waste of space.*

**watch** so/sth **like a hawk** *Fig.* to watch someone or something very closely. (Hawks have very good eyesight and watch carefully for prey.) □ *The teacher didn't trust me. During tests, she used to watch me like a hawk.*

**water over the dam** AND **water under the bridge** *Fig.* past and unchangeable events. □ *Your quarrel with Lena is water over the dam, so you ought to concentrate on getting along with her.* □ *George and I were friends once, but that's all water under the bridge now.*

**water under the bridge** Go to previous.

**wax angry** AND **wax wroth** *Fig.* to speak in anger and with indignation. □ *Seeing the damage done by the careless children caused the preacher to wax wroth at their parents.*

**wax eloquent** *Fig.* to speak with eloquence. □ *Perry never passed up a chance to wax eloquent at a banquet.*

**wax poetic** *Fig.* to speak poetically. □ *I hope you will pardon me if I wax poetic for a moment when I say that your lovely hands drift across the piano keys like swans on the lake.*

**wax wroth** Go to wax angry.

**We all gotta go sometime.** *Inf.* We all must die sometime. (As jocular as possible.) □ *Sorry to hear about old Bubba, but we all gotta go sometime.*

**the weak link (in the chain)** *Fig.* the weak point or person in a system or organization. □ *Joan's hasty generalizations about the economy were definitely the weak link in her argument.*

**wear and tear** *Fig.* damage to something through use. □ *This old couch shows some wear and tear, but generally, it's in good shape.*

**wear** so **to a frazzle** *Fig.* to exhaust someone. □ *Taking care of all those kids must wear you to a frazzle.*

**well up in years** *Euph.* aged; old. □ *Jane's husband is well up in years. He is nearly 75.*

**well-fixed** Go to next.

**well-heeled** AND **well-fixed; well-off** *Fig.* wealthy; with sufficient money. □ *My uncle can afford a new car. He's well-heeled.*

**well-off** Go to previous.

a **wet blanket** *Fig.* a dull or depressing person who spoils other people's enjoyment. □ *Jack's fun at parties, but his brother's a wet blanket.*

**whale the tar out of** so *Inf.* to spank or beat someone. □ *I'll whale the tar out of you when we get home if you don't settle down.*

**What can I say?** *Inf.* I have no explanation or excuse. What do you expect me to say? □ *Bob: You're going to have to act more aggressive if you want to make sales. You're just too timid. Tom: What can I say? I am what I am.*

**What can I tell you?** *Inf.* I haven't any idea of what to say. (Compare this with **What can I say?**) □ *John: Why on earth did you do a dumb thing like that? Bill: What can I tell you? I just did it, that's all.*

**What I wouldn't give for a** sth! I would give anything for something. □ *What I wouldn't give for a cold drink about now.*

**What** so **said.** *Sl.* I agree with what someone just said, although I might not have been able to say it as well or so elegantly. □ *What John said. And I agree 100 percent.*

**What you see is what you get.** *Fig.* The product you are looking at is exactly what you get if you buy it. □ *It comes just like this. What you see is what you get.*

**What's cooking?** *Inf.* What is happening?; How are you? □ *Bob: Hi, Fred! What's cooking? Fred: How are you doing, Bob?*

**What's the catch?** *Sl.* What is the drawback?; It sounds good, but are there any hidden problems? □ *Sounds too good to be true. What's the catch?*

**What's the damage?** *Sl.* What are the charges?; How much is the bill? □ *Bill: That was delicious. Waiter, what's the damage? Waiter: I'll get the check, sir.*

**What's the world coming to?** There are too many changes, and they are all bad. □ *Look at how people speed down this street now. What's the world coming to?*

**wheel and deal** *Fig.* to take part in clever (but sometimes dishonest or immoral) business deals. □ *Jack got tired of all the wheeling and dealing of big business and retired to a farm out west.*

**when the chips are down** *Fig.* at the final, critical moment; when things really get difficult. □ *When the chips are down, I know that I can depend on Jean to help out.*

**when the dust settles 1.** *Fig.* when the dust falls out of the air onto the ground or floor. □ *When the dust settles, we will have to begin sweeping it up.* **2.** *Fig.* when things have calmed down. (Fig. on ①.) □ *When the dust settles, we can start patching up all the hurt feelings.*

**where** so's **head is at** *Inf.* the state of one's mental well-being. □ *As soon as I figure where my head is at, I'll be okay.*

**where** one **is coming from** *Fig.* one's point of view. □ *I think I know what you mean. I know where you're coming from.*

**where the rubber meets the road** *Fig.* at the point in a process where there are challenges, issues, or problems. □ *Now we have* *spelled out the main area of dissent. This is where the rubber meets the road.*

**Where there's smoke, there's fire.** *Fig.* Where there is evidence of an event, the event must have happened. □ *She found lipstick on his collar. Knowing that where there's smoke, there's fire, she confronted him.*

a **whipping boy** *Fig.* someone who is punished for someone else's misdeeds. □ *The president has turned out to be the whipping boy for his party.*

**whistle in the dark** *Inf.* to guess aimlessly; to speculate as to a fact. □ *She was just whistling in the dark. She has no idea of what's going on.*

**white knuckle** sth *Fig.* to survive something threatening through strained endurance, that is to say, holding on tight. □ *The flight from New York was terrible. We had to white knuckle the entire flight.*

**white-collar** *Fig.* of the class of salaried office workers or lower-level managers. □ *His parents were both white-collar employees and had good-paying jobs.*

**whole bag of tricks** *Fig.* everything; every possibility. □ *Well now. I've used my whole bag of tricks, and we still haven't solved this.*

the **whole enchilada** *Inf.* the whole thing; everything. (From Spanish.) □ *Nobody, but nobody, ever gets the whole enchilada.*

the **whole kit and caboodle** *Inf.* a group of pieces of equipment or belongings. (The word *caboodle* is used only in this expression.) □ *When I bought Bob's motor home, I got furniture, refrigerator, and linen—the whole kit and caboodle.*

the **whole shebang** *Inf.* everything; the whole thing. □ *Mary's all set to give a fancy dinner party. She's got a fine tablecloth, good crystal, and silverware, the whole shebang.*

the **whole wide world** *Fig.* everywhere; everywhere and everything. □ *I've searched the whole wide world for just the right hat.*

**\*wide of the mark 1.** *Fig.* far from the target; [falling] short of or to the side of the goal. (\*Typically: **be** ~**; fall** ~.) □ *Tom's shot was wide of the mark.* □ *The arrow fell wide of the mark.* **2.** *Fig.* inadequate; far from what is required or expected. (\*Typically: **be** ~**; fall** ~.) □ *Jane's efforts were sincere, but wide of the mark.*

a **wide place in the road** *Inf.* a very small town. □ *The town is little more than a wide place in the road.*

a **wild-goose chase** a worthless hunt or chase; a futile pursuit. □ *I wasted all afternoon on a wild-goose chase.*

**will be the death of** so/sth **(yet)** *Fig.* [the thing named] will be the end or ruin of someone or something. □ *This job will be the death of me!* □ *These rough roads will be the death of these tires.*

a **window of opportunity** *Fig.* a brief time period in which an opportunity exists. □ *This afternoon, I had a brief window of opportunity when I could discuss this with the boss, but she wasn't receptive.*

**window-shopping** *Fig.* the habit or practice of looking at goods in shop windows or stores without actually buying anything. □ *Mary and Jane do a lot of window-shopping in their lunch hour, looking for things to buy when they get paid.*

**wine and dine** so *Fig.* to treat someone to an expensive meal of the type that includes fine wines; to entertain someone lavishly. □ *The lobbyists wined and dined the senators one by one in order to influence them.*

**winner take all** *Fig.* a situation where the one who defeats others takes all the spoils of the conflict. □ *The contest was a case of winner take all. There was no second place or runner-up.*

**wishful thinking** *Fig.* believing that something is true or that something will happen just because one wishes that it were true

with bells on (one's toes)

or would happen. □ *Hoping for a car as a birthday present is just wishful thinking.*

**with a vengeance** *Cliché* with determination and eagerness. □ *Bill ate all his dinner and gobbled up his dessert with a vengeance.*

**with all due respect** not meaning to be disrespectful. □ *With all due respect, your honor, I think you are making a mistake.*

**with bated breath** *Fig.* while holding one's breath; with one's breathing suspended or abated. (Often spelled incorrectly as *baited*. *Bated* is from *abated* and only appears in this phrase, which appeared first in Shakespeare's *The Merchant of Venice*. It means holding one's breath.) □ *We stood there with bated breath while the man hung onto the side of the bridge.*

**with bells on (**one's **toes)** *Fig.* eagerly, willingly, and on time. □ *Oh, yes! I'll meet you at the restaurant. I'll be there with bells on.*

□ *All the smiling children were there waiting for me with bells on their toes.*

**with flying colors** Cliché easily and excellently. (A ship displaying flags and pennants presents itself with flying colors.) □ *John passed his geometry test with flying colors.*

**with gay abandon** with complete and oblivious abandon or innocent carelessness. (This has nothing to do with *gay* = homosexual.) □ *She ran through her homework with gay abandon and still got an A in every subject.*

**with (great) relish** *Fig.* with pleasure or enjoyment. (Often seen as a pun as if this were pickle relish.) □ *John put on his new coat with great relish.* □ *We accepted the offer to use their beach house with relish.*

**(with) hat in hand** *Fig.* with humility. (Fig. on the image of someone standing, respectfully, in front of a powerful person, asking for a favor.) □ *We had to go hat in hand to the committee to get a grant for our proposal.*

**with the best will in the world** *Fig.* however much one wishes to do something or however hard one tries to do something. □ *With the best will in the world, Jack won't be able to help Mary get the job.*

**with the naked eye** *Fig.* with eyes that are not aided by telescopes, microscopes, or binoculars. □ *Bacteria are too small to be seen with the naked eye.*

**within** one's **means** *Fig.* affordable. □ *I think that a TV set with a smaller screen would be more within our means.*

**without further ado** without any more being said or done; without any additional introductory comments. (Sometimes in fun or ignorance *without further adieu* = without any more good-byes.) □ *Without further ado, here is the next president of the club!*

**without question** *Fig.* absolutely; certainly. □ *She agreed to help without question.*

*one's **wits about** one *Fig.* [keeping] calm making one's mind work smoothly, especially in a time of stress. (*Get* = to acquire and *have, keep* = retain. *Typically: **get** ~; **have** ~; **keep (all)** ~.) □ *Let me get my wits about me so I can figure this out.* □ *If Jane hadn't kept her wits about her during the fire, things would have been much worse.*

a **wolf in sheep's clothing** *Fig.* a dangerous person pretending to be harmless. □ *Carla thought the handsome stranger was gentle and kind, but Susan suspected he was a wolf in sheep's clothing.*

**won't hold water** *Fig.* to be inadequate, insubstantial, or ill-conceived. □ *Sorry, your ideas won't hold water. Nice try, though.*

the **woods are full of** so/sth *Fig.* there are lots and lots of people or things. □ *The woods are full of nice-looking guys who'll scam you if you aren't careful.*

**wool-gathering** daydreaming. (From the practice of wandering along collecting tufts of sheep's wool from hedges.) □ *I wish my new secretary would get on with the work and stop wool-gathering.*

**word by word** *Fig.* one word at a time. □ *We examined the contract word by word to make sure everything was the way we wanted.*

**word for word** *Fig.* in the exact words; verbatim. □ *I can't recall word for word what she told us.*

one's **word is** one's **bond** *Fig.* one's statement of agreement is as sound as a posting of a performance bond. □ *Of course, you can trust anything I agree to verbally. My word is my bond. There's no need to get it in writing.*

a **word to the wise** *Fig.* a good piece of advice; a word of wisdom. □ *If I can give you a word to the wise, I would suggest going to the courthouse about an hour before your trial.*

**work** one's **fingers to the bone** *Cliché* to work very hard. □ *I worked my fingers to the bone so you children could have everything you needed. Now look at the way you treat me!*

**work its magic on** so/sth *Fig.* [for something] to charm, influence, or transform someone or something, usually in some trivial way.

□ *You will be pleased at how Jimson's Wax works its magic on your floors and woodwork.* □ *The beautician worked her magic on Mrs. Uppington, and she looked two years younger.*

**work out for the best** *Fig.* [for a bad situation] to turn out all right in the end. □ *Don't worry. Everything will work out for the best.*

**work wonders (with** so/sth**)** *Fig.* to be surprisingly beneficial to someone or something; to be very helpful with someone or something. □ *This new medicine works wonders with my headaches.*

a **working stiff** *Fig.* someone who works, especially in a non-management position. (Originally and typically referring to males.) □ *But does the working stiff really care about all this economic stuff?*

The **world is** one's **oyster.** *Fig.* One rules the world.; One is in charge of everything. □ *The world is my oyster! I'm in love!*

**worried sick (about** so/sth**)** *Fig.* very worried or anxious about someone or something. □ *Oh, thank heavens you are all right. We were worried sick about you!*

**worship the ground** so **walks on** *Fig.* to honor someone to a great extent. □ *She always admired the professor. In fact, she worshiped the ground he walked on.*

**worth** one's **salt** *Fig.* worth (in productivity) what it costs to keep or support one. □ *We decided that you are worth your salt, and you can stay on as office clerk.*

**worthy of the name** *Fig.* deserving to be so called; good enough to enjoy a specific designation. □ *Any art critic worthy of the name would know that painting to be a fake.*

**wouldn't dream of** doing sth *Fig.* would not even consider doing something. □ *I wouldn't dream of taking your money!*

**wrack and ruin** *Cliché* complete destruction or ruin. □ *They went back after the fire and saw the wrack and ruin that used to be their house.*

**\*wrapped up (with** so/sth**)** *Fig.* involved with someone or something. (\*Typically: **be** ~**; get** ~.) □ *She is all wrapped up with her husband and his problems.*

**wreak vengeance (up)on** so/sth *Cliché* to seek and get revenge on someone by harming someone or something. □ *The general wanted to wreak vengeance on the opposing army for their recent successful attack.*

**wring** one's **hands 1.** to nervously rub one's hands as if one were washing them. □ *He was so upset that he was actually wringing his hands.* **2.** *Fig.* to do something ineffective while one is very upset. (Fig. on ①.) □ *Don't just stand there weeping and wringing your hands! Call the police!*

**writ large** *Fig.* magnified; done on a larger scale; made more prominent. (Formal or learned.) □ *As the child grew bigger, his behavior grew worse, and too soon the man was but the flawed boy writ large.*

**writer's block** *Fig.* the temporary inability for a writer to think of what to write. □ *I have writer's block at the moment and can't seem to get a sensible sentence on paper.*

**\*the wrong number 1.** an incorrect telephone number. (\*Typically: **get** ~**; have** ~**; dial** ~**; give** so ~.) □ *When a young child answered, I knew I had the wrong number.* **2.** *Fig.* [a state of being] incorrect, late, inaccurate, etc. (\*Typically: **get** ~**; have** ~**; give** so ~.) □ *Boy, do you have the wrong number! Get with it!*

**wrote the book on** sth *Fig.* to be very authoritative about something; to know enough about something to write the definitive book on it. (Always in past tense.) □ *Ted wrote the book on unemployment. He's been looking for work in three states for two years.* □ *Do I know about misery? I wrote the book on misery!*

# Y

**Ye gods (and little fishes)!** *Inf.* What a surprising thing! □ *Ye gods and little fishes! Someone covered my car with broken eggs!*

a **yoke around** SO's **neck** *Fig.* something that oppresses people; a burden. □ *John's greedy children are a yoke around his neck.*

**You and what army?** Go to next.

**You and who else?** AND **You and what army?** *Inf.* a phrase that responds to a threat by implying that the threat is a weak one. □ *Bill: I'm going to punch you in the nose! Bob: Yeah? You and who else?*

**You are only young once.** You might as well do a thing, since you may never have the chance again. (Typically said to a younger person and jocular when said to an older person.) □ *Of course, you should go backpacking to Europe. You're only young once.*

**You are what you eat.** You are made up of the nutritional content of the food you eat. □ *You shouldn't eat pizza and hamburgers every day. After all, you are what you eat!*

**You asked for it! 1.** *Fig.* You are getting what you requested. □ *The waiter set a huge bowl of ice cream, strawberries, and whipped cream in front of Mary, saying apologetically, "You asked for it!"* **2.** *Inf.* You are getting the punishment you deserve! □ *Bill: The tax people just ordered me to pay a big fine. Bob: The careless way you do your tax forms caused it. You asked for it!*

**You could have knocked me over with a feather.** *Inf.* I was extremely surprised.; I was so surprised that it was as if I was disoriented and could have been knocked over easily. □ *When she told me she was going to get married, you could have knocked me over with a feather.*

**You go to your church, and I'll go to mine.** You do it your way, and I'll do it mine. □ *Yes, you are faster, but I am more exact. You go to your church, and I'll go to mine.*

**You'll get the hang of it.** *Fig.* Don't worry. You will learn soon how it is done. □ *Mary: It's harder than I thought to glue these things together. Tom: You'll get the hang of it.*

**\*young at heart** *Fig.* having a youthful spirit no matter what one's age. (\*Typically: **act** ~; **be** ~; **keep** so ~; **stay** ~.) □ *I am over 70, but I still feel young at heart.*

**You're on!** *Fig. Inf.* The bet, challenge, or invitation is accepted! □ *Q: What about a few beers at the club? A: You're on!*

**You're the doctor.** *Inf.* You are in a position to tell me what to do.; I yield to you and your knowledge of this matter. (Usually jocular; the person being addressed is most likely not a physician.) □ *Bill: Eat your dinner, then you'll feel more like playing ball. Get some energy! Tom: Okay, you're the doctor.*

**You've got another think coming.** AND **You can (just) think again.** *Inf.* You will have to rethink your position. (Both of the entry heads are usually found with a conditional phrase, such as "If you think so-and-so, then **you've got another think coming.**" The first entry head is also heard as *thing* rather than *think*.) □ *Rachel: If you think I'm going to stand here and listen to your complaining all day, you've got another think coming!*

**zero in (on** so/sth**)** *Fig.* to aim directly at someone or something. □ *The television camera zeroed in on the little boy scratching his head.* □ *Mary is very good about zeroing in on the most important and helpful ideas.*

**zero tolerance** *Fig.* absolutely no toleration of even the smallest infraction of a rule. □ *Because of the zero-tolerance rule, the kindergartner was expelled from school because his mother accidentally left a table knife in his lunch box.*

**Zip (up) your lip!** AND **Zip it up!** *Inf.* Be quiet!; Close your mouth and be quiet! □ *"I've heard enough. Zip your lip!" hollered the coach.* □ *Andy: All right, you guys. Shut up! Zip it up! Bob: Sorry. Andy: That's better.*

# Hidden Key Word Index

Always try to look up the phrase that you want in the regular dictionary. Sometimes it is useful to try to locate a phrase using a key word WITHIN the phrase. This is an index of those (non-initial) "hidden" key words. None of the initial key words are listed in this index.

**abandon** with gay abandon
**ABCs** know one's ABCs
**abet** aid and abet so
**account** call so to account
**ace** come within an ace of sth
**Achilles** Achilles' heel
**act** clean one's act up ♦ get in(to) the act
**action** all talk (and no action) ♦ out of action ♦ suit one's actions to one's words
**activity** hum with activity ♦ a hive of activity
**Adam** not know so from Adam
**ado** without further ado
**advice** sage advice
**advocate** play (the) devil's advocate
**affair** settle so's affairs
**again** on again, off again ♦ Run that by (me) again.
**age** Act your age! ♦ a ripe old age
**agenda** a hidden agenda
**agog** all agog
**ahead** dead ahead ♦ quit while one is ahead
**air** a breath of fresh air ♦ build castles in the air ♦ clear the air ♦ come up for air ♦ dance on air ♦ leave so up in the air ♦ leave sth up in the air ♦ one's nose is in the air ♦ up in the air (about so/sth)
**alike** share and share alike
**alive** more dead than alive
**all** away from it all ♦ downhill all the way ♦ get it (all) together ♦ have all the time in the world ♦ have all one's marbles ♦ It takes all kinds (to make a world). ♦ It'll all come out in the wash. ♦ It's written all over one's face. ♦ jack of all trades ♦ know all the angles ♦ know where all the bodies are buried ♦ laugh all the way to the bank ♦ let it all hang out ♦ the mother of all sth ♦ not for all the tea in China ♦ out of (all) proportion ♦ play it for all it's worth ♦ pull all the stops out ♦ put all one's eggs in one basket ♦ ride off in all directions ♦ run on all cylinders ♦ That's all folks! ♦ warts and all ♦ We all gotta go sometime. ♦ winner take all ♦ with all due respect
**allowances** make allowance(s) (for so/sth)

**alone** let well enough alone
**amendment** take the Fifth (Amendment)
**amount** to the tune of some amount of money
**angle** know all the angles
**angry** wax angry
**annal** go down in the annals of history
**another** a horse of another color ♦ It's six of one, half a dozen of another. ♦ You've got another think coming.
**anymore** not a kid anymore
**apart** poles apart
**apology** make no apologies
**appearance** keep up appearances
**appetite** lose one's appetite
**apple** American as apple pie ♦ compare apples and oranges ♦ in apple-pie order ♦ a rotten apple ♦ The Big Apple ♦ upset the apple cart
**arm** bear arms ♦ keep at arm's length from so/sth ♦ lay down one's arms ♦ put the arm on so ♦ a shot in the arm ♦ strong-arm tactics
**armor** a knight in shining armor
**army** You and what army?
**arrangement** make the arrangements
**arrest** under arrest
**arrow** straight as an arrow
**art** state of the art
**ash** rise from the ashes
**ask** You asked for it!
**ass** kiss so's ass
**attached** strings attached
**attention** the center of attention
**attitude** have a bad attitude ♦ wait-and-see attitude
**automatic** on automatic (pilot)
**awkward** main strength and awkwardness ♦ place so in an awkward position

**axe** have an ax(e) to grind (with so)

# B

**baby** leave so holding the baby
**back** back to the salt mines ♦ a crick in one's back ♦ give so the shirt off one's back ♦ on the back burner ♦ scratch so's back ♦ take a back seat (to so/sth) ♦ turn back the clock
**backroom** the boys in the backroom
**bacon** bring home the bacon
**bad** (It's) not half bad. ♦ come to a bad end ♦ good riddance (to bad rubbish) ♦ have a bad attitude ♦ leave a bad taste in so's mouth
**bag** the cat is out of the bag ♦ a doggy bag ♦ leave so holding the bag ♦ let the cat out of the bag ♦ whole bag of tricks
**bait** fish or cut bait
**balance** checks and balances
**ball** behind the eight ball ♦ drop the ball ♦ Great balls of fire! ♦ keep one's eye on the ball ♦ on the ball
**balloon** send up a trial balloon ♦ trial balloon
**ballot** stuff the ballot box
**ballpark** in the ballpark ♦ out of the ballpark
**band** strike up the band ♦ to beat the band
**bandwagon** on the bandwagon
**bank** break the bank ♦ can take it to the bank ♦ laugh all the way to the bank
**banker** keep banker's hours
**bar** behind bars ♦ Katie bar the door ♦ raise the bar
**bark** more bark than bite
**barn** all around Robin Hood's barn ♦ can't hit the (broad) side of a barn ♦ hit the (broad) side of a barn

**barrel** let so have it (with both barrels) ♦ lock, stock, and barrel ♦ over a barrel ♦ scrape the bottom of the barrel

**base** get to first base (with so/sth) ♦ reach first base (with so/sth) ♦ steal a base

**basic** back to basics

**basket** can't carry a tune (in a bushel basket) ♦ go to hell in a hand basket ♦ put all one's eggs in one basket

**bat** have bats in one's belfry ♦ like a bat out of hell

**bated** with bated breath

**bath** take a bath (on sth)

**battery** recharge one's batteries

**beam** broad in the beam

**bean** don't know beans (about sth)

**bear** loaded for bear

**beat** to beat the band

**beauty** Age before beauty.

**beaver** eager beaver

**beck** at so's beck and call

**bed** in bed with so ♦ put so to bed with a shovel ♦ should have stood in bed

**bee** the birds and the bees

**beeline** make a beeline for so/sth

**beg** go begging

**behold** a marvel to behold

**belfry** have bats in one's belfry

**believe** not believe one's ears ♦ not believe one's eyes

**bell** can't unring the bell ♦ Hell's bells (and buckets of blood)! ♦ ring a bell ♦ with bells on (one's toes)

**belt** tighten one's belt

**bend** on bended knee

**best** one's best bib and tucker ♦ put one's best foot forward ♦ with the best will in the world ♦ work out for the best

**bet** Don't bet on it! ♦ hedge one's bets

**better** (I've) seen better. ♦ build a better mousetrap ♦ for better or (for) worse ♦ have seen better days ♦ take a turn for the better

**big** play in the big leagues ♦ too big for one's britches

**bird** early bird ♦ eat like a bird ♦ for the birds ♦ kill two birds with one stone ♦ A little bird told me.

**birth** give birth to sth

**birthday** in one's birthday suit

**bite** more bark than bite

**blanche** carte blanche

**blanket** a wet blanket

**bless** count one's blessings

**blind** turn a blind eye (to so/sth)

**bliss** Ignorance is bliss.

**block** a chip off the old block ♦ a mental block (against sth) ♦ the new kid on the block ♦ put one's head on the block (for so/sth) ♦ writer's block

**blood** (some) new blood ♦ bad blood (between people) ♦ blue blood ♦ draw blood ♦ Hell's bells (and buckets of blood)! ♦ make so's blood boil ♦ make so's blood run cold ♦ smell blood ♦ take so's blood pressure

**bloom** a late bloomer

**blue** black and blue ♦ feel blue ♦ like a bolt out of the blue ♦ singing the blues ♦ talk a blue streak

**blush** at first blush

**board** back to the drawing board ♦ go by the board ♦ room and board

**body** enough to keep body and soul together ♦ keep body and soul together ♦ know where all the bodies are buried ♦ Over my dead body! ♦ warm body

**boil** come to a boil ♦ make so's blood boil

**bolt** get down to the nuts and bolts ♦ like a bolt out of the blue ♦ nuts and bolts

**bond** one's word is one's bond

**bone** bag of bones ♦ bare-bones ♦ have a bone to pick (with so) ♦ make no bones about sth ♦ work one's fingers to the bone

**bonnet** a bee in one's bonnet

**book** crack a book ♦ every trick in the book ♦ go down in the history books ♦ have one's nose in a book ♦ Not in my book. ♦ not to judge a book by its cover ♦ one for the (record) books ♦ read so like a book ♦ throw the book at so ♦ wrote the book on sth

**boom** lower the boom on so

**boondocks** in the boondocks

**boonies** in the boonies

**boot** to boot

**bootstrap** pull oneself up by one's (own) bootstraps

**born** to the manner born

**both** burn the candle at both ends ♦ have it both ways ♦ land (up)on both feet ♦ let so have it (with both barrels)

**bother** hot and bothered

**bottle** chief cook and bottle washer

**bottom** scrape the bottom of the barrel

**bound** know no bounds

**box** go home in a box ♦ inside the box ♦ open Pandora's box ♦ outside the box ♦ stuff the ballot box ♦ think inside the box ♦ think outside the box

**boy** a whipping boy

**brain** beat one's brains out (to do sth) ♦ pick so's brain(s) ♦ rack one's brain(s)

**brake** slam the brakes on

**branch** hold out the olive branch

**brass** top brass

**breach** step in(to the breach)

**bread** the greatest thing since sliced bread

**break** die of a broken heart ♦ Give me a break! ♦ make or break so ♦ a tough break

**breakdown** a (nervous) breakdown

**breast** make a clean breast of sth (to so)

**breath** (all) in one breath ♦ a breath of fresh air ♦ catch one's breath ♦ Don't waste your breath. ♦ hold one's breath ♦ save one's breath ♦ Take a deep breath. ♦ take so's breath away ♦ waste one's breath ♦ with bated breath

**brick** drop a brick ♦ knock one's head (up) against a brick wall ♦ like a ton of bricks

**bridge** burn one's bridges (behind one) ♦ cross that bridge before one comes to it ♦ cross that bridge when one comes to it

**britches** too big for one's britches

**broad** can't hit the (broad) side of a barn

**brow** by the sweat of one's brow

**brown** do sth up brown

**brute** by brute strength

**bubble** burst so's bubble

**bucket** can't carry a tune in a bucket ♦ go to hell in a bucket ♦ Hell's bells (and buckets of blood)!

**bulge** battle of the bulge

**bull** cock-and-bull story ♦ take the bull by the horns

**bullet** bite the bullet

**bump** like a bump on a log

**bunch** thanks a bunch

**burn** do a slow burn ♦ fiddle while Rome burns ♦ get one's fingers burned ♦ Money burns a hole in so's pocket. ♦ on the back burner ♦ on the front burner ♦ slash and burn

**bury** know where all the bodies are buried

**bushel** can't carry a tune (in a bushel basket) ♦ hide one's light under a bushel

**bushy** bright-eyed and bushy-tailed

**business** do a land-office business ♦ get down to business ♦ (just) taking care of business ♦ land-office business ♦ mix business with pleasure ♦ open for business ♦ strictly business

**bustle** hustle and bustle

**butter** look as if butter wouldn't melt in one's mouth

**button** push so's buttons

**bygone** Let bygones be bygones.

**byway** highways and byways

# C

**cab** hail a cab

**caboodle** the whole kit and caboodle

**cage** rattle so's cage

**Cain** raise Cain

**cake** the icing on the cake

**calf** kill the fatted calf

**call** answer the call ♦ at so's beck and call ♦ Don't call us, we'll call you. ♦ have a close call ♦ on call ♦ a place to call one's own ♦ a tough call

**campaign** a smear campaign (against so)

**camper** a happy camper

**campus** big man on campus

**can** in the can ♦ live out of cans

**canary** look like the cat that swallowed the canary

**candle** burn the candle at both ends

**cannon** a loose cannon

**canoe** paddle one's own canoe

**cap** a feather in one's cap

**card** a house of cards ♦ in the cards ♦ play one's trump card ♦ the the race card

**care** (just) taking care of business ♦ not have a care in the world ♦ take care of number one

**carpet** the red-carpet treatment

**carry** can't carry a tune (in a bushel basket) ♦ can't carry a tune in a bucket ♦ can't carry a tune in a paper sack ♦ card-carrying member

**cart** upset the apple cart

**case** a basket case ♦ get down to cases ♦ an open-and-shut case

**cash** cold, hard cash

**castle** build castles in Spain ♦ build castles in the air

**cat** let the cat out of the bag ♦ look like the cat that swallowed the canary ♦ look like sth the cat dragged in ♦ not enough room to swing a cat ♦ play cat and mouse with so ♦ rain cats and dogs

**catch** What's the catch?

**caution** throw caution to the wind

**cent** For two cents I would do sth.

**center** dead center ♦ on dead center ♦ take center stage

**century** the turn of the century

**ceremony** Don't stand on ceremony. ♦ stand on ceremony

**certain** dead certain

**chain** ball and chain ♦ the weak link (in the chain)

**chair** play first chair

**challenge** pose a challenge

**chance** a ghost of a chance ♦ on the off-chance

**change** and change ♦ a chunk of change ♦ have a change of heart ♦ a sea change ♦ small change

**character** out of character ♦ a shady character

**chart** off the charts

**daylight** begin to see daylight
**dead** at a dead end ♦ dead from the neck up ♦ give so up for dead ♦ in a dead heat ♦ more dead than alive ♦ on dead center ♦ Over my dead body! ♦ roll over and play dead ♦ stop (dead) in one's tracks ♦ take so for dead ♦ wake the dead
**deadwood** cut the deadwood out
**deaf** fall on deaf ears ♦ turn a deaf ear (to so/sth)
**deal** a shady deal
**death** a brush with death ♦ at death's door ♦ dance with death ♦ have a death wish ♦ lie at death's door ♦ nickel and dime so (to death) ♦ sick to death (of so/sth) ♦ sign one's own death warrant ♦ sound the death knell ♦ the kiss of death ♦ will be the death of so/sth (yet)
**debt** owe so a debt of gratitude
**deck** play with a full deck
**deep** Take a deep breath.
**defeat** snatch victory from the jaws of defeat
**degree** to the nth degree
**deliver** signed, sealed, and delivered
**denial** in denial
**dent** make a dent in sth
**desk** away from one's desk
**determine** bound and determined
**devil** give the devil his due ♦ play (the) devil's advocate ♦ sell one's soul (to the devil)
**dibs** have dibs on sth ♦ put one's dibs on sth
**difference** same difference ♦ split the difference
**different** a horse of a different color
**dilemma** on the horns of a dilemma

**dime** get off the dime ♦ nickel and dime so (to death) ♦ stop on a dime ♦ turn on a dime
**dine** wine and dine so
**dip** skinny dip
**direction** ride off in all directions
**dirt** dig some dirt up (on so)
**dirty** quick and dirty
**disagree** agree to disagree
**disaster** flirt with disaster ♦ spell disaster
**disease** shake a disease or illness off
**dividend** pay dividends
**doctor** just what the doctor ordered ♦ spin doctor ♦ You're the doctor.
**dog** rain cats and dogs ♦ a shaggy-dog story ♦ the tail wagging the dog ♦ throw so to the dogs
**doggo** lie doggo
**doghouse** in the doghouse
**dole** on the dole
**dollar** sound as a dollar ♦ the almighty dollar ♦ the sixty-four-dollar question
**doom** gloom and doom
**door** at death's door ♦ beat a path to so's door ♦ get one's foot in the door ♦ Katie bar the door ♦ keep the wolf from the door ♦ lie at death's door
**doorstep** lay sth at so's doorstep
**dot** sign on the dotted line
**doubt** the benefit of the doubt
**dozen** It's six of one, half a dozen of another. ♦ a baker's dozen
**drab** in dribs and drabs
**drag** knock-down-drag-out fight ♦ look like sth the cat dragged in
**draw** back to the drawing board ♦ beat so to the draw ♦ the luck of the draw ♦ quick on the draw
**dream** The American Dream ♦ broken dreams ♦ a pipe dream ♦ wouldn't dream of doing sth

**drib** in dribs and drabs
**drift** if you get my drift
**drive** backseat driver ♦ in the driver's seat ♦ Sunday driver
**drop** at the drop of a hat ♦ wait for the other shoe to drop
**dry** cut and dried ♦ dry run ♦ hang so out to dry ♦ keep one's powder dry ♦ leave so high and dry ♦ not a dry eye (in the place)
**duck** lame duck
**dudgeon** in high dudgeon
**due** give the devil his due ♦ with all due respect
**dull** keep it down (to a dull roar)
**dunk** slam dunk
**duration** for the duration
**dust** bite the dust ♦ when the dust settles
**dye** dyed-in-the-wool

## E

**ear** all ears ♦ all eyes and ears ♦ assault the ear ♦ fall on deaf ears ♦ go in one ear and out the other ♦ not believe one's ears ♦ pull in one's ears ♦ set some place on its ear ♦ turn a deaf ear (to so/sth)
**earth** like nothing on earth ♦ move heaven and earth to do sth ♦ the salt of the earth ♦ to the ends of the earth
**easy** breathe easy ♦ on easy street ♦ take things easy ♦ That's easy for you to say.
**eat** I could eat a horse! ♦ I hate to eat and run. ♦ I'll eat my hat. ♦ You are what you eat.
**edge** lose one's edge ♦ moist around the edges ♦ on the edge ♦ set so's teeth on edge
**effect** or words to that effect
**effigy** burn so in effigy
**effort** an all-out effort
**egg** have egg on one's face ♦ put all one's eggs in one basket ♦

teach one's grandmother to suck eggs
**eggshell** walk on eggshells
**eight** behind the eight ball
**elbow** elbow grease ♦ rub elbows (with so) ♦ some elbow room ♦ use some elbow grease
**eloquent** wax eloquent
**else** (So) what else is new? ♦ in so else's shoes ♦ You and who else?
**enchilada** the whole enchilada
**end** at a dead end ♦ at loose ends ♦ at the end of the day ♦ at the end of one's rope ♦ at one's wit's end ♦ burn the candle at both ends ♦ the business end of sth ♦ come to a bad end ♦ no end in sight ♦ not the end of the world ♦ some loose ends ♦ to the ends of the earth
**enemy** one's own worst enemy
**enough** let well enough alone ♦ not enough room to swing a cat ♦ not know enough to come in out of the rain
**envelope** pushing the envelope
**epic** a disaster of epic proportions
**errand** on a fool's errand
**error** see the error of one's ways ♦ a rounding error
**escape** avenue of escape
**eve** on the eve of sth
**event** chain of events
**every** hang on (so's) every word
**evil** the lesser of two evils
**examine** one needs to have one's head examined
**exhibition** make an exhibition of oneself
**expense** spare no expense
**extreme** go from one extreme to the other
**eye** a bird's-eye view ♦ a black eye ♦ a feast for the eyes ♦ all eyes and ears ♦ bright-eyed and bushy-tailed ♦ have a roving eye

255

◆ have eyes in the back of one's head ◆ in one's mind's eye ◆ keep one's eye on the ball ◆ look at so cross-eyed ◆ not a dry eye (in the place) ◆ not believe one's eyes ◆ out of the public eye ◆ pull the wool over so's eyes ◆ put so's eye out ◆ a sight for sore eyes ◆ some shut-eye ◆ the naked eye ◆ turn a blind eye (to so/sth) ◆ with the naked eye

**eyeteeth** cut one's (eye)teeth on sth

## F

**face** can't see one's hand in front of one's face ◆ cut off one's nose to spite one's face ◆ get out of one's face ◆ give so a red face ◆ have egg on one's face ◆ It's written all over one's face. ◆ not show one's face ◆ on the face of it ◆ put a smile on so's face ◆ put one's face on ◆ a slap in the face ◆ a smack in the face ◆ a straight face

**fact** after the fact ◆ face (the) facts ◆ get down to the facts ◆ in point of fact

**factor** fudge factor

**faint** damn so/sth with faint praise

**faith** article of faith ◆ take sth on faith ◆ an act of faith

**fall** just fell off the turnip truck ◆ let the chips fall (where they may) ◆ riding for a fall ◆ take the fall

**fame** so's claim to fame

**family** (all) in the family ◆ run in the family

**fancy** flight of fancy

**fantastic** trip the light fantastic

**fast** life in the fast lane ◆ on the fast track

**fat** kill the fatted calf ◆ live off the fat of the land

**fate** seal so's fate

**favor** curry favor with so ◆ return the favor ◆ Thank God for small favors.

**fear** in fear and trembling ◆ put the fear of God in(to) so

**feast** a movable feast

**feather** in fine feather ◆ knock so over (with a feather) ◆ ruffle so's feathers ◆ smooth (so's) ruffled feathers ◆ tar and feather so ◆ You could have knocked me over with a feather.

**feed** chicken feed ◆ spoon-feed so

**feel** gut feeling

**feeler** put out (some) feelers (on so/sth)

**fence** on the fence (about sth) ◆ sit on the fence ◆ straddle the fence

**few** a man of few words

**field** have a field day ◆ a level playing field ◆ out in left field

**fifth** take the Fifth (Amendment)

**fifty** go fifty-fifty (on sth)

**fight** knock-down-drag-out fight ◆ Them's fighting words!

**figure** a ballpark figure

**file** rank and file

**fill** back and fill ◆ smoke-filled room

**find** nowhere to be found

**fine** in fine feather

**finger** at one's fingertips ◆ get one's fingers burned ◆ have sticky fingers ◆ have one's finger in too may pies ◆ point the finger at so ◆ put one's finger on sth ◆ work one's fingers to the bone

**fire** ball of fire ◆ baptism of fire ◆ Great balls of fire! ◆ play with fire ◆ pull sth out of the fire ◆ set the world on fire ◆ under fire ◆ Where there's smoke, there's fire.

**firm** take a firm grip on so/sth

**first** at first blush ◆ cast the first stone ◆ get to first base (with so/sth) ◆ of the first water ◆ play

**first** chair ♦ reach first base (with so/sth)
**fish** a fine kettle of fish ♦ like a fish out of water ♦ neither fish nor fowl ♦ smell fishy ♦ Ye gods (and little fishes)!
**fist** hand over fist ♦ rule with an iron fist
**fit** the survival of the fittest
**fix** well-fixed
**fixture** a regular fixture
**flame** go down in flames ♦ shoot so down in flames
**flash** quick as a flash
**flesh** a pound of flesh
**floor** in on the ground floor ♦ take the floor
**fly** drop like flies ♦ It'll never fly. ♦ no flies on so ♦ on the fly ♦ time flies (when you're having fun) ♦ with flying colors
**foe** friend or foe
**fog** able to fog a mirror
**folks** That's all folks!
**fool** nobody's fool ♦ not suffer fools gladly ♦ not suffer fools lightly ♦ on a fool's errand
**foot** bound hand and foot ♦ drag one's feet (on or over sth) ♦ get one's foot in the door ♦ have one foot in the grave ♦ have the shoe on the other foot ♦ have two left feet ♦ I wouldn't touch it with a ten-foot pole. ♦ knock one off one's feet ♦ land (up)on both feet ♦ let grass grow under one's feet ♦ not let the grass grow under one's feet ♦ the patter of tiny feet ♦ put one foot in front of the other ♦ put one's best foot forward ♦ shoot oneself in the foot ♦ sit at the feet of so ♦ six feet under ♦ stand on one's (own) two feet ♦ think on one's feet ♦ vote with one's feet ♦ wait on so hand and foot
**football** a political football
**footsie** play footsie with so

**footwork** fancy footwork
**force** by force of habit
**fore** bring sth to the fore
**forever** lost and gone forever
**forgotten** gone but not forgotten
**form** in rare form ♦ true to form
**fortune** a small fortune
**forward** put one's best foot forward
**foundation** shake the foundations of sth
**four** the sixty-four-dollar question
**fowl** neither fish nor fowl
**fray** above the fray
**frazzle** wear so to a frazzle
**free** give free rein to so
**freeze** until hell freezes over
**fresh** a breath of fresh air
**friend** have friends in high places ♦ user friendly
**fringe** on the fringe
**frog** a big frog in a small pond
**front** can't see one's hand in front of one's face ♦ on the front burner ♦ put one foot in front of the other
**fruit** bear fruit ♦ low-hanging fruit
**fruition** bring sth to fruition
**fry** small fry
**full** chock full of sth ♦ come full circle ♦ play with a full deck ♦ the woods are full of so/sth
**fun** Getting there is half the fun. ♦ poke fun at so/sth ♦ time flies (when you're having fun)
**funeral** It's your funeral.
**further** without further ado

## G

**gain** No pain, no gain
**game** ahead of the game ♦ at the top of one's game ♦ back in the game ♦ fun and games
**gamut** run the gamut
**gander** take a gander (at so/sth)
**gangbusters** like gangbusters
**gap** bridge the gap

**gas** out of gas
**gasp** at the last gasp
**gather** wool-gathering
**gauntlet** run the gauntlet ✦ throw down the gauntlet
**gay** with gay abandon
**gear** swing into high gear
**genius** a stroke of genius
**George** Let George do it.
**ghost** give up the ghost
**giant** a sleeping giant
**gift** look a gift horse in the mouth
**give** Don't give up the ship! ✦ a lot of give and take ✦ What I wouldn't give for a sth!
**glad** not suffer fools gladly
**glove** rule with a velvet glove ✦ take one's gloves off
**go** All systems (are) go. ✦ easy come, easy go ✦ good to go ✦ have a good thing going ✦ lost and gone forever ✦ slow going ✦ touch and go ✦ We all gotta go sometime. ✦ You go to your church, and I'll go to mine.
**God** put the fear of God in(to) so ✦ Thank God for small favors. ✦ Ye gods (and little fishes)!
**gold** have a heart of gold ✦ sitting on a gold mine ✦ a pot of gold
**good** all to the good ✦ as good as one's word ✦ have a good thing going ✦ I'm good. ✦ in good company ✦ keep in good with so ✦ look good on paper ✦ make good money ✦ make good time ✦ No news is good news. ✦ the picture of (good) health ✦ Thank goodness! ✦ twelve good men and true ✦ up to no good
**goose** cook so's goose ✦ send so on a wild-goose chase ✦ a wild-goose chase
**gown** town-and-gown
**grab** up for grabs

**grain** against the grain ✦ take sth with a grain of salt
**grandmother** teach one's grandmother to suck eggs
**grape** belt the grape ✦ sour grapes
**grass** let grass grow under one's feet ✦ not let the grass grow under one's feet ✦ snake in the grass
**gratitude** owe so a debt of gratitude
**grave** dig one's own grave ✦ from the cradle to the grave ✦ have one foot in the grave ✦ take it to one's grave
**gravy** ride the gravy train
**grease** elbow grease ✦ quick as (greased) lightning ✦ use some elbow grease
**great** at great length ✦ no great shakes ✦ set great store by so/sth ✦ with (great) relish
**green** have a green thumb
**grief** come to grief
**grind** the daily grind ✦ have an ax(e) to grind (with so)
**grindstone** keep one's nose to the grindstone ✦ put one's nose to the grindstone
**grip** come to grips with so/sth ✦ take a firm grip on so/sth
**gritty** get down to the nitty-gritty
**ground** break ground (for sth) ✦ break new ground ✦ cover a lot of ground ✦ cut the ground out from under so ✦ in on the ground floor ✦ on moral grounds ✦ on shaky ground ✦ one's old stamping ground ✦ riveted to the ground ✦ worship the ground so walks on
**grow** let grass grow under one's feet ✦ not let the grass grow under one's feet
**guard** let one's guard down
**guest** Be my guest.

**guinea** serve as a guinea pig
**gums** beat one's gums
**gun** beat the gun ♦ going great guns ♦ jump the gun ♦ the smoking gun
**gut** blood and guts ♦ a kick in the guts
**gutter** have (got) one's mind in the gutter

## H

**habit** by force of habit
**hair** a bad hair day ♦ get out of so's hair ♦ let one's hair down ♦ part so's hair ♦ plaster one's hair down ♦ split hairs
**half** (It's) not half bad. ♦ cheap at half the price ♦ Getting there is half the fun. ♦ how the other half lives ♦ It's six of one, half a dozen of another. ♦ That's not the half of it!
**hand** (with) hat in hand ♦ bound hand and foot ♦ by a show of hands ♦ can't see one's hand in front of one's face ♦ fall into the wrong hands ♦ go to hell in a hand basket ♦ have clean hands ♦ live from hand to mouth ♦ not lay a hand on so/sth ♦ on (the) one hand ♦ on the other hand ♦ put one's hand to the plow ♦ a show of hands ♦ sit on its hands ♦ sit on one's hands ♦ take the law into one's own hands ♦ take one's life into one's (own) hands ♦ time hangs heavy (on so's hands) ♦ wait on so hand and foot ♦ wash one's hands of so/sth ♦ wring one's hands
**hang** let it all hang out ♦ low-hanging fruit ♦ time hangs heavy (on so's hands) ♦ You'll get the hang of it.
**happen** it'll be a cold day in Hell when sth happens
**happy** fat and happy

**hard** cold, hard cash ♦ fall on hard times ♦ the school of hard knocks
**hardball** play hardball (with so)
**harm** out of harm's way
**hasty** beat a (hasty) retreat
**hat** at the drop of a hat ♦ eat one's hat ♦ I'll eat my hat. ♦ pass the hat (around) (to so) ♦ take one's hat off to so ♦ (with) hat in hand
**hatch** batten down the hatches ♦ count one's chickens before they hatch
**hatchet** bury the hatchet
**hate** I hate to eat and run. ♦ a love-hate relationship ♦ pet hate
**haw** hem and haw (around)
**hawk** watch so/sth like a hawk
**hay** make hay (while the sun shines)
**haywire** go haywire
**head** (right) off the top of one's head ♦ bite so's head off ♦ bring sth to a head ♦ crazy in the head ♦ have eyes in the back of one's head ♦ hit the nail (right) on the head ♦ keep a civil tongue (in one's head) ♦ knock some heads together ♦ knock one's head (up) against a brick wall ♦ laugh one's head off ♦ need sth like a hole in the head ♦ Not able to make head or tail of sth ♦ one needs to have one's head examined ♦ a price on one's head ♦ put ideas into so's head ♦ put one's head on the block (for so/sth) ♦ put people's heads together ♦ rear its ugly head ♦ run around like a chicken with its head cut off ♦ snap so's head off ♦ soft in the head ♦ stand on one's head ♦ turn some heads ♦ where so's head is at
**health** in the pink (of health) ♦ the picture of (good) health
**hear** cannot hear oneself think

**heart** break so's heart ♦ die of a broken heart ♦ eat one's heart out ♦ have a change of heart ♦ have a heart of gold ♦ have a heart of stone ♦ have one's heart in one's mouth ♦ have one's heart stand still ♦ makes one's heart sink ♦ pour one's heart out to so ♦ set one's heart against sth ♦ set one's heart on so/sth ♦ warm the cockles of so's heart ♦ young at heart

**heartbeat** a heartbeat away from being sth

**heat** in a dead heat

**heaven** in hog heaven ♦ in seventh heaven ♦ move heaven and earth to do sth

**heavy** time hangs heavy (on so's hands)

**heel** Achilles' heel ♦ drag one's heels (or or over sth) ♦ kick one's heels up ♦ well-heeled

**hell** come hell or high water ♦ go to hell in a bucket ♦ go to hell in a hand basket ♦ it'll be a cold day in Hell when sth happens ♦ like a bat out of hell ♦ a living hell ♦ until hell freezes over

**help** seek professional help

**hero** unsung hero

**herring** a red herring

**hide** tan so's hide

**high** come hell or high water ♦ have friends in high places ♦ hit the high spots ♦ in high dudgeon ♦ it's high time ♦ leave so high and dry ♦ on one's high horse ♦ swing into high gear

**hind** get up on one's hind legs

**hip** shoot from the hip

**history** ancient history ♦ go down in the annals of history ♦ go down in the history books ♦ The rest is history.

**hither** come-hither look

**hock** out of hock

**hog** call hogs ♦ go whole hog ♦ in hog heaven ♦ road hog

**hold** leave so holding the baby ♦ leave so holding the bag ♦ not hold water ♦ won't hold water

**hole** full of holes ♦ Money burns a hole in so's pocket. ♦ need sth like a hole in the head ♦ out of the hole ♦ a square peg (in a round hole)

**hollow** have a hollow leg

**homage** pay homage to so/sth

**home** (un)til the cows come home ♦ bring home the bacon ♦ bring sth home to so ♦ come home (to roost) ♦ go home in a box ♦ nothing to write home about

**honor** do the honors ♦ put one on one's honor

**hood** all around Robin Hood's barn ♦ look under the hood

**hook** off the hook

**hoop** jump through a hoop ♦ shoot (some) hoops

**hope** set one's hopes on so/sth

**horizon** on the horizon

**horn** lock horns (with so) ♦ on the horns of a dilemma ♦ take the bull by the horns

**hornet** stir up a hornet's nest

**horse** (straight) from the horse's mouth ♦ drive a coach and horses through sth ♦ eat like a horse ♦ I could eat a horse! ♦ look a gift horse in the mouth ♦ on one's high horse

**hot** blow hot and cold

**hotcakes** sell like hotcakes

**hour** after hours ♦ all hours (of the day and night) ♦ keep banker's hours ♦ keep late hours

**house** bring the house down

**housekeeping** set up housekeeping

**how** no matter how you slice it

**Hoyle** according to Hoyle

**human** the milk of human kindness
**humble** eat humble pie ♦ in my humble opinion
**hump** over the hump
**hunt** hunt-and-peck
**hurt** cry before one is hurt
**Hyde** Jekyll and Hyde

## I

**ice** break the ice ♦ cut no ice (with so) ♦ on ice ♦ on thin ice ♦ skate on thin ice ♦ walk on thin ice
**iceberg** the tip of the iceberg
**idea** flirt with the idea of doing sth ♦ put ideas into so's head
**illness** shake a disease or illness off
**immemorial** since time immemorial
**impact** upon impact
**impartial** fair and impartial
**impression** leave an impression (on so) ♦ make an impression on so
**inch** come within an inch of doing sth ♦ Give one an inch and one will take a mile.
**indeed** A friend in need is a friend indeed.
**indoor** the greatest thing since indoor plumbing
**infinite** in so's infinite wisdom
**information** a gold mine of information
**inhumanity** man's inhumanity to man
**interest** a vested interest in sth
**ironed** get the kinks (ironed) out
**issue** take issue with so ♦ take issue with sth
**ivory** in an ivory tower ♦ tickle the ivories

## J

**jackpot** hit the jackpot

**jaw** snatch victory from the jaws of defeat
**jaybird** naked as a jaybird
**jerk** a knee-jerk reaction
**job** do a snow job on so ♦ on the job ♦ patient as Job ♦ a snow job ♦ walk off the job
**joke** able to take a joke ♦ the butt of a joke ♦ crack a joke ♦ a standing joke
**Joneses** keep up with the Joneses
**jowl** cheek by jowl
**joy** pride and joy
**judge** not to judge a book by its cover
**judgment** pass judgment (on so/sth) ♦ sit in judgment (up)on so/sth
**juice** cow juice ♦ stew in one's own juice
**jump** a hop, skip, and a jump
**juncture** at this juncture
**jungle** It's a jungle out there.
**justice** do justice to sth ♦ a miscarriage of justice ♦ a travesty of justice

## K

**keep** enough to keep body and soul together ♦ One is known by the company one keeps.
**keg** sitting on a powder keg
**ken** beyond one's ken
**kettle** a fine kettle of fish
**kid** not a kid anymore ♦ the new kid on the block
**kill** make a killing
**kimono** open (up) one's kimono
**kind** It takes all kinds (to make a world). ♦ nothing of the kind
**kindness** kill so with kindness ♦ the milk of human kindness
**kingdom** till kingdom come
**kink** get the kinks (ironed) out
**kiss** blow so a kiss ♦ right in the kisser

**kit** the whole kit and caboodle
**kitten** have kittens
**kitty** feed the kitty
**knee** on bended knee
**knell** sound the death knell
**knife** go under the knife
**knock** the school of hard knocks
♦ You could have knocked me
over with a feather.
**knot** tie the knot
**know** (It) takes one to know
one. ♦ don't know beans (about
sth) ♦ Lord knows I've tried. ♦ not
know enough to come in out of
the rain ♦ not know so from
Adam ♦ One is known by the
company one keeps.
**knuckle** white knuckle sth

# L

**labor** the fruits of one's labor(s)
**lam** take it on the lam
**lamb** in two shakes of a lamb's
tail ♦ like lambs to the slaughter
**land** do a land-office business ♦
the lay of the land ♦ live off the
fat of the land
**lane** life in the fast lane
**language** speak the same
language ♦ speak so's language
**lap** in the lap of luxury
**lard** tub of lard
**large** by and large ♦ living large ♦
writ large
**last** at the last gasp ♦ at the last
minute ♦ famous last words ♦
head for the last roundup
**late** Better late than never. ♦
keep late hours
**laugh** die laughing ♦ no laughing
matter
**laughter** gales of laughter ♦ split
one's sides (with laughter)
**laurels** look to one's laurels ♦ rest
on one's laurels
**lavender** lay so out in lavender

**law** above the law ♦ bend the
law ♦ lay down the law (to so)
(about sth) ♦ the long arm of the
law ♦ on the wrong side of the
law ♦ take the law into one's own
hands
**lay** not lay a hand on so/sth
**lazy** born lazy
**league** in the same league as
so/sth ♦ play in the big leagues
**leash** on a tight leash ♦ strain at
the leash
**least** follow the line of least
resistance
**left** have two left feet ♦ out in
left field
**leg** an arm and a leg ♦ get up on
one's hind legs ♦ have a hollow
leg ♦ not have a leg to stand on
♦ shake a leg ♦ stretch one's legs
**length** at great length ♦ keep at
arm's length from so/sth
**less** in less than no time
**lesson** learn one's lesson ♦ teach
so a lesson
**letter** to the letter
**liberty** take the liberty of doing sth
**lie** a little white lie ♦ a pack of
lies
**life** all walks of life ♦ breathe
new life into sth ♦ claim a life ♦
every walk of life ♦ the facts of
life ♦ in the prime of (one's) life ♦
lead the life of Riley ♦ make life
miserable for so ♦ the seamy side
of life ♦ sign one's life away ♦
take one's life into one's (own)
hands ♦ That's the story of my
life.
**lifetime** a legend in one's own
(life)time
**light** all sweetness and light ♦
hide one's light under a bushel ♦
not suffer fools lightly ♦ see the
light (of day) ♦ trip the light
fantastic
**lightning** quick as (greased)
lightning

**limb** life and limb ♦ tear so/animal limb from limb

**line** follow the line of least resistance ♦ read between the lines ♦ sign on the dotted line ♦ step out of line

**link** the weak link (in the chain)

**lip** Loose lips sink ships. ♦ None of your lip! ♦ read so's lips ♦ Zip (up) your lip!

**liquor** hold one's liquor

**little** Ye gods (and little fishes)!

**live** how the other half lives ♦ Pardon me for living!

**loan** float a loan ♦ take out a loan

**log** like a bump on a log

**loggerheads** at loggerheads (with so) (over sth)

**long** not long for this world

**look** come-hither look ♦ not much to look at

**loose** at loose ends ♦ on the loose ♦ some loose ends

**lose** make up for lost time ♦ a two-time loser

**lot** carry (a lot of) weight (with so/sth) ♦ cover a lot of ground

**loud** think out loud

**love** not for love nor money ♦ a labor of love

**low** lay so low ♦ low man on the totem pole ♦ low-hanging fruit

**luck** have more luck than sense ♦ No such luck.

**lurch** leave so in the lurch

**luxury** in the lap of luxury

# M

**mad** method in one's madness ♦ stark raving mad ♦ steaming (mad) ♦ tap dance like mad

**madding** far from the madding crowd

**made** not made of money

**magic** work its magic on so/sth

**main** main strength and awkwardness

**make** history in the making ♦ It takes all kinds (to make a world). ♦ Not able to make head or tail of sth ♦ That makes two of us.

**man** big man on campus ♦ hatchet man ♦ high man on the totem pole ♦ low man on the totem pole ♦ odd man out ♦ a straw man

**manger** dog in the manger

**manner** to the manner born

**many** have one's finger in too many pies ♦ in so many words

**marble** have all one's marbles

**mare** by shank's mare

**mark** off the mark ♦ toe the mark ♦ wide of the mark

**market** on the market ♦ play the (stock) market

**master** a past master at sth

**match** strike a match

**matter** as a matter of course ♦ no laughing matter ♦ no matter how you slice it

**McCoy** the real McCoy

**mean** lean and mean ♦ no offense meant ♦ within one's means

**measure** beyond measure

**medication** on medication

**medicine** take one's medicine

**meet** Fancy meeting you here! ♦ where the rubber meets the road

**melt** look as if butter wouldn't melt in one's mouth

**member** card-carrying member

**memory** commit sth to memory ♦ jog so's memory

**men** twelve good men and true

**mend** on the mend

**mental** make a (mental) note of sth

**mercy** at the mercy of so

## N

**nail** hit the nail (right) on the head

**naked** with the naked eye

**name** take (some) names ♦ worthy of the name

**nape** by the nape of the neck

**nature** let nature take its course

**neck** by the nape of the neck ♦ a crick in one's neck ♦ dead from the neck up ♦ in some neck of the woods ♦ a millstone about one's neck ♦ a yoke around so's neck

**need** A friend in need is a friend indeed. ♦ one needs to have one's head examined

**needle** on pins and needles

**nerve** a lot of nerve

**nest** feather one's (own) nest ♦ stir up a hornet's nest

**net** surf the Net

**new** (So) what else is new? ♦ (some) new blood ♦ break new ground ♦ breathe new life into sth ♦ No news is good news. ♦ ring in the new year

**niche** carve out a niche

**night** all hours (of the day and night) ♦ one-night stand ♦ ships that pass in the night

**nitty** get down to the nitty-gritty

**noise** make noises about sth

**nonsense** stuff and nonsense

**nook** every nook and cranny

**North** up North

**nose** blow one's nose ♦ cut off one's nose to spite one's face ♦ have one's nose in a book ♦ hold one's nose ♦ keep one's nose out of sth ♦ keep one's nose to the grindstone ♦ one's nose is in the air ♦ put one's nose to the grindstone

**note** make a (mental) note of sth ♦ a hell of a note

**nothing** all or nothing ♦ like nothing on earth ♦ sweet nothings

**notice** serve notice (on so)

**nowhere** Flattery will get you nowhere. ♦ in the middle of nowhere

**number** take care of number one ♦ the wrong number

**nut** get down to the nuts and bolts

**nutshell** put sth in a nutshell

## O

**oat** sow one's wild oats

**oath** take an oath ♦ under oath

**offense** no offense meant ♦ no offense taken

**office** do a land-office business ♦ take office

**oil** burn the midnight oil ♦ pour oil on troubled water(s)

**old** a chip off the old block ♦ for old time's sake ♦ one's old stamping ground ♦ ring out the old (year) ♦ a ripe old age ♦ the same old story

**olive** hold out the olive branch

**omega** alpha and omega

**once** all at once ♦ You are only young once.

**one** (all) in one breath ♦ back to square one ♦ go from one extreme to the other ♦ go in one ear and out the other ♦ have one foot in the grave ♦ It's six of one, half a dozen of another. ♦ (It) takes one to know one. ♦ kill two birds with one stone ♦ on (the) one hand ♦ put all one's eggs in one basket ♦ put one foot in front of the other ♦ speak with one voice ♦ take care of number one

**only** You are only young once.

**open** crack sth (wide) open ♦ an open-and-shut case

**operation** a mopping-up operation

**opinion** in my humble opinion

**opportunity** a golden
opportunity ✦ a photo
op(portunity) ✦ a window of
opportunity
**orange** compare apples and
oranges
**orbit** in orbit
**order** in apple-pie order ✦ just
what the doctor ordered ✦ made
to order ✦ out of order
**ordinary** out of the ordinary
**other** drop the other shoe ✦ go
from one extreme to the other ✦
go in one ear and out the other
✦ have the shoe on the other
foot ✦ how the other half lives ✦
on the other hand ✦ put one
foot in front of the other ✦ turn
the other cheek ✦ wait for the
other shoe to drop
**overboard** go overboard
**overdrive** into overdrive
**own** afraid of one's own shadow ✦
cut one's (own) throat ✦ dig one's
own grave ✦ feather one's (own)
nest ✦ keep one's own counsel ✦ a
legend in one's own (life)time ✦
line one's own pocket(s) ✦ paddle
one's own canoe ✦ a place to call
one's own ✦ pull oneself up by one's
(own) bootstraps ✦ sign one's
own death warrant ✦ stand on
one's (own) two feet ✦ stew in
one's own juice ✦ take the law
into one's own hands ✦ take one's
life into one's (own) hands ✦
under one's own steam
**oyster** The world is one's oyster.

## P

**pace** a change of pace
**paddle** up the creek (without a
paddle)
**pain** feeling no pain ✦ No pain,
no gain ✦ a royal pain ✦ take
pains with so/sth
**paint** close as two coats of paint
**pale** beyond the pale

**pall** cast a pall on sth
**Pandora** open Pandora's box
**pants** ants in one's pants ✦ by the
seat of one's pants ✦ catch one
with one's pants down ✦ charm
the pants off so
**paper** can't carry a tune in a
paper sack ✦ look good on paper
**par** above par
**parade** rain on so's parade
**paradise** a fool's paradise
**parry** thrust and parry
**party** a certain party ✦ the life of
the party
**pass** come to a pretty pass ✦
ships that pass in the night
**past** a thing of the past
**paste** cut and paste
**path** beat a path to so's door ✦ the
primrose path
**patience** try so's patience
**Paul** rob Peter to pay Paul
**pay** the price one has to pay ✦ put
paid to sth ✦ rob Peter to pay
Paul
**pea** like (two) peas in a pod
**peace** at peace ✦ keep the peace
✦ make (one's) peace with so ✦
rest in peace
**pearl** cast (one's) pearls before
swine
**peck** hunt-and-peck
**peculiar** funny peculiar
**pedal** put the pedal to the metal
**pedestal** on a pedestal
**peeve** pet peeve
**peg** a square peg (in a round
hole)
**penalty** pay the penalty
**penny** a bad penny
**people** bad blood (between
people)
**perish** publish or perish
**Peter** rob Peter to pay Paul
**phrase** coin a phrase
**pick** have a bone to pick (with
so)
**pickle** in a (pretty) pickle

**picnic** one sandwich short of a picnic

**picture** out of the picture ♦ the (very) picture of sth

**pie** American as apple pie ♦ eat humble pie ♦ have one's finger in too many pies ♦ in apple-pie order

**piece** pick sth to pieces ♦ the villain of the piece

**pig** buy a pig in a poke ♦ serve as a guinea pig

**pill** on the pill

**pillar** from pillar to post

**pilot** on automatic (pilot)

**pin** on pins and needles

**pinch** take sth with a pinch of salt

**pincher** a penny-pincher

**pink** in the pink (of condition) ♦ in the pink (of health)

**pipe** a lead-pipe cinch ♦ Put that in your pipe and smoke it! ♦ a set of pipes

**pipeline** in the pipeline

**piper** pay the piper

**place** have friends in high places ♦ in the right place at the right time ♦ the toast of some place ♦ a wide place in the road

**plague** avoid so/sth like the plague

**plank** walk the plank

**plate** step up to the plate

**platter** on a silver platter

**play** a game that two can play ♦ a level playing field ♦ a power play ♦ roll over and play dead ♦ a team player

**please** the disease to please

**pleasure** mix business with pleasure

**pledge** take the pledge

**plow** put one's hand to the plow

**plug** pull the plug (on sth) ♦ put a plug in (for so/sth)

**plumbing** the greatest thing since indoor plumbing

**plunge** take the plunge

**pocket** line one's own pocket(s) ♦ Money burns a hole in so's pocket. ♦ pick so's pocket

**pod** like (two) peas in a pod

**poetic** wax poetic

**point** belabor the point ♦ a case in point ♦ in point of fact ♦ stretch a point

**poke** buy a pig in a poke

**pole** high man on the totem pole ♦ I wouldn't touch it with a ten-foot pole. ♦ low man on the totem pole

**polish** apple-polisher ♦ spit and polish

**politic** the body politic ♦ play politics

**pond** a big frog in a small pond

**pony** dog and pony show

**poor** poor as a church mouse

**position** jockey for position ♦ place so in an awkward position

**possum** play possum

**post** from pillar to post ♦ keep so posted

**poster** a poster child (for sth)

**pot** sweeten the pot ♦ throw sth in(to) the pot

**potato** a couch potato ♦ meat-and-potatoes ♦ small potatoes

**potshot** take a potshot at so/sth

**powder** keep one's powder dry ♦ sitting on a powder keg ♦ take a powder

**practice** out of practice

**praise** damn so/sth with faint praise

**prayer** on a wing and a prayer

**premium** at a premium

**present** There's no time like the present.

**pressure** take so's blood pressure

**pretty** come to a pretty pass ♦ in a (pretty) pickle ♦ sitting pretty

**prevent** take steps (to prevent sth)

**price** cheap at half the price

**pride** swallow one's pride
**prime** in the prime of (one's) life
**principle** a matter of principle
**print** out of print
**private** in private
**prize** booby prize
**professional** seek professional help
**profile** a low profile
**profit** turn a profit
**program** get with the program
**proportion** out of (all) proportion ♦ a disaster of epic proportions
**prowl** on the prowl
**public** out of the public eye
**pull** like pulling teeth
**punch** beat so to the punch ♦ pull one's punches ♦ telegraph one's punches
**punishment** a glutton for punishment ♦ a sucker for punishment
**purge** binge and purge
**purpose** at cross-purposes
**put** to put it mildly

## Q

**quarrel** patch a quarrel up
**quartered** drawn and quartered
**question** leading question ♦ pose a question ♦ the sixty-four-dollar question ♦ without question

## R

**race** off to the races ♦ the rat race ♦ a tight race
**radar** below so's radar (screen) ♦ on so's radar (screen)
**rag** from rags to riches
**rain** not know enough to come in out of the rain
**rampant** run rampant
**range** at close range
**rank** break ranks with so/sth ♦ close ranks ♦ pull rank on so

**ransom** a king's ransom
**rap** take the rap (for sth)
**rare** in rare form
**rat** smell a rat
**rave** rant and rave (about so/sth) ♦ stark raving mad
**reaction** gut reaction ♦ a knee-jerk reaction
**reality** lose touch with reality
**reaper** the grim reaper
**rear** bring up the rear
**reason** listen to reason ♦ neither rhyme nor reason ♦ stand to reason
**record** off the record ♦ one for the (record) books
**red** cut through red tape ♦ give so a red face
**rein** give free rein to so ♦ keep a tight rein on so/sth ♦ take over the reins (of sth)
**relationship** a love-hate relationship
**relish** with (great) relish
**reputation** carve out a reputation
**resistance** follow the line of least resistance ♦ a pocket of resistance
**respect** with all due respect
**response** gut response
**rest** Give it a rest! ♦ lay so to rest ♦ No rest for the wicked.
**retreat** beat a (hasty) retreat
**rhyme** neither rhyme nor reason
**rib** stick to one's ribs
**rich** from rags to riches ♦ stinking rich ♦ strike it rich
**riddance** good riddance (to bad rubbish)
**ride** a free ride ♦ take so for a ride
**ridiculous** from the sublime to the ridiculous
**right** hit the nail (right) on the head ♦ in the right place at the right time ♦ on the right track ♦

(right) off the top of one's head ♦ see (right) through so/sth

**Riley** lead the life of Riley

**ring** like a three-ring circus ♦ a (dead) ringer (for so)

**road** middle-of-the-road ♦ a rocky road ♦ where the rubber meets the road ♦ a wide place in the road

**roar** keep it down (to a dull roar)

**Robin** all around Robin Hood's barn

**rock** on the rocks

**rocket** not rocket science

**roll** heads will roll ♦ ready to roll

**Rome** fiddle while Rome burns

**roof** go through the roof ♦ live under the same roof (with so)

**room** not enough room to swing a cat ♦ smoke-filled room ♦ some elbow room

**roost** come home (to roost) ♦ rule the roost

**rope** at the end of one's rope

**rose** a bed of roses ♦ Everything's coming up roses. ♦ smell like a rose

**rot** spoiled rotten

**rough** a diamond in the rough

**round** a square peg (in a round hole)

**roundup** head for the last roundup

**rove** have a roving eye

**royal** a battle royal

**rub** There's the rub.

**rubber** where the rubber meets the road

**rubbish** good riddance (to bad rubbish)

**ruffle** smooth (so's) ruffled feathers

**rug** pull the rug out (from under so)

**ruin** lie in ruins ♦ wrack and ruin

**rule** bend the rules

**run** cut and run ♦ dry run ♦ I hate to eat and run. ♦ make so's blood run cold ♦ off to a running start ♦ up and running

**rut** in a rut

## S

**sack** can't carry a tune in a paper sack

**safe** better safe than sorry ♦ on the safe side

**sake** for old time's sake

**salad** toss a salad

**salt** back to the salt mines ♦ rub salt in a wound ♦ take sth with a grain of salt ♦ take sth with a pinch of salt ♦ worth one's salt

**same** by the same token ♦ cast in the same mold ♦ in the same league as so/sth ♦ live under the same roof (with so) ♦ on the same wavelength ♦ speak the same language

**sandwich** one sandwich short of a picnic ♦ a knuckle sandwich

**sardine** pack so/sth (in) like sardines

**sassy** fat and sassy

**savings** dip into one's savings

**say** Smile when you say that. ♦ That's easy for you to say. ♦ What can I say? ♦ What so said.

**scapegoat** make so the scapegoat for sth

**science** not rocket science

**score** settle a score with so

**scrape** bow and scrape

**scratch** from scratch ♦ start from scratch

**screen** below so's radar (screen) ♦ on so's radar (screen)

**seal** signed, sealed, and delivered

**seat** by the seat of one's pants ♦ in the driver's seat ♦ take a back seat (to so/sth)

**second** on second thought

**see** begin to see daylight ♦ can't see one's hand in front of one's face ♦ have seen better days ♦ (I've) seen better. ♦ (I've) seen worse. ♦ They must have seen you coming. ♦ wait-and-see attitude ♦ What you see is what you get.

**sell** soft sell

**sense** come to one's senses ♦ have more luck than sense

**service** press so/sth into service

**settle** when the dust settles

**seven** at sixes and sevens

**seventh** in seventh heaven

**sex** the opposite sex

**shabby** not too shabby

**shadow** afraid of one's own shadow

**shake** in two shakes of a lamb's tail ♦ more so/sth than one can shake a stick at ♦ no great shakes ♦ two shakes of a lamb's tail

**shaky** on shaky ground

**shank** by shank's mare

**shape** bent out of shape ♦ take shape

**share** Thank you for sharing.

**shave** have a close shave

**shebang** the whole shebang

**shed** not shed a tear

**sheep** a wolf in sheep's clothing

**shell** out of one's shell

**shine** a knight in shining armor ♦ make hay (while the sun shines) ♦ Rise and shine!

**ship** abandon ship ♦ Don't give up the ship! ♦ jump ship ♦ Loose lips sink ships. ♦ run a taut ship ♦ run a tight ship ♦ Shape up or ship out.

**shirt** give so the shirt off one's back ♦ keep one's shirt on ♦ lose one's shirt

**shoe** drop the other shoe ♦ have the shoe on the other foot ♦ in so else's shoes ♦ wait for the other shoe to drop

**shoestring** on a shoestring

**shop** close up shop ♦ talk shop ♦ window-shopping

**short** one sandwich short of a picnic

**shoulder** carry the weight of the world on one's shoulders ♦ rub shoulders with so ♦ straight from the shoulder

**shovel** put so to bed with a shovel

**show** by a show of hands ♦ dog and pony show ♦ not show one's face

**shut** an open-and-shut case ♦ Put up or shut up! ♦ some shut-eye

**sick** worried sick (about so/sth)

**side** can't hit the (broad) side of a barn ♦ the dark side of so/sth ♦ hit the (broad) side of a barn ♦ on the safe side ♦ on the wrong side of the law ♦ the seamy side of life ♦ split one's sides (with laughter)

**sight** no end in sight ♦ out of sight ♦ raise one's sights

**signal** send out the wrong signals

**silence** break silence ♦ break the silence

**silver** born with a silver spoon in one's mouth ♦ on a silver platter

**since** the greatest thing since indoor plumbing ♦ the greatest thing since sliced bread

**sink** Loose lips sink ships. ♦ makes one's heart sink

**six** at sixes and sevens ♦ It's six of one, half a dozen of another.

**size** That's about the size of it.

**sketch** a thumbnail sketch

**skin** by the skin of one's teeth ♦ get under so's skin

**skip** a hop, skip, and a jump

**sky** pie in the sky

**stop** The buck stops here. ✦ pull all the stops out

**store** set great store by so/sth

**stork** a visit from the stork

**story** break a story ✦ cock-and-bull story ✦ fish story ✦ the same old story ✦ a shaggy-dog story ✦ That's the story of my life.

**straight** set so straight ✦ vote a straight ticket

**strain** crack under the strain

**straw** draw straws for sth

**streak** a mean streak ✦ talk a blue streak

**street** the man in the street ✦ on easy street ✦ put sth on the street ✦ a two-way street

**strength** by brute strength ✦ main strength and awkwardness

**stretch** at a stretch

**strike** two strikes against one

**stuff** the right stuff

**style** cramp so's style

**sublime** from the sublime to the ridiculous

**substance** sum and substance

**such** No such luck.

**suck** teach one's grandmother to suck eggs

**suffer** not suffer fools gladly

**suit** follow suit ✦ in one's birthday suit ✦ monkey suit

**suitcase** live out of a suitcase

**sun** make hay (while the sun shines) ✦ under the sun

**sundry** all and sundry

**sunshine** a ray of sunshine

**surface** scratch the surface

**suspicion** under a cloud (of suspicion)

**swallow** look like the cat that swallowed the canary

**sweat** blood, sweat, and tears ✦ break out in a cold sweat ✦ by the sweat of one's brow

**sweep** a clean sweep

**sweet** all sweetness and light ✦ have a sweet tooth ✦ short and sweet

**swim** in the swim of things ✦ sink or swim

**swing** not enough room to swing a cat

**switch** asleep at the switch ✦ bait and switch

**sword** cross swords (with so)

**system** All systems (are) go. ✦ get sth out of one's system

## T

**table** get so around the table ✦ under the table

**tactic** strong-arm tactics

**tail** bright-eyed and bushy-tailed ✦ heads or tails ✦ in two shakes of a lamb's tail ✦ Not able to make head or tail of sth ✦ two shakes of a lamb's tail

**take** (It) takes one to know one. ✦ able to take a joke ✦ can take it to the bank ✦ Give one an inch and one will take a mile. ✦ It takes all kinds (to make a world). ✦ (just) taking care of business ✦ let nature take its course ✦ a lot of give-and-take ✦ no offense taken ✦ on the take ✦ winner take all

**tale** fish tale ✦ an old wives' tale

**talk** all talk (and no action)

**tangent** off on a tangent

**tape** cut through red tape ✦ red tape

**tar** whale the tar out of so

**taste** leave a bad taste in so's mouth

**taut** run a taut ship

**taxi** hail a taxi

**tea** just one's cup of tea ✦ not for all the tea in China ✦ not one's cup of tea

**teacup** a tempest in a teacup

**teapot** a tempest in a teapot

**top** at the top of one's game ♦ come out on top ♦ (right) off the top of one's head ♦ sitting on top of the world ♦ take it from the top

**totem** high man on the totem pole ♦ low man on the totem pole

**touch** I wouldn't touch it with a ten-foot pole. ♦ Keep in touch. ♦ lose touch with reality ♦ soft touch

**tough** hang tough (on sth)

**tower** in an ivory tower

**town** all over town ♦ go to town

**track** on the fast track ♦ on the right track ♦ on the wrong track ♦ stop (dead) in one's tracks

**trade** jack of all trades ♦ tools of the trade ♦ tricks of the trade

**tradition** break with tradition

**trail** a paper trail

**train** lose one's train of thought ♦ ride the gravy train ♦ so's train of thought

**treatment** the red-carpet treatment ♦ the royal treatment

**tree** bark up the wrong tree

**trembling** in fear and trembling

**trial** send up a trial balloon

**triangle** the eternal triangle

**tribulation** trials and tribulations

**trick** bag of tricks ♦ do the trick ♦ every trick in the book ♦ turn a trick ♦ whole bag of tricks

**trifle** a mere trifle

**trigger** quick on the trigger

**trolley** slip one's trolley

**trooper** swear like a trooper

**troth** plight one's troth to so

**trouble** borrow trouble ♦ fish in troubled waters ♦ pour oil on troubled water(s) ♦ spell trouble ♦ teething troubles

**truck** just fell off the turnip truck

**true** ring true ♦ show one's (true) colors ♦ twelve good men and true

**trump** play one's trump card

**truth** the naked truth

**try** Lord knows I've tried.

**tucker** one's best bib and tucker

**tune** can't carry a tune (in a bushel basket) ♦ can't carry a tune in a bucket ♦ can't carry a tune in a paper sack ♦ change so's tune ♦ in tune with so/sth ♦ to the tune of some amount of money

**turf** surf and turf

**turkey** go cold turkey ♦ talk turkey

**turn** take a turn for the better ♦ take a turn for the worse

**turnip** just fell off the turnip truck

**turtle** turn turtle

**twice** think twice (before doing sth) ♦ think twice about so/sth

**two** close as two coats of paint ♦ fall between two stools ♦ For two cents I would do sth. ♦ a game that two can play ♦ have two left feet ♦ in two shakes of a lamb's tail ♦ It cuts two ways. ♦ kill two birds with one stone ♦ the lesser of two evils ♦ like (two) peas in a pod ♦ of two minds (about so/sth) ♦ put two and two together ♦ stand on one's (own) two feet ♦ That makes two of us.

## U

**ugly** rear its ugly head

**umbrage** take umbrage at sth

**uncle** I'll be a monkey's uncle!

**unglued** come unglued

**unring** can't unring the bell

**unturned** leave no stone unturned

**usual** business as usual

## V

**velvet** rule with a velvet glove

**vengeance** with a vengeance ◆ wreak vengeance (up)on so/sth
**verse** chapter and verse
**vicious** in a vicious circle
**victory** snatch victory from the jaws of defeat ◆ a landslide victory
**view** a bird's-eye view
**vigor** vim and vigor
**violet** a shrinking violet
**vision** tunnel vision
**voice** speak with one voice
**void** null and void
**volume** speak volumes
**vote** cast one's vote

# W

**wag** cause (some) tongues to wag ◆ set tongues (a)wagging ◆ the tail wagging the dog
**walk** all walks of life ◆ every walk of life ◆ talk the talk and walk the walk ◆ worship the ground so walks on
**wall** climb the wall(s) ◆ a hole in the wall ◆ knock one's head (up) against a brick wall ◆ off-the-wall
**wallet** vote with one's wallet
**wane** on the wane
**wanted** know when one is not wanted
**warhorse** an old warhorse
**warrant** sign one's own death warrant
**wash** chief cook and bottle washer ◆ come out in the wash ◆ It won't wash! ◆ It'll all come out in the wash.
**waste** Don't waste your breath.
**watch** on so's watch
**water** bread and water ◆ come hell or high water ◆ fish in troubled waters ◆ like a fish out of water ◆ not hold water ◆ of the first water ◆ pour oil on troubled water(s) ◆ test the water(s) ◆ tread water ◆ turn so's water off ◆ won't hold water

**waterfront** cover the waterfront
**waterworks** turn on the waterworks
**wave** make waves
**wavelength** on the same wavelength
**way** downhill all the way ◆ have a way with words ◆ have it both ways ◆ It cuts two ways. ◆ know one's way around ◆ laugh all the way to the bank ◆ out of harm's way ◆ see the error of one's ways ◆ take the coward's way out ◆ a two-way street
**wear** none the worse for wear
**weather** under the weather
**weep** read it and weep
**weight** carry (a lot of) weight (with so/sth) ◆ carry the weight of the world on one's shoulders
**well** let well enough alone
**were** as it were
**whale** have a whale of a time
**wheel** asleep at the wheel ◆ a fifth wheel ◆ reinvent the wheel ◆ a set of wheels ◆ spin one's wheels
**whistle** bells and whistles ◆ blow the whistle (on so/sth)
**white** black and white ◆ a little white lie
**who** You and who else?
**whole** go whole hog
**wicked** No rest for the wicked.
**wide** all wool and a yard wide ◆ crack sth (wide) open ◆ far and wide ◆ the whole wide world
**wife** an old wives' tale
**wild** send so on a wild-goose chase ◆ sow one's wild oats
**wildfire** spread like wildfire
**willing** ready, willing, and able
**wind** gone with the wind ◆ throw caution to the wind
**windmill** tilt at windmills
**window** out the window
**wing** on a wing and a prayer

**wink** forty winks ♦ quick as a wink

**wire** have one's wires crossed

**wisdom** in so's infinite wisdom

**wise** a word to the wise

**wiser** sadder but wiser

**wish** have a death wish

**wit** at one's wit's end ♦ live by one's wits ♦ one's wits about one ♦ a sharp wit

**woe** tale of woe

**wolf** cry wolf ♦ keep the wolf from the door ♦ throw so to the wolves

**wonder** a seven-day wonder ♦ work wonders (with so/sth)

**woods** A babe in the woods ♦ in some neck of the woods ♦ the woods are full of so/sth

**woodwork** out of the woodwork

**wool** all wool and a yard wide ♦ dyed-in-the-wool ♦ pull the wool over so's eyes

**word** as good as one's word ♦ by word of mouth ♦ eat one's words ♦ famous last words ♦ hang on (so's) every word ♦ have a way with words ♦ in so many words ♦ the last word in sth ♦ a man of few words ♦ mince (one's) words ♦ Mum's the word. ♦ one's word is one's bond ♦ or words to that effect ♦ put words in(to) so's mouth ♦ spread the word ♦ suit one's actions to one's words ♦ take the words out of so's mouth ♦ Them's fighting words!

**work** all in a day's work ♦ get down to work ♦ grunt work ♦ a lick of work ♦ throw a (monkey) wrench in the works

**world** bring so into the world ♦ carry the weight of the world on one's shoulders ♦ come down in the world ♦ come into the world ♦ have all the time in the world ♦ It takes all kinds (to make a world). ♦ not have a care in the world ♦ not long for this world ♦ not the end of the world ♦ set the world on fire ♦ sitting on top of the world ♦ What's the world coming to? ♦ with the best will in the world

**worm** a can of worms

**worry** Not to worry.

**worse** (I've) seen worse. ♦ for better or (for) worse ♦ none the worse for wear ♦ take a turn for the worse

**worst** one's own worst enemy

**worth** play it for all it's worth

**wound** rub salt in a wound

**wrench** throw a (monkey) wrench in the works

**wring** put so through the wringer

**wrinkle** get the wrinkles out (of sth)

**write** It's written all over one's face. ♦ nothing to write home about

**wrong** bark up the wrong tree ♦ fall into the wrong hands ♦ on the wrong side of the law ♦ on the wrong track ♦ send out the wrong signals

# Y

**yard** all wool and a yard wide

**yarn** spin a yarn

**year** ring in the new year ♦ ring out the old (year) ♦ twilight years ♦ well up in years

**York** a New York minute